MARK HERRMANN

AUTHOR OF *THE CURMUDGEON'S GUIDE TO PRACTICING LAW*

INSIDE STRAIGHT

ADVICE ABOUT LAWYERING, IN-HOUSE AND OUT, THAT ONLY THE INTERNET COULD PROVIDE

INSIDE STRAIGHT

Printed in the United States of America.

15 14 13   5 4 3 2

Library of Congress Cataloging-in-Publication Data

Herrmann, Mark.
 Inside straight : advice about lawyering, in-house and out that only the Internet could provide / by Mark Herrmann.
    p. cm.
 Includes bibliographical references and index.
 ISBN 978-1-61438-539-4 (alk. paper)
 1. Corporate legal departments--United States. 2. Corporate lawyers--United States--Handbooks, manuals, etc. I. Title.
 KF1425.H47 2012
 658.1'2--dc23
                    2012019419

CONTENTS

FOREWORD

In August 2010, Above the Law celebrated its fourth birthday. The site, devoted to providing news and commentary about the legal profession, was thriving, with hundreds of thousands of readers and millions of pageviews per month. But it also needed to evolve. We had excellent market penetration in large law firms and law schools, as well as among younger readers, who have a preference for consuming their news online. If we wanted the site to continue growing, however, we needed to reach new constituencies. We decided to add offerings that would appeal to these communities, including in-house lawyers and attorneys at small law firms, as well as older readers.

Part of this evolution, my colleagues and I decided, would involve a subtle shift in tone. Above the Law—or "ATL," as it has become known—historically spoke in a cheeky, irreverent, truth-telling voice. We did not want to lose our reputation for insight and candor, which has been integral to ATL's success. In order to reach older readers, however, we realized that we would need to add some content with greater seriousness and gravitas, to complement the humorous and edgy stories for which the site was well-known.

That month—on August 17, 2010, to be precise—we published a post entitled "Help Wanted: Above the Law Seeks In-House Counsel Columnist." We received numerous enthusiastic responses. Choosing between them would have been difficult had we not received a response from Mark Herrmann—a senior in-house lawyer (and former law firm partner), a rock star of the legal blogging world, and a perfect fit for what we were hoping to achieve with the new column.

Herrmann's reputation preceded him. After a long and distinguished career in private practice, Herrmann left a partnership at Jones Day to become the global head of litigation at Aon, the world's largest insurance and reinsurance brokerage. He had almost 100 articles in the legal and popular press to his name, as well as two books: a treatise on the state court analogues to federal multidistrict litigation, and *The Curmudgeon's Guide to Practicing Law*, which should be required reading for all young lawyers aspiring to successful legal careers. And he had extensive blogging experience, having founded and co-hosted—for three years, which is a long time in the blogosphere—the widely read and respected Drug and Device Law Blog (which we would regularly link to from Above the Law). Herrmann's retirement from the blogosphere in late 2009, shortly before he left Jones Day to join Aon, was met with much dismay. We couldn't pass up the opportunity to bring him back to the blogosphere.

We had high expectations for Herrmann—which he has not only met but exceeded. Since "Inside Straight" launched in the fall of 2010, it has become one of Above the Law's most popular offerings. In its first sixteen months, the twice-weekly column generated over 800,000 pageviews, for an average of over 6,000 pageviews per column. His most well-trafficked column—discussing the plight of an unemployed former editor-in-chief of a law review (who subsequently found employment, thanks to Herrmann's coverage)—has received approximately 20,000 pageviews as of this writing. As any legal blogger can tell you, very few blog posts receive anywhere close to that kind of traffic. (At the first legal blog that I started, Underneath Their Robes—a site providing "news, gossip, and colorful commentary about the federal judiciary"—a good day for the entire site would involve 2,000 to 3,000 pageviews.)

The traffic generated by "Inside Straight" grows more impressive when one considers the limitations under which Herrmann writes. Writing online for a large audience while continuing to practice law—at a very high level, as a senior legal officer at a publicly traded company—can be tricky. One way to gain traction in the online world is by advocating an extreme opinion, but such a column might offend readers with opposing views. An in-house lawyer at a corporation that does a great deal of business for the Fortune 500 can't risk alienating colleagues or clients, current or future, in such a way. Another way to generate traffic is to cover a tale of a lawyer acting unethically or illegally; but Aon places insurance for law firms, and Herrmann's columns can't offend potential clients. Those of us who write full-time for Above the Law, or our outside contributors who write under pseudonyms, do not have to worry about such concerns. The fact that Herrmann, using his real name in his byline, can write such engaging columns—columns that can generate as much traffic or even more traffic than stories about far racier fare—testifies to his insight and talent as a writer.

Herrmann's column has garnered not just traffic but respect. Partners at major law firms send out firm-wide emails directing their colleagues to read particular "Inside Straight" posts for their wisdom. We receive regular requests to reprint Herrmann's columns for purposes of continuing legal education events. Readers frequently praise his work—"enlightening and informative," "right on target," full of "great client service nuggets"—over email, in posts on other blogs, and on Twitter (even though Herrmann himself has raised questions about the effectiveness of Twitter, most memorably in a column entitled "Empirical Proof That Twitter Doesn't Work"). In this book, you can check out Herrmann's advice for yourself, on topics ranging from office politics to business development to how to be a good boss (or how to avoid being a bad one). This volume can be seen as a sequel to Herrmann's last book: if *The Curmudgeon's Guide* speaks to law students and young lawyers, *Inside Straight* addresses the people who supervise them, like senior in-house attorneys and partners at law firms.

Respect for "Inside Straight" has not been universal: as you will see, Above the Law's cantankerous commenters have not spared Herrmann from criticism (although the reader comments on his posts tend to be among the most positive and the most thoughtful for any of our writers). The commenters represent a small minority of our readership—comment-related traffic accounts for anywhere from two to five percent of ATL's total traffic on a given day—so they should not be taken as representative of the site's readership as a whole; many of our visitors never post comments or even read them (one has to specifically click into the comments in order to view them). But because the commenters can and do speak out, in frequently colorful and sometimes outrageous ways, and because they are a notoriously tough crowd, they inevitably attract notice. In the pages that follow, you'll be exposed to selected examples of both their insight and their impudence. To quote Justice Clarence Thomas, the ATL commenters "ain't evolving."[1]

Above the Law, though, is definitely evolving—and as we had hoped when we brought Herrmann on board, his column has contributed to the desired expansion and transformation of ATL. The site has transcended its origins as a one-man blog focused mainly on commentary and grown into a comprehensive source for legal news and opinion that employs four full-time writers and a dozen outside contributors. ATL continues to grow and currently has a record number of readers—and many of these readers come from the senior ranks of corporate legal departments and the partnerships of major law firms, thanks in large part to Herrmann's column.

Growing up isn't always fun. Just like people, websites can lose their youthful energy, edge, and exuberance. But aging is not without its consolations. If growing older will bring another writer like Mark Herrmann to the pages of Above the Law, then we welcome it.

David Lat
Managing Editor, Above the Law
April 2012

---

1 Jane Mayer and Jill Abramson, *Strange Justice: The Selling of Clarence Thomas* 360 (1994).

PREFACE

We tried to keep this book honest.

For the most part, this book consists of the verbatim text of some of the "Inside Straight" columns that appeared on the Above the Law blog between November 2010 and April 2012.

We did, however, cheat here and there. We slightly revised the titles of a few columns to make the material better fit the format of this book. We also gently edited certain columns where we found small errors in the original versions or simply couldn't resist improving upon a poor choice of words or phrasing.

We had to be more ruthless with the "comments" than we were with the columns themselves. We aggressively culled the comments, selecting only a tiny percentage for publication. We did that for reasons of length (the book would be impossibly long if we had included all of the comments), comprehension (with all due respect to the commenters, their contributions are occasionally unintelligible and often go off on wild tangents), and clarity (we altered the grammar or style of some of the comments). We had to be similarly aggressive in eliminating four-letter words from the comments, either by deleting those words or replacing them with synonyms better suited to appear in a book published by the American Bar Association. What can we say? The commenters occasionally got carried away with their emotions; we calmed things down (slightly).

You will notice two oddities created when we changed on-line text into manuscript form. First, we necessarily deleted all hyperlinks that had been imbedded in the on-line text. On-line, those links allowed us to offer, just a click away, an explanation of certain obscure words or phrases. That possibility does not exist in a hard-copy book. Second, the on-line versions of these essays began with a few paragraphs of text, followed by a link that invited readers to click and "continue reading." That format explains why the third or fourth paragraph of many posts ends with an ellipsis or a question mark—we were inviting the on-line readers to click and continue reading. We've left those ellipses and question marks in the text of this book, to provide context, although they serve no purpose here.

For the most part, however, as we said, the book is honest. We hope you enjoy it.

FLOTSAM

THINGS MY SON SAID ...

... at age five, when I was driving him to kindergarten one morning:

"Dad, you're a lawyer, right?"

"Yes, Jere."

"So you've read all the laws?"

"Oh, no, Jeremy. No one could ever read all the laws. There are way too many laws for anyone to read them all."

Pause.

"Hey, Dad: How are you supposed to obey all the laws if you haven't read them all?"

Longer pause.

"That's a good question, son. When you get home tonight, ask your mother."

* * *

At age seven, after we walked back from watching a baseball game on a miserably hot Sunday afternoon to my law firm's nearby parking garage, where we'd left the car. We stopped in the cafeteria and bought soft drinks from a vending machine before getting in the car:

"Hey, Dad, you've got a pretty good job."

"Why's that, Jere?"

"Because it's air-conditioned, and you can get a root beer whenever you want one."

[Think about that the next time you're sitting in your office cursing a colleague, opposing counsel, a client, or a judge: "It's air-conditioned, and I can get a root beer whenever I want one."]

* * *

At age 12, when the phone rang at 5 a.m., and the kids ran into our bedroom, saw me talking on the phone, and watched me transform from Dad-Dad into Lawyer-Dad and head to the closet to pull on a suit:

"Dad, what happened?"

"A MedEvac helicopter just crashed over at University Hospital."

Horrified: "Was anyone hurt?"

"Yes, Jere. Two people were killed. A third's in the hospital."

Pause.

"What are they calling *you* for?"

[No kidding, Jere. In a sane world, they'd be calling a doctor, or a priest, or a florist, or a mortician. But it's the United States in the year 2002. They called a lawyer.]

* * *

At age 19, sophomore spring at college, when he called to discuss his choice of major:

"Dad, I have to pick my major, and that's made me think about what I want to do with my life."

"Yes, Jere?"

"I know I want to do good for people. I want to help others, and I want to be satisfied when I'm old that I've made a difference. And I'm thinking about what job I might pick."

"Yes, Jere?"

"I thought about being a lawyer. You know, Dad, I really love you. But basically you help big companies that did it get off the hook."

The little turd's in medical school now. I sure love him.

COMMENTS

HELPFUL CAREER TIPS: He should have been an auto mechanic. Less school, less baseless malpractice litigation and more prestige.

ELIE: If I'm ever in a helicopter crash, I hope it crashes into a hospital.

STEVE: In the particular incident referred to in the post, the crashing into the hospital part likely wasn't the worst of it. Complicating matters was the fact that the helipad where the helicopter was taking off was on top of a 20-some story building. I think the 200+ foot fall significantly reduced the odds of passenger survival.

The incident referred to was, at least in part, the inspiration for the scene in "ER" where one of the doctors was crushed by a falling, burning helicopter (the hospital in "ER" also had a rooftop helipad).

GUEST: Informal Survey: "Like" this comment if you wish it were Mark in the helicopter.

INTRODUCTION

ABOVE THE LAW LAUNCHES A NEW COLUMN FOR IN-HOUSE COUNSEL (11.16.2010)

We are pleased to announce the launch of a new column, titled "Inside Straight" (for the poker aficionados among you). As its name suggests, the column will cover the world of corporate counsel with all of the candor and insight that you've come to expect from Above the Law.

Our columnist—a former law firm partner, current in-house lawyer, and author of a well-received book on legal practice—should be familiar to longtime followers of the world of legal blogging….

Here's the press release, which has all the details about our new offering:

ABOVE THE LAW LAUNCHES NEW COLUMN FOR IN-HOUSE COUNSEL

The legal profession is currently experiencing sweeping and dramatic change, marked by such developments as the rise of alternatives to the billable hour and the increased use of outsourcing. Many of these changes reflect a larger trend: exploring how law firms can provide high-quality legal services in a timely and cost-effective manner, by focusing on the needs of their clients. In light of this renewed emphasis on the client, and in response to the demand for additional coverage of corporate legal departments, Above the Law ("ATL") is launching a new column aimed at corporate counsel.

"Covering the in-house counsel world has always been a crucial part of Above the Law's mission," said ATL managing editor David Lat. "But based on the return of the spotlight to the client, as well as what we were hearing from our readers, it became clear that there was an even greater hunger for coverage of the corporate legal world. Adding a dedicated in-house column is just a natural extension of the Above the Law brand."

Above the Law's new column, to be called "Inside Straight," will be written by Mark Herrmann, vice president and chief counsel for litigation at Aon, the world's leading provider of risk management services and human capital consulting. A leading commentator on the legal profession, Herrmann—a former partner at Jones Day, and the author of *The Curmudgeon's Guide to Practicing Law*—is no stranger to the world of blogging. He blogged from 2006 to 2009 at Drug and Device Law Blog, the leading blog in its area of law. Inside Straight will appear twice a week, on Mondays and Thursdays.

"I've been out of blogging for nearly a year, and I was starting to suffer withdrawal symptoms," said Herrmann. "I'm delighted to get back in the game. ATL is one of the most widely read legal blogs in the country, and I'm flattered to have been asked to contribute."

"There's so much to write about now in the in-house world," said ATL editor Elie Mystal, "including changing relationships with outside counsel, alternate fee agreements, and the politics of corporate legal departments. We're thrilled to have Mark joining us to cover this fascinating and dynamic environment, with his invaluable insider perspective."

If you have questions about Above the Law's enhanced in-house coverage or want to learn more about how to reach in-house readers through advertising on ATL, feel free to contact us.

COMMENTS

BENNY: Homophobic title.

GUEST: Rich partner writing for ATL? He hurting for money?? Is Aon in good financial shape? Oh my God, I am worried.

ZOOLANDER: Mark Herrmann couldn't decide whether to do some writing on the side, or male modeling. . .

TIPS: And, honestly, Mark, from looking at you, I have grave doubts you've got what it takes to roll here. Nothing would bring more delight to me (and, I expect, the vast majority of my fellow sharp-toothed brethren) than taking a former partner to task for any lazy, boring, or poorly written post you happen to cobble together. For every associate everywhere, I look forward to excoriating you at every opportunity you present.

GUEST: This is a good idea but it can't possibly work if we know the identity of the blogger. There's no way he can be candid now.

GLADGUEST: I'm excited! A regular column written by a real lawyer who has done real law stuff for longer than a year or two and is still doing real law stuff! Exactly what I'm looking for on a law blog! I might have to start visiting you regularly again, ATL.

THE INSIDE STORY (11.18.2010)

On Friday, you were a litigator: You wrote briefs, argued motions, took depositions, and tried cases.

On Monday, you were a litigator: You identified loss contingencies, minimized them, quantified them, and removed them from a balance sheet.

What happened?

Don't give me, "You died and went to Hell."

The correct answer is, "You went in-house."

And an in-house lawyer views things from a different perspective than an outside lawyer does.

I'll use this column to share with you that different perspective and to discuss the distinct concerns that intrigue (or infuriate) in-house lawyers.

What exactly does that mean?

Heck if I know.

I'll say whatever springs to mind about the concerns of in-house counsel, the mistakes outside counsel make, alternate fee agreements, outsourcing, cronyism, and the issues du jour.

You can't fuel a column on a blog with the few discrete ideas that you have before you write your first post; you can fuel the thing only by observing the world around you and seeing the wisdom, or humor, tucked into events.

There are surely plenty of things that happen in the lives of in-house counsel that are filled with wisdom or humor. I've been in-house for only ten months (after more than 25 years in private practice), and I've already seen first-hand (or heard from in-house lawyers elsewhere) a bundle.

I've heard reactions to flat-fee billing arrangements for litigation ("I had no idea that [name of AmLaw 20 firm redacted] had that many first-year associates."); listened to presentations at beauty contests ("If you hire me, you get one of the outstanding corporate litigators in America."); received phone calls from old colleagues ("I know we haven't spoken for nearly 20 years, but I thought maybe we could do some business together."); and on and on.

Where it goes, nobody knows.

But I'm glad to join the gang here at ATL. Feel free to contact me—with questions, comments, or story suggestions—by e-mail, at inhouse@abovethelaw.com.

COMMENTS

LEARNED PAW: On Friday, you were a contract attorney: You sat in front of a computer, skimmed documents, clicked buttons, and tried looking for another job.

On Monday, you were a contract attorney: You sat in front of a computer, skimmed documents, clicked buttons, and tried looking for another job.

What happened? You died and went to Hell.

GUEST: This actually seems like it might be interesting and useful. Are you sure you want to do it on Above the Law?

GUEST: Wow—the writer actually separates each sentence into its own paragraph. Kudos!

GUEST: Hey Mark, I Know You're New And All That. But for some reason, you really annoy me.

HOULIHAN: I have seen this guy speak at seminars, and he is really, really funny, so please give him a chance.

BL1Y: Mark, would you mind asking your mom not to post in the comments?

INHOUSEGUEST: Lat, fire this moron. As an in-house attorney, I can assure you that when the company randomly brings in some former partner douchebag to head the department, the general reaction is that this guy is completely out of touch and over-compensated. He's a puppet for the board to play with, and is extremely well paid in stock options for the privilege. He has no clue what the real in-house attorneys deal with on a daily basis, the ways in which our clients annoy us, the things we love about our jobs, etc.

As an aside, talk about poor judgment. The guy wasn't hired to be a celebutard blogger. Anything interesting he writes will cause us to pass judgment on him as a professional, in his current role, or on his colleagues, etc. There's just no up-side. Which means he craves fame (he clearly doesn't need the money, even if you're offering it) and wants to prove how cool he is. I predict major failure.

REMINISCENCE, AFTER FOUR WEEKS (12.16.2010)

Look: If Lat and Mystal are silly enough to let me write a column about in-house lawyers when I've worked in-house for just ten months, then surely I can reminisce about blogging at Above the Law after just four weeks on the job. Fair is fair, guys.

So here are three thoughts, after four weeks of typing. First:

On November 15, Lat published the post announcing that my column would start in three days. Lat wrote the post; I had nothing to do with it. He promptly sent me a link to that post, telling me that we were up. I hung up the phone after finishing a business call and clicked on the link, viewing the post within ten minutes of its publication. Incredibly, the "commenters" were already out in force.

I scrolled through the comments and immediately learned that I'm (1) homophobic, (2) a failure in Big Law, (3) desperate for money, and (4) ugly.

Before I'd written a word.

Fortunately, an old friend sent me an e-mail providing emotional support: "Hey, Mark, you're not homophobic."

Second…

In the four weeks since I actually started writing stuff, the most frequent critique of my work has been (mercifully, I suppose) that I have an odd writing style, because I write many paragraphs that are only one sentence long.

That critique is correct: I do use many one-sentence paragraphs. And, on reflection, that's odd, because when I write in traditional media, I write traditional multi-sentence paragraphs. But somehow long paragraphs seem less appealing in blog posts, which are, by their nature, so short.

In any event, you'll have to deal with it.

Because that's how I write these things.

And I'm at the keyboard.

Not you.

Got it?

Third:

Writing this column for Above the Law, and keeping it funny, is going to be awfully hard. Who will I tease?

I can't tease my employer (even if I wanted to, and I don't) for obvious reasons.

I can't tease law firms (even if I wanted to, and I don't), because my employer is the world's leading insurance broker for law firms. If I start making fun of the clients, there'll be brokers with pitchforks lined up at my office door.

So that leaves only one object for humor: Me.

(At least it's an easy target.)

It's gonna be a long, self-deprecating slog.

I can hardly wait.

COMMENTS

MEAN GIRLS: Homophobic or not, you are still (1) a failure in Big Law, (2) desperate for money, and (3) ugly.

MEAN GIRLS: But I'm pretty sure you're homophobic.

J777: You have to have a thick skin to read this blog, much less write for it. About 3/4 of the comments should be deleted. Or perhaps 3/4 of the commenters should be deleted? (Excellent writing so far, BTW.)

AATIPS: I'm not surprised that you've run out of things to say, given that you've only been in-house since lunchtime last Tuesday. But I would have thought you'd have scruples enough just to go quiet until you came up with some revelation about how the in-house cafeteria compares to a law firm's cafeteria, or how wide you set the margins on Word documents.

And yet here you are with another post that doesn't tell anyone anything they don't already know: It's going to be a long slog, alright.

JETSAM

MY WISTFUL DAY

I'm fast approaching the two-year anniversary of my move in-house, and I don't often look back wistfully on my former life as a partner at one of the world's largest law firms.

But last Tuesday was different. Please bear with me.

For 25 years, I practiced, and tried to develop new business, in the complex litigation space. I worked at a firm that wasn't interested in defending companies in one-off pharmaceutical product liability or Automobile Dealers' Day In Court Act cases. Those cases were frequently insured (and the carriers often wouldn't agree to pay our rates) or otherwise too small to fry. But the moment one of those silly little cases morphed into something real—a mass tort or a Dealers' Act class action—we were champing at the bit to get retained.

It's tricky to market into that niche: "I don't want your 'drug caused an injury' case until you have 1,000 of them. Then, even though I spurned you before, I want you to hire me to displace (or, at a minimum, supplement) your existing counsel on the cases." The existing lawyer already knows the facts and the law, and ignorant you, who showed no interest before, now wants to butt in. How do you pitch that?

I figured the answer was to develop a reputation at the point where small cases transmogrified into big ones: the filing of a class action, the filing of enough cases that a motion for multidistrict litigation (or "MDL") became likely, and advising companies how to respond when "60 Minutes" or "20/20" called for an interview. I thus spent an awful lot of time writing about those topics and speaking at any conference that would give me a lectern and a worthwhile audience.

Then I moved in-house and changed my focus entirely. Until last Tuesday . . .

Last Tuesday, the general counsel of an international company called me. The company was being joined as a defendant in a bunch of cases that fell precisely into my private-practice power alley. The GC knew my reputation from private practice, had poked around on-line, and realized that he (or she) needed a lawyer with just my experience. Because I was no longer available, would I spend a few minutes kibitzing about who the company should retain to defend litigation that once was small but now was large?

What a wonderful set of cases they were! Class actions! An MDL! Statewide co-ordinated proceedings! Thorny constitutional issues! We chatted generally about the cases and specifically about lawyers who might be able to lead the defense. I was generous with my time, because my juices were flowing. I got off the phone all pumped up.

If I were still in private practice, what a day this would have been! Get copies of the complaints! Start thinking about motions to dismiss that could save your client and make you a hero! Think hard about class certification! Gin up arguments, including novel constitutional ones, that we'd be arguing within a few months! Advise a client about the pros and cons of participating in an MDL or state court analogues! Deal with public relations issues!

I could hardly contain myself. What a day it would have been! I wiped away a tear.

What a day it would have been: Do a conflict check. Receive back a foot-high conflict clearance form that was lit up like a Christmas tree. Try, to no avail, to get your colleagues to respond to conflict clearance e-mails. Nudge the last guy in the Taiwan office daily for a response to the conflict check, and still get ignored. Apologize repeatedly to the client about your inability to actually accept the work.

Decide you'll start doing the work before every last conflict cleared—with the client's consent, of course, but aware that you might have to give up the work (and forfeit any related fees) if a conflict proved insoluble.

And then it would turn out the client wanted to negotiate discounted fees. Run endless bureaucratic traps for weeks trying to satisfy the competing desires of your exciting new client and your existing partners.

Fight with your colleagues about which decent associates can be spared to work on your new matter.

Fly around the country like a lunatic to handle emergency hearings and meet with witnesses. Don't see your family for weeks on end. Sleep too little. Eat poorly, mainly at the Gate Eight Cafe at Reagan National.

Suffer through endless silly phone calls with opposing counsel who won't agree to the dates or locations of depositions. Meet and confer with a series of sociopaths about meaningless discovery spats.

Read opposing counsel's motions seeking to imprison your client, disbar you, and sanction your grandmother and your cat.

Have your bills cut randomly by an unthinking computer and a college kid who has to prove his value by hacking fees.

At year-end, transmit your firm's message that rates are going up seven percent across-the-board, and have the client tell you that times are tough, and fees are frozen.

What a day it would have been, indeed.

On reflection, I'm staying in-house.

VIVE LA DIFFÉRENCE: LIFE AS IN-HOUSE VERSUS OUTSIDE COUNSEL

INSIDE STRAIGHT: VIVE LA DIFFÉRENCE

When I moved in-house ten months ago, my phone started to ring off the hook—and not just from folks I hadn't spoken to in years, who thought that I'd now be itching to retain them. I also got a few calls from people who were simply curious about the difference between working in-house and working at a law firm.

One of the differences is self-evident: You arrive at work on your first day at a corporation, and you devote that day entirely to ministerial crap. You spend an hour completing immigration forms, spend an hour having your photograph taken for various ID cards, fill out your health insurance and retirement benefit forms, create passwords for a dizzying array of computer databases, set up your computer to receive corporate training, and then realize that everyone is heading home.

Ouch! Another wasted day! You didn't do a minute of billable work. You might as well have been on vacation today, because you did nothing that could legitimately be charged to a client.

But wait…

For the first workday since, in my case, October 15, 1984, you did not have to fill out a timesheet. For reasons not entirely clear, today would not be recorded as a vacation day. This day somehow, miraculously, counted as work.

No timesheets. Thank the lawdy.

There are other differences between private practice and in-house life that are less self-evident. These include, for example, your level of concern for the work quality of the folks who are helping you.

At a law firm, senior lawyers give junior lawyers a chance—or two, or maybe three—to prove themselves. If the junior lawyer's work is top-notch, then you clutch that lawyer to your breast, never letting him or her escape. If the junior lawyer's work is okay, you work with the lawyer a couple of times, to see if he or she is educable. If the junior lawyer's work is bad, you cut that person out of your life.

In the law firm environment, cutting a person out of your life is generally easy and painless. You just don't ask the junior person to help you any more.

Voilà! No muss, no fuss, and no more crappy drafts!

And the junior lawyer pays only the gentlest price for this. The lawyer is not fired. The lawyer simply goes on to work with other people. Some of those other people may actually approve of the lawyer's work. If so, a decade from now, you may be surprised to see your junior colleague join you as a partner.

Even if the junior lawyer impresses no one, the firm probably won't decide to fire the lawyer for years. Your decision not to work with the junior lawyer had essentially no ramifications.

Not so in-house.

At a corporation, you'll have some small and immutable number of "direct reports," who make your department run, and for whom you are responsible. If you're unhappy with the quality of work performed by someone in your team, you can't easily excise that person from your life. For the most part, you have two choices: Train the person, or "transition him out" (which is corporate-speak for "fire him").

Firing a person, unlike choosing not to work with a person (and thus simply foisting him off on your partners), is a big deal; only the most heartless would fire someone casually. The realities of corporate life force you to work with your folks pretty closely.

I'm not passing judgment here. Maybe the law firm approach is too callous; maybe the in-house approach is too forgiving; maybe I'm missing the ball completely.

But if you're thinking about moving to an in-house position, you should be aware that the structure of your professional life—whom you support, and who supports you—can be far more rigid in a corporation than it is in a large professional partnership.

Vive la différence.

COMMENTS

GUEST: The guy can write, and this is an interesting topic. Why does it seem like he used a dozen paragraphs to say absolutely nothing?

IN-HOUSE GUEST: As a fellow in-house attorney, I welcome this column and look forward to your advice and that of other in-house lawyers who comment. I hope that in time you will write at least an article or two on a phenomenon I have encountered in corporate attorney-client relations after nine years of in-house practice with three different employers. There are two categories of clients law firm attorneys may never see, who corporate attorneys try to avoid. The first are the clients who fear the advice they may get from lawyers and therefore try to avoid us. These clients view us as impediments to their business and try to get corporate initiatives through under the legal radar screen, to avoid them from being slowed down or stopped by us on account of those pesky things we call "laws." The second group of clients comes from an opposite pole. These clients are risk averse to an extreme, do not trust their own judgment and know we in-house lawyers are free of charge to their business units. They therefore call or e-mail us seemingly every time they want to sign any document, send any e-mail, talk to any person, blow their noses, wipe their . . . . well, you get my point. In an environment where there is always plenty of work to be done and triage is required every day, the challenge is to get your clients to come to you—but not every minute. Striking this balance without annoying people can be tricky. I'd love to hear your thoughts and those of other readers.

WHY: "I also got a few calls from people who were simply curious about the difference between working in-house and working at a law firm."

Protip: Those people were just sucking up to you, too. They just wanted to be more subtle about it (evidently it worked).

BENEDICK: What Mark left out of his first-day description was that, when he realized everyone was heading home, he probably wasn't among them (or if he was, he wasn't going home simply to crack open a cold one and unwind).

In-house litigators (I am one) increasingly work very long hours—this is particularly the case for those of us at global companies. I have clients and in-house colleagues (and cases and outside counsel) around the world, which frequently means after-hours (or before-hours) conference calls.

I do manage to get out of the office at a pretty reasonable hour, but I then do a lot of working from home (and while on vacation). The key difference from when I was in a law firm (aside from no longer billing time) is the kind of work that I'm doing, not how much time I spend working.

If I'm up late, it's no longer finalizing a summary judgment brief or preparing for an argument. It's more likely trying to coordinate a document-production strategy involving five subsidiaries in five time zones, four countries, and three languages. Or trying to convince skeptical senior management (who only have time to talk to me for 5 minutes at 2:00 a.m. EST because they're in meetings in Japan) why it makes sense to spend $X million to settle a case we all agree is frivolous.

VIVE LA DIFFÉRENCE, PART II

Which lawyers are important at large law firms? Let's set aside for a moment the guy who controls the tickets to the loge at the Lakers' games, and think more generally. Who matters at law firms?

First, partners with big clients. Those folks have power. They influence decisions within the firm, have the capacity to push new people into the partnership, and have work to share with others, which keeps the others busy.

Partners with clients count. Who else counts?

Great lawyers. Sometimes, you just need a really smart person to help you solve a problem for a client. Good lawyers are generally adept at identifying great lawyers. If you're a great lawyer, your colleagues at a big firm will come to you for advice.

(Sometimes, the lawyers with big clients are also great lawyers; sometimes, not. That should be self-evident. It is, in any event, grist for some other mill.)

Who counts in in-house legal departments?

Not lawyers with clients.

Every in-house lawyer has a client—the corporation for whom she works—so attracting clients is no longer a relevant metric.

How about great lawyers?

Maybe, maybe not.

First, it's awfully hard for business folks to identify great lawyers. A good tax lawyer can quickly identify a great tax lawyer; it takes just a couple of hours of interaction to distinguish Einstein from Bozo. But a good tax lawyer can't identify a great dentist. The tax lawyer knows whether the dentist hurts him and knows whether the dentist seems like a nice guy, but the tax lawyer is clueless whether dental work is actually necessary and performed properly.

It's hard to identify greatness outside of your area of expertise.

What's the likelihood that someone in a corporate business unit—a head of sales, or a head of research and development, or someone with a Ph.D. in mechanical engineering—can identify a great lawyer? Not so high.

Business folks in a corporation may not be able to identify great lawyers, so great lawyers may not automatically be in demand.

Moreover, business folks may not always want to identify great lawyers.

Don't get me wrong: Responsible business people want good legal advice, and they will seek it out.

But a less responsible business person—the sales rep with some cockamamie, and probably illegal, get-rich-quick scheme—may not be searching for a great in-house lawyer. The sales rep may be searching for the weakest link in the legal department—the lawyer who will unthinkingly sign off on anything—who is the easiest route for obtaining any necessary "approval from legal."

What, then, makes in-house lawyers valuable?

Two things: First, you must get along with the business folks. You must be sufficiently personable that the business people will be willing, or maybe even anxious, to give you a call. (Satisfying this requirement is particularly tough for me.)

Second, you must be a problem-solver. You can't be widely known as the lawyer who always says "no." In a corporate setting, developing that reputation will quickly make you lonelier than the Maytag repairman.

Instead of being the person who says "no," you must be the person who says, "No, but. . ." You must identify legal problems in business proposals, analyze alternative possibilities, and give the client two or three alternatives that could achieve the client's goals with less legal risk.

That's an attractive in-house lawyer.

Those characteristics—people skills and problem solving—that corporations value do not match up precisely to the characteristics that large law firms treasure.

If you're considering making a move from a firm to the in-house world, you might consider how your skill set matches the implicit demands likely to be imposed by your new employer.

COMMENTS

GUEST: This is useful and duly self-effacing. This is the first adult-level post I've read on here in a while.

NO: I cannot quite figure out. What it is that makes reading this column so annoying. Maybe I will figure it out at some point.

PROLATARIAT: Before you go praising the golden musings of ATL's in-house "special" blogger, I hope you all realize that this isn't new information, it is just common sense.

> **FROZT:** That's kind of what a musing is. It's why you rarely hear the final results of investigations or scientific studies referred to as a musing.

WENTINHOUSE: I think what you said is true for in-house attorneys in smaller companies where the legal department is small. When you get to bigger in-house departments (think Microsoft or Exxon), the "being a great attorney" quality becomes important again as your customer is frequently a more senior attorney on staff, not a marketing, finance or other business person in the company.

IN-HOUSE LAWYER: The General Counsel of a Fortune 500 company where I used to work in-house once said, "Clients don't know good; they only know fast." I think this is generally true of less sophisticated clients. Smarter, more experienced and better educated clients (think Wharton and Harvard MBAs with 10+ years of corporate experience under their belts) do know when they're getting good legal advice and when they're not. And those are the clients in-house lawyers should most want to work for—the clients who challenge us and make us better lawyers.

MSMMMSMMPLS: Herrmann's comments are about as revelatory as stating that most cars need fuel to make them go. What's not elementary about this? I think in-house counsel insights of substance would be valuable—but this is barely pap.

GUEST: OK, maybe his points are common sense, but sometimes people get "off-track" when they start thinking there is some secret complicated answer when there isn't one. If you are at a firm, start thinking about how to get clients and build specialized legal knowledge. If you are in-house, start building relationships with other business groups and learning how to solve business problems (not something that just comes naturally; it requires some experience). The answers may be simple, but if they are correct, then they are correct, and you will find more success focusing on those points than by searching for some mysterious answer. Also, the objective of the post may be to get the ball rolling, so in-house attorneys can add experiences and advice in the comments. If you have something that is counterintuitive or more helpful that you could share, please do.

IN THE HOUSE: You are absolutely correct that problem-solving is highly valued in an in-house environment. I've run into many in-house lawyers (usually newly arrived from law firms) who think that explaining why something cannot or should not happen in a highly detailed memo is a mark of a great lawyer. Most clients understand the answer is sometimes "no," but they want you to work with them to try to get to "yes." They also want you to respect their prerogative to make business decisions with which you may not agree after you've provided your input. Know and understand your role in the process and you will do well in-house. I'd argue that anyone who can't make this adjustment, their total mastery of securities law or whatever notwithstanding, isn't actually a great lawyer.

WHERE LAW IS NOT KING

There are many advantages to working for a corporation instead of a law firm: You learn a business from the inside out; work regularly with business people, rather than other lawyers; are spared the daily insanity of quibbling with opposing counsel about whether the deposition will be taken in Houston or Denver; can often avoid blowing up the week between Christmas and New Year's because some clown dropped a TRO on your client on December 24; and on and on.

But it's much too easy to write about that. So I've decided to explore the other side of the coin: I've asked several litigators who recently went in-house what they missed most about private practice. I generally heard two things in response.

First: Many litigators enjoy litigating. A common refrain is this: "I miss doing it!"

"I can't believe I have to sit in the back of a courtroom and watch other guys give opening statements. And over lunch, I'm just kibitzing from the sidelines, hoping the trial lawyers listen to my suggestions."

Or, "There's a huge difference between flying to Chicago to argue in the Seventh Circuit and flying to Chicago to watch your outside counsel argue. One is a real event. For the other, you call an old friend to set up dinner the night before, watch the end of Monday Night Football in your hotel room, and then roll down to the courthouse in the morning. Your pulse rate never goes above 60."

If you love the spotlight (as many litigators do), you may not like stepping out of it. You may miss doing it....

Second, some people say that they miss working at a place where law is king.

At a law firm, law is king.

Raise a legal issue, and everyone's interested. People mull it over in their offices or chat about it over lunch. People may do a little on-line research (on their own time, out of interest) to get a better grasp of the issue. The firm celebrates favorable jury verdicts on its website and in its press releases and promotional materials. The managing partner sends around memos bestowing kudos on the champions.

At a corporation, law is not king. Or queen, or jack, or ten. Law is a department.

At a law firm, when the court grants your motion to exclude the other side's expert, you give each other high fives. You go out for a celebratory beer.

In a corporate law department, when your client wins a jury trial, the folks in the law department congratulate each other for having picked the right case to try and having staffed it correctly. But then you report the victory to the business unit, and you may hear, "That's nice. But our stock price is down today."

It's all a matter of emphasis.

Corporations celebrate things, but often not the same things that law firms celebrate.

People go to law school for different reasons. Some think it's a route to a good career. Some think it's the best alternative, because they can't stand the sight of blood and don't want to be unemployed Ph.Ds. Some figure they'll put a law degree to use in some non-legal way. But some go to law school out of genuine interest and may well prefer to work in an environment in which law is king.

So do a little soul-searching before moving in-house. Think about your likes and dislikes. And bear in mind that, if you make the switch, you may miss two things about your old life: Doing it, and working in a place where law is king.

COMMENTS

COMMON CENTS: Mark, you are seriously in a downward spiral of navel gazing. Seriously, I'm a young in-house attorney, and I find your "revelations" humorous—if for no other reason than you come across like the corporate law equivalent of a 1L; "wow, dudes, listen to what I just realized!" In other news, I've noticed that it's colder in the winter than in the summer.

The most interesting part of your piece is the subtext at the end—that you've realized you just aren't cut out for and don't enjoy in-house practice. I'm just amazed you're so blatantly honest about this. How long until your stock options vest? Safe to assume you're gonna hit the road after that?

EPM145: Maybe you should present your own insights if you think Mark's are so uninspired. I love it when people criticize a position, opinion, legislative bill, *etc.*, and don't offer anything as an alternative. What do you miss most about Big Law?

FORMER SECONDEE: Another side of the "law is not king" point is that by going inside, you cease to be a fee earner and become a cost. That really changes the importance/priority given to your work. In a law firm, the staff orbits around the lawyers and makes sure they have all the resources to keep billing relentlessly. Not so much on the in-house front.

EGIAN: Mark, you missed the main point—your legal skills deteriorate. I know you're an in-house newbie, but that is probably the most important issue for people deciding to work in-house—your skills will deteriorate. If you're a litigator, soon you will no longer be competent (or confident) enough to go back to a real litigation practice. This applies to many areas of law as well. You become trapped and unable to transition back into private practice. Frankly, it is scary and demoralizing, especially if you liked being a "real" lawyer. In-house you're not discussing the case law as it evolves or other issues attendant to law and you become stale and then wholly obsolete.

Mark, if you ever want to go back to real law in private practice, you'll need to do it within 5 years, and even then you'll find it daunting.

> **GUEST:** I disagree. Your skills don't deteriorate, they simply shift. Your expertise moves from just the vacuum of legal analysis to that of an effective corporate advisor. Corporations aren't interested in case law, but they do want and value practical advice from their legal advisors.

One of my ongoing frustrations with law firms is that they are not adept at providing advice in the context of achieving our business objectives. In-house attorneys become experts at developing advice, and often systems and procedures that limit risk to the company while improving its path to financial success.

In general, most lawyers don't know how to make money outside of a fee agreement.

SAMIAM: Agreed. Five years after going in-house as a mid-to-senior level associate means you often come back in as a partner. Partners must give practical advice to their clients who, as "guest" points out, don't want to hear about case law. This is why partners generally leave case law research and analysis to associates. Partners might read a few cases to double-check their associates' work (and pad the bill), but their job is to give practical advice to in-house counsel or the C-level officers of a client. In-house counsel don't generally have the time (or unlimited Westlaw or Lexis-Nexis access) to do the research on their own.

All of the foregoing notwithstanding, I sometimes miss litigation in the private practice context. There is a certain intellectual challenge about crafting the legal argument, finding the "perfect" case law to support your point(s), and persuasively putting everything down on paper in such a way that the judge doesn't use your brief to cure his insomnia. There's nothing like hearing that the judge granted your motion to justify the late night(s) and weekends you spent in the office.

ANOTHER VOICE: Wow, you nailed it! After being outside counsel for 23 years, I came in-house. I would not go back (for a lot of the reasons you cited as advantages of being in-house), but watching litigation is not the same as doing litigation. Luckily, I still get to litigate as much as I want, which is great about my department—but I never thought about the "law is king" aspect, which is totally lacking.

TEXJUDGE: Out of law school I practiced briefly on my own and spent (before becoming a judge) the next 12 years in-house, the main reason initially being that, with 2 young kids, I needed a good health plan that only major companies offer. However, I grew to appreciate life in-house as I did not have to work 70-80 hours a week, put up with unreasonable partners who can fire you at any time for often whimsical reasons and spend years reaching for the nirvana of a partnership knowing that less than 25% of associates at Big Law achieve it. The work I did was interesting and I got to travel around the country giving presentations, *etc.*, and helping our company acquire new accounts. Sure, I would have made more money as a Big Law associate though, on a per-hour basis, the gap was quite small factoring in taxes. Most important, I had a life and was able to see sunrises and sunsets, play sports and spend time with the family and not have to worry about spending Christmas reviewing some dumb M and A document that no one, outside of greedy investment bankers, cares about.

ON LAWYERS' GARNITURES

Lawyers in private practice collect things.

The lawyers use those collections to adorn professional biographies that appear on firm web pages. The garnitures generally include (1) experiences (which are trumpeted in the form of "deal lists" or "representative engagements"), (2) publications, and (3) speaking engagements. After you pick off a case in the Second Circuit, or publish an article in the *National Law Journal*, or give a talk to an industry group, you go home and polish your on-line image; you update your bio.

When you're in private practice, it makes sense to do this. You are, after all, trying to attract business, so your on-line bio is essentially your calling card. Strangers may visit the website and see your bio; you may send a link to potential clients; you may print the bio and hand it out during a beauty contest.

In an odd way, for many people, assembling these collections marks the passage of time. ("2005? I was up to my eyeballs in MDL 1150." "1997? That was when we tried the *Doe* case.") You're nuts, of course, if those professional moments even begin to approach the significance of truly important stuff—marriage, the birth of a child, a death in the family—but those events mark time, in the same way that changing seasons do.

Ultimately, who's to say that collecting stuff is wrong? People collect stamps, and coins, and books, and they take some pleasure there. Maybe collecting experiences, or achievements, fills the same psychic need. Or maybe the need to achieve, and to prove your achievements to the world, is hard-wired into many people who spent their early years in college, law school, and law firms, pursuing a succession of brass rings....

Reasonable minds can differ over the value of lawyers' garnitures. Relevant experience matters, so it makes good sense for lawyers in private practice to track that closely. Beyond that, however, personal relationships and the quality of your work largely determine how much new business you'll attract. The other stuff matters, but you do it primarily to raise your personal profile, and you deploy the results primarily around the edges. Once in a blue moon, your law review article on "naming trade associations as defendants in lawsuits pleading industry-wide conspiracies" will become the centerpiece of some pitch that you're making, but don't hold your breath. More often, you'll simply include lists of articles and speeches, or a reprint or two, in a client handout, basically to imply that, since you've written (or spoken) about a subject, you must know what you're talking about. Maybe, at the end of the pitch, you'll mention in passing that you're widely published and naturally listed in all of the usual publications that rate the country's leading lawyers. First, you collect; then, you deploy.

If you're a collector at heart—if you take some satisfaction in attaining and cataloging achievements—you may miss your hobby if you go in-house.

In-house lawyers don't collect things or, at a minimum, don't collect things as publicly as outside counsel do.

Once you're in-house, you're no longer marketing your services to the world at large. There's no reason to post your bio on your corporation's website. Your colleagues who work in business units will seek your advice for many reasons, but the quantity of your speaking engagements and quality of your publications won't be high on the list. No one will care very much if you were listed in the Best Lawyers in America or profiled in *Chambers*.

When you move in-house, you stop collecting. Gathering experience takes care of itself; after a few years at a corporation, you'll probably have a decent sense of your industry. You can continue to write articles or give talks, but you won't do this to generate business. (You may do these things for other reasons, such as to share a thought with the world or influence a public debate, to accommodate a friend or colleague who needs a speaker, or to raise the profile of your corporation or its law department. Those motivations, however, often seem less urgent than the need to attract new business that permeates private practice.)

Even if you continue to speak and write after you go in-house, there will be little need to track those accomplishments; they simply don't serve the purpose they once did.

So think about that.

Now that I'm in-house (and writing this column), I've been contacted by a fair number of folks in private practice seeking advice about whether (and how) to make a similar move. Some of those people have a knack for writing articles, being invited to give talks, and otherwise maintaining a high public profile. Those people may regret leaving private practice and thus losing the impetus to maintain their hobby—to keep expanding their collections in the future.

COMMENTS

REASON: I couldn't disagree more. Your public persona is important when you go in-house, but for different—or maybe a sub-category of—reasons vs. outside counsel.

I've been in-house for six years, and I continue to speak and write articles. While I don't post these events on my company's website, the motivation is not much different from that of outside counsel. In a company, personal branding is very important. There is a constant drive to be both a legal expert and a "business partner," whatever that means. But the politics of a corporation are such that in order to advance, you have to be seen as a leader. And people who have never met you in your own company need to know your name. The best way to accomplish this is to continue speaking and writing. Representing the company at speaking engagements has the indirect benefit of letting the people who you work with, and for, know that you are a leader. Internally, offering trainings, sharing "best practices" memos on how to "add value" to the company from a legal perspective, and speaking up in meetings with senior management are all important to career growth.

Rest assured that the nose-to-the-grindstone types become pigeon-holed as experts at what they do, but are considered incapable of driving the business forward. Soft skills, strategy creation, and image are much more important on this side of the fence.

As evidence, please note that Mark Herrmann is a VP and Chief Counsel of his company yet blogs for ATL.

GUEST: It depends on your career level. As a general counsel, you may not need to prove your expertise. As a corporate associate, it may be very desirable for a future employer to see some specialization in certain areas, particularly in companies that have very large legal departments.

I don't think it would hurt to have some Labor Relations articles on best practices for responding to unionization for certain large retailers. Or perhaps, to have experience on managing recall decisions were you to join a large consumer manufacturer.

Trade publications are good for exposure and they also keep you current—especially if you're in a really niche field (which can be supported/desired by larger companies which essentially have internal law firms).

NON-LAWYERS AS CLIENTS

I never noticed this before I went in-house, because it never made a difference to me: When you're an outside litigator, representing corporations in significant disputes, your clients are lawyers.

This may not be true for all outside lawyers. If you're representing a small business, the business may not have inside counsel, so you may report to the business people. If you're a transactional lawyer, perhaps your clients are more often business folks. But, as an outside litigator representing big companies, your client contacts are generally lawyers.

This matters. The client contacts have been through four years of college and three years of law school. That may not mean much, but it means something. Tautologically, it means that they've had lots of years of formal education. ("If I'm still dumb now, it's my fault.") Practically, it means that your client contacts have learned how lawyers think and, to some extent, the words that lawyers use. (When I was outside counsel, not all of my clients knew what an "MDL" was. If the client had the misfortune to be dragged into one of those puppies, I might have spent a little time explaining. But basically all of my client contacts knew what the words "complaint," or "discovery," or "summary judgment" meant. We shared a common vocabulary.) And lawyers as a group probably care more about legal issues than non-lawyers do.

To be sure, outside litigators often *work* with non-lawyers. We've all had to prepare for depositions senior executives who were way too self-assured, or people whose view of the facts wasn't exactly confirmed by the documents, or witnesses who required a lot of time and effort because they were slightly slow on the uptake. But, as outside counsel litigating cases for big companies, it was typically the in-house lawyers who ultimately supervised and evaluated our work.

Once you move in-house, that is no longer true. We're the lawyers; our clients are not….

Some business folks are extraordinarily sophisticated or well-versed in the law. Others are not. Some managers graduated from top colleges and spent two years in business school. Others went into business straight from high school and rose meteorically due to their innate aptitude for business. Yet others have little formal education, are currently performing mid-level roles at small business units, and are unlikely ever to advance from there. As an in-house lawyer, you have to be sensitive to your audience when you communicate.

Among other things, don't slip into lawyer-speak. Business people want to understand what you're saying; they won't be impressed by fancy legal words or doctrines. Write, and speak, comprehensibly.

Many of the business folks are ferociously busy and not particularly interested in the details of your legal problems. Keep that in mind as you communicate. You don't need an hour-long meeting or a 15-page document to resolve a legal tangent to a business issue.

Be prepared for questions that have nothing to do with what you know. Business folks may not appreciate that you're an intellectual property lawyer and don't know anything about securities law. You're in the law department, so you're supposed to answer the legal questions. (My father immigrated to the United States from Austria and was fluent in German, French, and English. He served in World War II as a translator, and the Army naturally shipped him off to the South Pacific. When the first group of Japanese prisoners came on board his ship, my father explained to the captain: "German. French. English. A little schoolboy Latin. What do you want me to do?" The captain knew: "You're the translator. Translate.")

You're legal. You answer the legal questions. If you can't, you'd better be able to explain in plain English why you'll need to wait for advice from someone else.

(Okay, I won't leave you hanging: One of the Japanese prisoners spoke English. Dad kept him close.)

Understand that many business folks will have very little appreciation for what you do, and they may have worked with lawyers only infrequently. Your relationship with those people will be very different from your previous relationship with an in-house lawyer who knew the game. Don't be arrogant. Don't be obstructionist. And don't expect the same level of responsiveness from all business folks that you previously got from lawyers. Doing things on time and right is the name of the game in the private practice of law; that's pretty much ingrained in every decent lawyer. Not so much so with some business folks. You'd better leave yourself enough time to adjust for late responses, and you'd better put a note on your own calendar to follow up with people to remind them a few days before the deadline they're supposed to meet.

Having business people as clients can be a refreshing change of pace. It can be educational. But, more than anything else, it's different.

It's just one more way that in-house life differs from life at a firm.

COMMENTS

GUEST: "Having business people as clients can be a refreshing change of pace."

I have definitely found this to be true in many cases. Granted, it can also be frustrating to explain the same things over and over, and what is important to you isn't always important to other business groups. Working with other business groups gives you perspective on a much broader set of business issues. Often advice from outside counsel can be very two-dimensional in that it may take a stand on legal issues, without really addressing those concerns in context. The in-house attorney then needs to add the context, figure out the cost of following the advice, and determine whether the advice is practical. I have received advice from outside advisors that has made me cringe because I feel like they haven't even considered whether their advice is practical—sometimes it seems like they are just trying to CYA, providing the most conservative/literal approach possible, rather than giving me options that I can actually present to my colleagues with an assessment of the costs and risks.

CAREFUL: I wonder if outside counsel might give more realistic advice orally, in a sauna steam room (to avoid wired recording)—where nothing can be blamed on them later. If you demand it in writing, then expect CYA.

RUFUS THE III: Outside counsel's job is to provide you the law that you do not know but need to know. It's your job to (i) apply that law to your business needs and (ii) explain the inherent risk in any course of action to your business people so they can make the decision. In-house counsel = risk manager. Otherwise, you're just a paper pusher.

WILL'S YAYA: Breaking news: The sky may be blue. More groundbreaking observations on their way once they have been suitably converted to unbearably long screed.

NON: Thought this column did a pretty good job in explaining the specifics of how communicating with non-lawyers differs from communicating with lawyers, and the different expectations with respect to issues of succinctness. The general point, that certain practices require more communication with non-lawyers, is a pretty obvious one, but the column did address how that differs from communicating with lawyers in sufficient detail to be useful.

GUEST: We went through a 3-year period of transformative education; it doesn't prevent us from communicating with other human beings. Unless, of course, you couldn't communicate with ordinary human beings before you went to law school.

> **NON:** Well it's true that legal education doesn't prevent us from communicating with other human beings, but it does change our vocabulary. This article does bring up the good point that lawyers do need to realize that when communicating with non-lawyers, they will need to simplify or explain things in more detail than if they're communicating with lawyers. Though this really isn't just a lawyer thing; my engineer friends simplify their explanations and use fewer acronyms and terms of art when they're trying to explain something technical to me, who has no engineering background.

SHISH: As a businessperson, let me say that it would be nice to occasionally meet in-house lawyers who understand that their salaries are paid not only by mitigating risk, but by helping me GET STUFF DONE!

THE OTHER SIDE OF PARADISE

I've received a couple of e-mails from associates at large firms saying that these folks sit at their desks dreaming about having in-house jobs: One client instead of many competing for your time. More manageable workload. A broader range of work. Less stress. An opportunity to think strategically instead of wallowing in minutiae. No more billable hours. No more timesheets. Bliss!

Please, these correspondents ask, write a column explaining the tribulations of in-house counsel.

This is tricky. First, the in-house life is pretty good. I wouldn't want to understate the advantages. Second, I don't hide behind a cloak of anonymity when I publish these columns. If I faced any tribulations (and I don't, of course), this wouldn't be a wise forum in which to let loose. Third, my own personal experience doesn't prove very much generally, and I hear a wide range of varied reactions from others who work in-house.

But I'll give it a shot....

One client instead of many competing for your time: This is true, but largely irrelevant. The question is not the number of clients competing for your time, but the number of tasks competing for your attention. When I was in private practice, there were times when I would work for years on end for a single client (as a mass tort ramped up, played itself out, and then reached a resolution). Those were by no means recreational times. I had only one client, but I had a great deal of work.

So, too, in-house. Although you'll theoretically have just one client, you'll have many internal clients—business folks in different business units, or within a single business unit, clamoring for your time, or your colleagues in the legal department coming to you for help. You'll still occasionally have fierce, and competing, demands on your time. Having just one "client" doesn't necessarily change the demand for your services.

More manageable workload: This depends. The head of litigation at a large pharmaceutical company (formerly a partner at an AmLaw 50 firm) tells me that he works harder now than he did in private practice. It's now seven days per week, every week, which is worse than the old life. But another person who recently moved in-house to help manage litigation at a different pharmaceutical company tells me that the whole in-house staff works 8:30 to 5:30, five days per week, period. Overall, the evidence (both anecdotal and the few empirics that I've seen) suggests that in-house life is less burdensome (perhaps in part because the crises can be handed to outside lawyers), but, as they say in the advertisements, your experience may vary.

A broader range of work: It depends on your job. A corporate lawyer serving a business unit is likely to become a generalist, being asked to handle whatever legal works needs doing in the business. But an in-house labor lawyer handling EEOC complaints may face a very different environment.

Moreover, some people are suited to handling a broad range of work and others are not. You can't be a specialist in everything. Folks who take comfort in knowing the details of every aspect of every matter may prefer life as a specialist. Folks who don't mind being set adrift may prefer working as generalists.

No matter your disposition, an in-house lawyer will live in only one industry, and only one business in that industry. If you want to think broadly about some set of issues or pursue a career in matters that cut across clients, it doesn't make sense to commit yourself to a single client. (I'm thinking, for example, of someone who wants to specialize in securities litigation. It would be a rare and unfortunate client indeed that had a steady diet of 10b-5 fraud cases brought against it. If you'd like to be a 10b-5 defense lawyer, it's unlikely that you could pursue that career in-house.)

Less stress: Different stress, anyway. Your clients in the C-suites may be quite demanding. Closing deadlines exist whether you work at a corporation or a law firm. Cases still go to trial and folks still pay close attention to the results. (At corporations where in-house lawyers try cases, the stress of trial is the same as in private practice. At corporations where in-house litigators supervise outside trial counsel, the stress level is quite different.) Moreover, in-house lawyers' days are occupied by internal meetings and attention to internal projects that outside lawyers are freed from.

An opportunity to think strategically: Again, it depends on your job. Higher-level in-house lawyers are further removed from the day-to-day aspects of particular issues. Those folks may think more strategically about legal issues. The percentage of your work that's strategic, rather than focused on particular projects, will vary by position. And remember: You can't do everything. People who are thinking strategically are unlikely to know the details of particular projects. Different people will have different tastes in jobs.

No more billable hours: This will probably be true. I'm told that some corporations do gently monitor lawyer time to allocate legal costs across business units, but I suspect that's a small minority of companies. For the most part, an in-house job frees you from the burden of billable hours. But that doesn't mean that corporations are ignoring the value provided by lawyers. People may not be tracking your hours, but they're surely looking to see if you're doing something productive. Being productive may be much harder than billing a few hours.

No more timesheets: On this, we can agree.

No more timesheets! Bliss, indeed.

COMMENTS

LIONEL: I work at a Fortune 500 IT company based in the Silicon Valley and I can tell you it's no less hours or stress than firm life, in fact perhaps more, and with a huge pay cut. The stock is doing well, but bonuses are trivial since they can get away with it in this economy (and they lied to me about this in hiring), and the "clients" are often disrespectful, don't listen to your advice, ignore company policy, deliberately conceal material facts from you, and insist that you must be available at all times–a single day off will result in snotty e-mails and calls to your cell phone.

If I had it to do over again, I wouldn't. In fact, after two Vault 20 firms and now several years in-house, that might go for law school generally, but in any event I would look VERY carefully at the corporate culture at any in-house gig you're considering. Ask questions of everyone you interview about the way they treat their attorneys, keeping in mind that they will likely be trying to be truthful while dodging the subject if the culture is less than great.

IN-HOUSE SECURE: I am in-house at a $1 billion company and love it. I leave with all the other employees at 4:45 every day, no nights or weekends. I eat dinner with my family every night and coach T-ball and soccer for my kids. I travel about once a month for mediations or trial. Work is interesting. You need to get used to the fact that lawyers are not the most important person in the company, as they were in the firm, but that is an easy adjustment. The one BIG downside for me is pay. I'm probably making half of what I would have had I stayed at my Vault 20 firm through partnership, but it is easily worth the trade-off.

IN-HOUSE: I also work in-house in litigation at a large pharma company. My thoughts:

First the Pros:

- Much better hours. 8:00-6:00 and rarely weekend work. Late night calls, etc. do occur but are manageable.
- No need to do "busy-work" like reviewing documents, preparing deposition outlines, etc.
- Largely a more strategic role (which is more interesting).
- Greater exposure to decision-makers and fewer layers to that level.

Cons:

- Need to review invoices/bills and stay inline with often unreasonable budgets. While this obviously also exists in a law firm, the repercussions are much more when in-house. If you miss the budget as outside counsel, it's no big deal if you end up winning the case. If you miss the budget and you're the in-house lawyer, you won't get your bonus. Big difference on a personal level.
- The stress is different and often worse. Rather than, "Why did you miss that document in review?" or "Why did you miss that question during a deposition?" you instead get "Why did 'you' (i.e., your outside counsel) lose that case?" While obviously many questions will overlap, your degree of "control" over the situation is much less when working in-house. Despite your requests,

your outside counsel will listen to only about half of your suggestions. You can't fire them because your GC is a golfing buddy with the firm's managing partner. As a result, you get the blame (and admittedly the reward) for events outside of your control. This can be very frustrating, especially since the client is looking for someone to blame and you're often only the messenger.

- The salary is much less. Depending on your level, you'll be kissing at least $100k good-bye compared to Big Law. In other words, you'll be foregoing an amount more than most American families make in a year (granted, you'll still be receiving six figures).

- (Often) Suburban working environments. This requires driving to work, working with more family-oriented people (who don't socialize outside of work) and succumbing to a "corporate culture." Many corporate people are there simply to wait it out until retirement. While this can be said for a few law firm employees, at a law firm there is a much stronger ethic and drive for results and to produce. Slackers at law firms often don't last very long (i.e., a year or two). Slackers at companies bounce around from job to job and don't leave until they're 65.

GUEST: One thing I think Mark didn't point out, which I think is important to highlight, is that being an in-house lawyer means having to be prepared to say yes without either the time or certainty that you had in private practice. If you say no too often or take too long to provide an answer, you'll be torn a new one. This leads me to the second crucial point—the role of an in-house lawyer is to be a business person who knows the law, not a lawyer who knows the business. If you are in Big Law and love writing 15 page memos on arcane points of law, then in-house is not for you, because when the CEO e-mails you he/she does not want to be kept waiting while you check something in a law review article.

FOULKE YU: Here's another important fact about in-house lawyers that I see play out all the time in my M&A practice–if your company gets acquired (and it happens all the time), you might find yourself "redundant" and out of a job. Of course, if you joined your company early enough, you might also get a nice payout for your stock pursuant to the acquisition. I've seen a ton of in-house lawyers get canned when their companies get acquired, though, and they don't always get a big payout (many of them join the company after it's mature and they don't get much stock, or they get it at a higher valuation).

ANONYMOUSE: I'm a former Big Law associate working for a Fortune 50 company in a large metro city. I've been in-house for 5 years and was at a Big Law firm for over 4. Would I make the switch over again? I'm not so sure. It is fewer hours overall. But as far as the workload goes, there are just fewer and fewer people here to do more and more work. I don't have one client. I have hundreds all within the business unit I work for...and with crazy deadlines. I do have a lot more independence and that I

LOVE. I also like my work on a day-to-day basis. But that's where it ends. The pay cut is H-U-G-E. I mean that I still make less than a 1st year at a Big Law firm. Yeah, that's right. Oh, and the raises...they are approximately 2% per year. Promotions? Unheard of. Non-existent and I have had stellar performance reviews. I thought the bureaucracy in a firm partnership was bad...this is SO MUCH worse. I also could not agree more with what another commenter said about the clients. They ARE often disrespectful, they don't listen to your advice, ignore company policy, deliberately conceal material facts from you, and then expect you to clean up the mess even after you advised them not to make it. I hate working with clients that are laypeople and have no respect for legal advice.

They both suck. But in the end I think I'd rather get paid more and work more than be totally overworked, underpaid and underappreciated.

GUEST: I arrived late to Mark's columns, but he is to be commended. This post and the many great comments that it generated amount to the most useful thing I have seen on ATL. The commentator who said "if you're in-house, you really should be interested in the company's business" nailed it. The key is to find an industry or niche that you really want to learn about, rather than pursuing an in-house role for the sake of avoiding the billable hour or leaving at 5.

In my case, I went in-house with a fund after 5 years in NY Big Law. Both comp and hours are considerably better. Trade-off is giving up the chance at the brass ring and the security of law firm life, but that's a trade I was happy to make.

IN-HOUSE CAREER PATHS

Career paths are easy at big law firms: As an associate, stay fully occupied doing great work, and become a partner. As a junior partner, stay fully occupied doing great work, and become a powerful partner. As a senior partner, generate enough business to keep you and others fully occupied, and become an even richer and more powerful partner.

These things may or may not be attainable, but everyone understands the career path.

Things are much trickier in-house. Corporations tend to have fewer lawyers than big law firms do, and in-house law departments tend to be flatter. Turnover tends to be less common. Six or eight people often report up to a single supervisor. In that environment, staying fully occupied and doing great work may not move you up the ranks. You can be fully occupied doing great work, but your boss is competent, happy in her job, not close to retirement age, and in good health. She's going nowhere, so you have nowhere to go in the corporation.

The corporation can actually be very good to its lawyers—investing in leadership and management training, using incentive or equity compensation, and employing other tools for recognizing achievements—but still fall short in actually creating career paths that make sense.

How do corporations create career paths for their in-house lawyers?

Corporate law departments tend to answer that question in two ways.

First, in-house lawyers can often "graduate" from the law department into the business. "You've worked diligently as our in-house real estate lawyer for five years. Congratulations! We're promoting you to being a site selection specialist who will work in the business unit to pick locations for our new stores."

That route can occasionally be a happy one. Lawyers who work in-house will naturally tend to learn the business in which they work, and they may develop an interest in working on the revenue-production side of the organization. But that's not a particularly satisfying career path for someone who went to law school because he wanted to be a lawyer. The corporation may view moving "up" into the business as a promotion, but the switch may involve changing the lawyer's career aspirations.

The second way that in-house law departments create career paths is by giving lawyers "stretch projects"—latching a specialist lawyer onto a different lawyer (or business person) to permit the specialist to learn new skills. For example, an intellectual property lawyer could be asked to serve as the business counsel for a small business unit, supported by one of the full-time counsels to another business unit. This would give the IP lawyer a chance to work more closely with his business (and inventors) and to learn the contract, employment, and other issues that arise in the business.

Stretch projects can be a win-win situation for the lawyer and the corporation. The lawyer learns more skills, and the corporation develops a more talented employee.

But that doesn't overcome the inherent limits on career paths imposed by a pyramidal structure—unless a job opens up, there's nowhere to go (except to a different corporation, which hardly serves the employer's interest).

Law firms, too, have pyramidal structures, and it's plainly not possible for the hordes at the bottom all to rise to the top. But it's easier for law firms to maintain the fiction of unlimited career opportunities, insisting that the partnership is open to all qualified associates and that a partner can always improve her lot through superior performance. Without the luxury of that fiction, in-house law departments must think more creatively about how to keep their lawyers satisfied with the progress of their careers.

COMMENTS

GUEST: When a corporation is unable to promote an in-house lawyer (because there is no open position), that person will likely move to another company. What I have observed is that most in-house lawyers who move up in position have to move from company to company to do it. If a corporation wants to keep talented individuals it will either have to open up positions for them (so they can progress in their careers) or watch them leave for a different company.

GUEST: Of course the down side is that the pyramid gets narrow at the top.

Say, for example you're assistant general counsel and the only step higher is for you go get promoted to General Counsel. The corporation can pay you more if they want to keep you, but the only way you get promoted is for the GC to leave.

The corporation might not want to lose you, but it's understood that you might look at a GC job elsewhere. The issue is that you'll usually end up taking a step down. A 2nd tier Assistant GC at a large corporation will more often than not end up taking a GC job at a smaller corporation. Then you move back up as a GC.

GUEST: As for getting learning ("stretch") experiences, my experience is that this is usually not too difficult when you are in-house. Managers don't usually have any problems with people who want to take on extra projects and help out in new areas. This is different from law firms that may feel pressure to keep the number of people working on a project/case limited (due to cost/relationship with client). I actually find that I can control what types of experiences I have and choose the types of projects I work on much better in-house than when I was in Big Law.

LATINTHUNDER: Yes, if only in-house legal departments were as good as law firms at laying out career paths, perhaps they would have the same fantastic morale and low turnover law firms do.

RECENT IN-HOUSE GUY: Don't forget the other, more positive side of the coin: a more limited career path means more security if you like what you are doing and want to just keep doing it.

Speaking as a recently minted in-house attorney (having made the jump from Big Law six months ago), I like the fact that I don't have to think constantly about how I am going to "advance" up the ladder in one year, or three, or five. In my new position I don't really get the opportunity to do "cutting edge" legal work, but my deals are manageable, my income is low six-figures, I have no billable requirement, I rarely work in excess of 40 hours a week, and I have a lot of time to live a life outside of work. I would just as soon keep going this way, and it would not be possible to do in the typical "up or out" environment of a law firm.

Will I get bored? Who cares? It's not like I have to spend a lot of my time at my job, and it pays the bills. Ask my colleague, who has been in my group for 10 years without much in the way of "advancement," how he likes his low stress, six-figure salary, and six weeks of true, paid vacation every year.

Advancing is just another word for "too much stuff to do."

GUEST: Being in-house gives you more options about your career path. You can be aggressive about moving up, which requires a bigger time commitment and more stress, or you can enjoy the stability and lifestyle benefits.

RECENT IN-HOUSE GUY: I know plenty of people (many of them my former Big Law colleagues) who would be bored to tears by my new job and would rue the day they left all that income, etc. on the table. Good for them, although I also know that theirs doesn't seem to be the way to happiness and fulfillment. To each his or her own.

THE ABSENCE OF GRIPING

At big law firms, people gripe. It's a way of life.

Junior associates gripe about being condemned to do scutwork. Senior associates complain about friends having been screwed out of partnership. Junior partners bellyache about not being invited to participate in client pitches. Senior partners grouse about their peers, who don't work very hard and aren't very good lawyers, being paid too much. The law firm's "owners"—the half-dozen guys who actually run the joint—moan that all those other lawyers should quit their whining and get back to work. And everyone kvetches about opposing counsel, unreasonable clients, and working too many hours.

(You'll note that nobody b*tches about anything. I offer the preceding paragraph as evidence that we needn't degrade the level of discourse to express ourselves.)

At corporations, this just doesn't happen. People occasionally whine, of course—there's a reason why they call it "work"—but griping is not the order of the day, every day, year in and year out.

Why not?

Perhaps it's the size of our teams. If a typical in-house lawyer is one of six or eight people reporting to a single boss, it's dangerous to carp too much. We're a small group, and word could get around.

Perhaps it's our longevity as a team. At law firms, cases (and transactions) come and go. Lawyers work with each other intensely for a few months (or, for big litigation matters, years) and then move on to work in other teams. At a corporation, we're bound together for a long, long time. A small band of in-house litigators will be handling all of the company's litigation until people change jobs, leave the company, or die. The same is true for in-house M&A lawyers. If you're likely to be working with the same people for many years, complaining can be dangerous business.

Perhaps it's the nature of our adversaries. At a law firm, high-testosterone lawyers who hammer the other side on a deal or a case may (unfortunately) be respected for their antics. In a corporate environment, people on the other side of a transaction may well be our customers; it pays to be civilized to them. If you badmouth the other side of a deal to your client in sales, the client may blame a lost opportunity on your bad attitude. Depending on a corporation's industry, even the corporation's opponents in litigation may be customers or potential customers.

Perhaps attitudes are simply perceived differently at corporations and law firms. Many people choose to be lawyers because they like arguing and make their career choices to match their personalities. People choose to work at corporations for many different reasons, but not often because they view their quarrelsome nature as a professional attribute.

Perhaps our jobs are better. If we have in fact reached nirvana by moving in-house, then we naturally wouldn't complain as much as those sorry others in our profession who remain trapped inside the barbed wire at law firms.

Or perhaps it's just me. I moved up through the ranks of a big law firm, so I saw (and heard) it all over the course of a couple of decades. I entered in-house life relatively late in the game, and not at a junior level, so perhaps I've simply lacked exposure to the realities of in-house life, or maybe I'm hopelessly out of the loop.

But, if fellow Big Law alums who've moved in-house share my perception, I'll be curious to hear their hypotheses as to why in-house lawyers grumble less than their outside peers.

COMMENTS

WORLDACCORDINGTOGRIPE: Dear Mark—I'm sure people gripe at your firm; you're just not included because they gripe about you.

SMALL-TIME PARTNER: My own experience is that in-house lawyers do gripe a ton, but about different issues. They gripe about corporate politics, boring dead-end jobs and pay. It's human nature to gripe. If you take a griper out of a 200K, 2000 hr associate job and stick him/her into a 200K, 9-5 job, the griper will love it at first, then gradually find stuff to complain about. I have worked in both environments, and I often find corporate lifestyle closely mimics "Office Space." I love the movie, but can't function in that environment. As crazy as it sounds, I feel that a law firm attorney has much more control over his life. I am a small firm partner (of the owner kind). I gripe (at the kitchen table) about some of the difficult personality issues of my partners and a little bit about associates', but overall being a partner/owner, i.e., being in control, is something that can deliver satisfaction.

INTERNET ATTORNEY: Having grown up in-house, I can attest that there is plenty of griping by the lower ranks in the legal department. But it's usually the same type of griping that all employees of a company do—Mike in accounting is a douche, we don't get enough vacation, blah, blah, blah. New attorneys fresh from the firm also complain about having to type their own letters and send their own mail because they're not usually afforded an assistant or paralegal—and if the department has one, he/she has her own responsibilities that doesn't include getting you coffee. Once you get to the level of being able to influence company policy the griping begins to stop. Although after 7 years in-house going from staff attorney to GC of a small company, I still have the occasional gripe session. It's good to vent sometimes.

DIGG: The level of discontent is unlikely to vary significantly between the two settings. In more intimate work environments, it's just less likely to be expressed. It's the difference between, for example, dating your cousin when you have a small extended family versus dating your cousin when you have a large extended family. Trust me, the latter is easier than the former.

ALE: Honestly, I think in-house is just a better job in so many ways. I was a paralegal in-house before law school and am now a Big Law junior associate. The emergencies, the fire drills, the supplemental briefing due Monday at 11 am–these are the firm's problem. In-house, you call your firm to do the stuff you don't have time or desire for. In-house, you have many and varied clients, and in my experience are less accountable to particular clients (it's not like you have to do client development) to where if you prioritize one over the other (letting one, say, wait until next week), it's not a big deal.

I think the level of griping also depends on how well the company is doing. When my company went through mergers and various reorgs, people, lawyers included, were pretty unhappy. Not so much when the stock price was skyrocketing.

GUEST: I have also noticed that people complain much less in-house than at firms. In fact, in retrospect most of my complaining continues to be with friends who are still at my old firm...about that firm. I think there are a few reasons for this—life is just a little more relaxed and flexible in-house (you don't feel backed into a corner all the time). Also, your value to the company is judged differently. In a firm, it is all about the billables. You can be a total anti-social jerk and still succeed. In a company, how you work with others can determine your success ... if you are a miserable jerk, nobody is going to go out of their way to help you when you need information or action items from them. Also, you will be invited into decision-making opportunities more often, if you are perceived as a team player. Ultimately, this results in a more collegial and positive environment. The law firm model does nothing to curb bad behavior— in some cases they seem to promote it. When you go to work and everybody treats you like crap (because everybody else is treating them that way), then you are going to be miserable and more likely to want to complain about everything. I think collegiality (or lack of collegiality) has a lot to do with the level of complaining.

ABC: Along lines suggested above, I wonder if people drawn to litigation gripe more because they are by nature adversarial–that's why they are litigators. It's not that transactional work isn't often adversarial; it's just that, at the end of the day, the lawyers have to work it out if the business people insist, so they are forced to find a way past differences almost every time. My own—highly anecdotal, of course – experience at a firm was that litigators griped more, about everything, than transactional lawyers.

GUEST: People don't gripe less in-house. You're just not in the circle, Mark–one of the benefits of being at the "top." I am new to in-house after coming from a big firm and all I hear about from my new fellow co-workers is 1) how underpaid we are, 2) how x, y, and z is stealing territory/responsibility for legal assignments, 3) being left out of the loop, 4) incompetent, disrespectful "clients" aka business people, 5) no chance of promotion, title change, etc. ... 6) no recognition for a job well done. What I don't hear about anymore is the crazy long nights and unbearable partners, unless someone sends me an e-mail from the firm!!

A REQUIEM FOR EPIPHANIES

In the first lawsuit (during the proxy fight), the judge held that certain statements made in proxy materials were false and misleading. That lawsuit settled. In the next lawsuit (the 10b-5 class action), plaintiffs explain that precisely the same statements appeared in an annual report, and it is now settled law that those words are false and misleading. How do you avoid the devastating effect of collateral estoppel in the second case?

I solved that puzzle back in 1990. Now I've moved in-house, and I fear that I'll never solve a similar puzzle again.

Have I lost my creativity? I don't think so. Does my job still require creativity? Yes—but different kinds of creativity. This column is a requiem for a type of thinking that an in-house job—or, at a minimum, my in-house job—doesn't seem to permit....

A very few times in your life, you may have a legal epiphany: You're doing battle with a legal issue. It's insoluble; your client is toast. The issue is tormenting you as you take a shower or drive to work. The issue has infected your dreams. The client is dead, and you can't help.

And then it comes to you! It's not just an answer, but the right answer! Your position is not simply plausible, but indisputably correct! Before you were in the darkness, and now it's light! How could you ever have been so blind?

Those are great moments. I wish I could say I've had them often, but that wouldn't be true. I've had those moments maybe a half dozen times over the course of 25 years of practicing law. I wish I could say those moments bathed me in glory. I can't say that, either. I shared one of those moments (back when I was an associate) with just one partner at my small firm in San Francisco. Only the partner and I had wrestled with the issue, and only he and I saw the darkness turn to light. I shared two of those moments with very small groups of lawyers at my huge firm in Cleveland. The clients were toast; we told the clients they were toast; and then I saw the light. The clients had never really wrestled with the issues, so the clients didn't truly appreciate the epiphanies. The only ones to savor your epiphanies are you and the one or two other people who had wandered with you in the darkness.

I fear those days are gone.

Why?

First, because in-house life is different from life at a law firm. In-house lawyers are typically dealing with a higher volume of cases and have less time to wrestle with one particular case or issue. In that environment, you're less likely to have a flash of legal inspiration. (That's not to say that in-house lawyers can't add value to cases, of course. You can suggest arguments that outside counsel may have overlooked or propose editorial revisions to improve the persuasive force of a brief. But an honest-to-God epiphany—solving a legal issue that has confounded you and others for days or weeks—is hard to come by in a faster-paced, more-distant-from-the-facts-and-law environment.)

Second, you're unlikely to have epiphanies because you don't know in advance where an epiphany is lurking. If you knew with certainty that your outside law firm had analyzed a legal question and overlooked a critical issue, and that you personally would spy the solution if only you devoted a week to fretting about the matter, then you'd spend your in-house life pursuing epiphanies. But those epiphanies occur only once in a blue moon; as an in-house lawyer, you could waste decades pursuing epiphanies and never have one. Most of the time, when competent outside counsel analyze an issue, they notice what's there; your personal concentrated effort wouldn't add value.

Third, at least in my job, epiphanies are hard to come by because many of our cases are fact-bound, and the kinds of epiphanies I'm talking about involve legal issues. Lawyers frequently unearth new facts as the lawyers work with witnesses, but that's the result of spadework, not inspiration. To have a legal epiphany, you must be obsessed with a tough legal question for some period of time, and then see the light. "Working up the facts" is not the same thing as legal inspiration, and fact-bound cases aren't fertile fields for legal epiphanies.

Please don't get me wrong here: Working as an in-house lawyer requires creativity, and it requires the same diligence and dedication involved in a law firm job. But the role of "managing many cases as they move to resolution" is quite different from the role of "fretting for days, consciously and subconsciously, about this one darned issue that spells death to your client and robs you personally of any chance of victory." Until you're facing the hangman's noose in that very personal and extended way, you're unlikely to have a legal epiphany. (Why do you think I'm not an academic? Put me in a tweed jacket smoking a pipe in the library, and I'd never again have a decent thought in my life. Angst, not necessity, is the true mother of invention.)

Legal epiphanies. I've had them all too rarely in my life, and I fear that I'll never have one again. *Requiescat in pace.*

Oh, yeah: After I solved the proxy fight puzzle, I published the answer in a law review. I enlisted as co-authors the partner who was supervising the 10b-5 case (back when I was an associate), and a more junior associate who did a nice job gussying up the thesis into law review format. If you're really interested in the answer, see John M. Newman, Jr., Mark Herrmann, and Geoffrey J. Ritts, "Basic Truths: The Implications of the Fraud-on-the-Market Theory for Evaluating the 'Misleading' and 'Materiality' Elements of Securities Fraud Claims," J. Corp. L. (1995). Enjoy!

COMMENTS

AMBER: Mark—you crack me up. I enjoy an epiphany and the euphoria that comes with solving a complex problem just as much as the next gal...maybe more with my type "A" personality. But, in my opinion, your fears are unwarranted. I would worry more about becoming stagnant and resistant to challenging myself on a daily basis or whether the Rockets are going to beat the Spurs. You don't need an epiphany to get that awesome feeling of truly accomplishing something great in your legal career. You most likely are the very reason why your company stays out of hot water or closes a particular deal. And that, sir, should give you the high you seek on a regular basis.

SAMIAM: There are fewer epiphanies for in-house than outside counsel. As in-house counsel, you're not paid to have epiphanies. Rather, you're paid to do the day-to-day legal work required by your client. Bet-the-company legal thinking is why you hire outside counsel, and why that outside counsel charges you a ridiculous amount of money to do the thinking for you.

If you miss having litigation epiphanies, I suggest you get back into private practice. Even being a prosecutor won't give you them, since you'll be overworked and unable to spend a week working non-stop on a single brief or case.

ENTITLED PARTNER: Mark, you are not a potted plant. If you cannot provide legal epiphanies, you are not adding value. You should be fired.

SAMIAM: As sarcastic as Entitled Partner meant to be, he has a point. If you're a senior-level in-house counsel, it's up to you to create situations where you must think deeply and creatively. In-house counsel do not have to be just overhead. They can find ways to make or save significant money for their company, and it is these activities that will offer epiphanies, as well as possible promotion and additional remuneration. A company can hire anyone to do its day-to-day legal work, but a lawyer who truly knows the company's business and can think like the owner(s) of that business—is worth his or her weight in gold.

FROLIC

HOW TO BE A CRAPPY PARTNER

I need your help here.

I occasionally give "book talks" about my silly little ditty, *The Curmudgeon's Guide to Practicing Law*. During those talks, I explain that my book is written in the voice of a jaded old coot who rants at young lawyers about how to do their jobs. I explain that I would have liked to include in the book a chapter called, "How To Be A Crappy Partner." That chapter would have been written in the voice of a young lawyer ranting at an older one about the ways the old guy messes up his job. I didn't include that chapter because it would have required changing the authorial voice from an old coot to a young one, and I couldn't figure out how to execute the switch.

(Why are there so many great words for nasty old men, but none for nasty young ones? We have "curmudgeon," "coot," "crank," "grouch," and probably a bunch of others for the old guy. But there are so few (that you can type in public) for the younger version of that character. I propose to add "snark" to the lexicon, meaning a nasty young coot.)

If I'd been able to include the missing chapter, I would have included many examples of how to be a crappy partner. For example….

"Please don't take phone calls on unrelated matters when we're meeting in your office. I shouldn't have to sit there, cooling my jets for fifteen minutes, while you blather on to some client on an unrelated matter. Either don't take the call, or apologize to me, say that you'll call me when you're free, and let me go back to my office and do some work."

Or:

"Please don't pull the rug out from under me when you introduce me to a client. When we enter a room, everyone sees that you're the old guy, and I'm the young one, and that makes people suspicious of my judgment before we even get started. It doesn't help matters if you then introduce me as your 'associate.' That just makes people question my judgment even more. Please introduce me simply as your 'colleague.' That accomplishes exactly the same purpose without hurting my credibility. Your 'colleague' will suffice."

Or:

"Why is it that you're always calling me to meet in your office, and you're never swinging by to talk to me in mine? Is that just coincidence? Or are you so decrepit that you can't handle the stairs? Or is this really a power thing, and the way you show your superiority is to summon me to make an appearance on your turf? If you're trying to build a relationship with someone, how about treating the person like a human being? Once—just once—you swing by my office. Okay?"

Or:

"If multiple senior people are going to edit my work, why don't you clowns work out your differences before you inflict them on me? I can't have one guy telling me to expand on our third argument and highlight it in the introduction to the brief while another guy is telling me that the third argument is frivolous and I should delete the thing. I can't satisfy both of you, and I shouldn't be caught between you. Figure out what you collectively want to achieve, and then tell me. But don't put me in the middle of your fight."

You get the idea.

In fact, I suspect that you don't just get the idea, but you've got a dozen other examples that you've been itching to unload for a long time now. So lay 'em on me in the comments. (I know that there were a gazillion things that infuriated me when I was a young lawyer, but I didn't make a list, and I've basically forgotten them all by now. As I said at the outset, I need your help.)

I'm not sure what I'll use your gripes for. Maybe I'll use your ideas in book talks that I give in the future. Or, if we get enough rants to fill an entire book, maybe I'll be tempted to put pen to paper. (This is fair warning: You're giving up your copyright interest in your words when you post them in the comments.) Or maybe a few senior lawyers will read your ideas, realize that they've wronged you, and change their ways.

Or maybe we'll just read your rants and laugh until we weep.

However it plays out, it could be a lot of fun. Have at it in the "comments."

COMMENTS

DEADLINES: The most egregiously annoying thing a partner can do is sit on an assignment that he could have told you about weeks ago, and then give you a very tight deadline. This happens constantly because the partner truly believes he's so busy and/or important that he can't take 10 minutes to discuss it with you. Brutal.

> **M6:** Or because he was really waiting for someone else to become freed up to do that assignment, but once it became clear that person was not going to be available by the deadline, he figured he'd have to settle for you doing it instead.

> **GUEST:** There is a variation on the same theme that's even worse, and it happened to me often (years ago) when I worked for one particular partner. The partner would give me a tight deadline for a draft. I'd meet the deadline, and then he'd sit on the draft for two weeks. Then he'd finally read it on a Friday afternoon and tell me it needed to be completely rewritten by Monday morning.

YOUNGBLOOD:

1. Learn how to use a computer. And I don't mean get your secretary to print out your e-mails so you can read them and dictate your replies back.
2. If you blow up my weekend/vacation/wedding plans in order to get a rush memo prepared, you sure better read it, review it and send it out to the client in a similar time frame. When it sits on your desk or inbox for 10 days after you've ruined my plans for the nth time this year, it makes me want to stab out your eyes with a pencil.
3. Case law has probably changed, maybe significantly, since the last time you dealt with certain issues. I can't just use an old memo to bang out a quick response to a similar question without doing research to update and check the authority of the cites you used back in 1975.
4. No one uses bound reporters anymore. It's called Lexis/Westlaw. See also #1 above.
5. I don't want to socialize with you outside of work, and I especially don't want you eyeballing my pretty young wife after you've had your fourth scotch and soda at the firm Christmas party. Go buy a mail order bride and get a prescription for Viagra.
6. Lastly, please die or retire soon so that I can have your office/partnership/ Chihuly sculpture.

NON: "Why do you have to forward me an e-mail from the client on Friday afternoon at 5:30 that says you need an answer for the client by Monday when I can see that the original e-mail from the client was sent to you on Tuesday morning? If you could have just forwarded me the e-mail on Tuesday morning, I could have given you an answer by Thursday and I'd have some time over the weekend to work on not getting a divorce or having my kids hate me."

GUESTY GUESTY:

1. Please include me in all aspects of the case/matter and not just an ill-defined subpart without context. The quality of my work will go up, and your blood pressure will go down.

2. Please include me on calls/meetings with the client, even if I can't bill because you don't want 3, 4, or 12 lawyers billing for the call. Your paraphrase of what the client wants—without context—doesn't help me get you what you need.

3. Please be as considerate of my time as I am of yours. I know you're busy . . . but so am I. And I get yelled at if I don't bill enough hours or if I don't get home in time to kiss my kid goodnight. Don't waste my time, and don't ask me to do something without billing for it. If you don't want to bill the client, then you write it off. Don't ask me to take a hit that you're not willing to take yourself.

4. This is a job. You are my boss. Act like it.

5. You're a grown man/woman. Do not act like a child. If you don't understand something, ask me. If you need help, ask me.

6. Please say "please" and "thank you." This may be a job, and you may be my boss, but I am not your slave. I may be replaceable—but you're replaceable in my life, too.

GUEST: Don't act like I'm too stupid to know that I'm not making partner, and neither are the guys on either side of me. I'm smart; that's why you hired me. I can do the math: Each year you make 4-6 new non-equity partners out of the 100 associates that were eligible. Those 4-6 were superstars from the beginning. I'm not as good as the other 10-20 superstars who didn't make it.

Don't act like I'm too stupid to see through your "unlike other firms, we haven't had any attorney layoffs" crap. I attended half-a-dozen going away happy hours. Some of them weren't all that happy, i.e., the ones where the associate didn't have anything else lined up.

Don't brag about our tenth year of record profits while laying off associates and staff. I know how much money you make, you don't have to be a jerk about it.

Don't pretend that you care about my "professional development" when we both know you don't care if I develop into a fully functional attorney so long as I can do the meaningless tasks assigned to associates at this firm. In fact, don't pretend that you care about your clients, your associates, or the staff any more than is necessary to maximize your profits, because we both know that is exactly where your interest in us stops.

5TH YEAR ASSOCIATE: I think the absolute worst is giving an arbitrary deadline causing me to work round-the-clock, then sitting on the assignment for weeks, then returning it the day before the real deadline, requiring me to once again stay late to do something that I could have done while sitting on my hands yesterday.

Second worst – asking me to do work that is obviously unnecessary (or could be done by a paralegal) but serves the sole purpose of racking up billables.

INSIDE STRAIGHT FAN: Please don't treat me like your secretary just because I happen to be female. Please don't make me incorporate your preferred language into a draft and, then, 24 hours later, review that draft and tell me that the preferred language added at your request "is not English." (Yeah, I know. That is why I didn't write it that way.)

JUNIORASSOC:

1. If this is truly a team environment (like you told me it was when you hired me), then you should keep me in the loop. I understand that I am a junior associate, but I don't feel like I am part of team when I know nothing about our cases other than the specific tasks that are assigned to me.

2. If it's a memo to file, does it really matter if my introduction is too long, or my conclusion is too short? Wouldn't we serve our clients better by billing less time on research memos? I can understand fleshing out ideas, and even reworking paragraphs for style, but once we get to a tenth draft on a memo to file (and the only changes being made are stylistic), don't you think we have gone a little overboard?

3. If the ultimate goal at this firm is to increase revenue (and profit), and the best way to do that is to develop business, wouldn't it make sense to train associates to develop business? Take me to a pitch or two every year. Run a few simulations, where I can practice on you. In a few years, let me go out and get some business for you. Why keep the whole process a secret? If you teach me these things, I will be loyal to you forever.

4. Just because you are a great lawyer, does not mean you are a great manager. Understand your strengths and weaknesses. Do something about them. It doesn't help my morale when you give me instructions, I follow them, and you don't like the result because I should have read your mind. If I were psychic, I wouldn't be here. I'd be on TV.

5. Take some time and think about how your actions affect my feeling of self worth. I am more valuable to you when I am happy than when I am unhappy. It should bother you that most associates are unhappy. You should obsess over why that is. You should fix it.

6. When you wait 3 to 4 weeks to get me comments on a memo, I can't just jump back in and make your changes. I have to re-read the cases (because I forgot what they say). I have to reorganize my thoughts. Sure, it takes less time than it did the first time, but don't you think it would make a little more sense if you turned the memo around a little quicker (3-4 days instead of 3-4 weeks)?

INSIDE STRAIGHT FAN: Please learn how to say thank you. If you could learn to praise loudly and criticize softly, I guarantee you will get more out of your associates and support staff.

GUESTY MCGUESTENSTEIN: Don't make me sit at your desk and watch you "correct" my project by replacing words with synonyms, and then tell me to "maybe take a CLE, or something, on how to write." Jerk.

GUEST: There are actually more comments on the substance of the post than complaints about the crappiness of the column, a first I believe. Probably because MH invites the commenters to complain about something else though.

GUEST: Most of the comments have it about covered.
1. Don't use me as your secretary.
2. Don't ask me to do work and then not bill for it.
3. Don't lie/shade the truth in your communications to me in the same way you do with courts and opposing counsel.
4. Don't give me fake deadlines.

CHECK YOU REALITY:
1. Somebody who knows what the document has to say needs to go through, combine comments, and clean up the draft. As between you and me, that's not me. You have a secretary, too; work with him or her, but it's your responsibility.
2. Again, seriously? You think I love to write off time because it makes you feel small instead of because I'm getting squeezed by the client? Even if I were just a moneygrubbing jerk, this grubs no money. Look around and see the big picture.
3. Maybe you work with liars, and if so that's a shame. You seem pretty clueless, though.
4. Deal. As long as you get everything in absolutely on time, which does not mean an hour before I have to send it out the door. I always gave real deadlines. Associates frequently missed them, and guess what? I'm not a big fan of staying until 3AM revising the draft you got around to delivering at 8:00 PM the day before it had to go out. Now I only do that for associates I can trust. Earn it.

ATTRACTING BUSINESS

THE INCUMBENCY ADVANTAGE

Think for a minute about business development for law firms.

Your firm wants to expand its litigation presence in a particular practice area.

What do you do?

Many firms figure they'll march out their superstars and knock a potential new client's socks off.

The firm will look to its heavy-hitters, none of whom has ever tried a case in the field in which the target client does business, or given a talk or written an article in the relevant field, or given the subject a moment's thought.

But the heavy-hitters will go into the conference room and explain that they are the world's finest trial lawyers, they have great trial experience, and litigation is, after all, just a toolkit. A person who can try one case can try 'em all. Hire us.

Will it work?

Not often.

The company has been defending cases against it (which naturally involve the company's particular products or services) for decades. The company has relationships with many law firms, and scores of lawyers, going back years. The incumbent lawyers know the company's products, processes, and personnel. The incumbents know the company's general corporate policies and whom to call to answer questions. The in-house lawyers are comfortable with the incumbents, because the company weeded out the uncomfortable lawyers years ago.

Why change?

Incumbents have a huge advantage, and outside firms often overlook that fact.

Moreover, even if the corporation wants to make a change, why should it change to you?

You say that your trial lawyers are great.

The firm that was in here last week said that its trial lawyers are great.

I see all of your lips moving, but who am I supposed to believe?

I know there's a newspaper article that says that one of your lawyers is a star. But the guy in here last week had a press clipping, too. And he's tried 150 cases to your 20. Or he's tried 20 to your 150, but the stakes were higher in his 20, so he says those trials matter more.

From the inside perspective, the incumbent is the preferred choice.

The challengers are a distant second-best, and picking from among the challengers is basically a crap shoot.

Judging from most beauty contests, law firms underestimate those two things—the incumbency advantage, and the need for something tangible that actually sets your firm apart. If firms were to think harder about those subjects, they might be more satisfied with their business development efforts.

COMMENTS

GUEST: The post should provide some advice on what law firms should do when they realize incumbents have an advantage. How do you win business even if you realize this?

MOONSHINEJOE: The implicit suggestion seems to be that firms need to tailor their sales pitch to highlight their understanding of the client's business or industry instead of focusing on the firm's own capabilities.

GUEST: People work with advisors who they trust. This trust could come from incumbency, but it could also come from having worked together in previous jobs. We use advisors from a number of firms, but my boss tends to like to work with people he worked with in his previous firm, and I like to choose advisors from the firms that I worked at. I know them, have worked with them, and I know which ones seem the most competent. I could rely on other people's recommendations, but I really don't know what I can expect from those recommendations. So a good place to start for building business is to search out your former colleagues—although if they don't give you any business, it may be a sign of what they thought about working with you in the past.

GUEST: I come from a long line of salespeople. My mother always said that her best sales pitch was to sit and listen. She'd ask "are you happy with your current provider?" If they said yes, she'd ask if there was anything about them they'd change. If they said "nope, not a thing" my mother would thank them for their time and head out the door. But if they said "well, there is one thing" my mother would sit and listen and then explain exactly how her company could do what the current provider does—PLUS address that nagging issue. My mother always had the best sales in her company and brought home every sales award in her division.

IN THE HOUSE: The best time to challenge an incumbent firm is when the lawyer or lawyers handling the corporation's work retire or otherwise leave the firm. You should also keep an eye out for big losses, as that's when corporations will be most receptive to replacing their incumbent counsel. That's when you make your pitch.

The single best way to unseat an incumbent firm? Have one of your senior partners serve on the corporation's board of directors.

GUEST: I'm GC of a mid-size corporation and completely agree with this. When looking for new outside counsel after our company had changed the location of its HQ, I was surprised how many big firms couldn't wait to tell me about all sorts of wonderful things they had done that had absolutely no bearing on what we do or what I would need them to do. In the end, I went with a small firm run by former in-housers in a similar field—because they said "you don't need x, y and z; you just need x, and here is why."

BUSINESS DEVELOPMENT: WHAT WORKS?

Business development: What works?

I was on the other side—the law firm side—of the business development coin for 25 years. And those 25 years taught me this about generating business: Raise your profile; stay in touch with people; and get lucky.

I was never once retained by dint of good looks or charm. (Anyone who's seen or met me won't find this to be surprising.)

And I don't play golf.

So what's a lawyer to do? What business development efforts worked for me, and what might work for you?

Here are three examples of what worked for me.

First: Four years out of law school, I wrote a law review article about the reviewability of federal trial court remand orders. A lawyer got himself sanctioned in connection with a remand order, stumbled across the article, and asked me to handle his appeal. (That first call, when a client comes to you—you!—for help with a legal matter, is awfully flattering.) Two years later, the same lawyer was outgunned by opposing counsel in a very large case, and he again called for help. We were pleased to oblige.

Raise your profile; get lucky.

Second: The CEO of a small company in Ohio needed a lawyer who could help with a case that had tentacles in both Cleveland and Los Angeles. He went to my firm's website, because he knew my firm had offices in both cities. He looked through on-line biographies for lawyers whose credentials he found to be acceptable. (I'm not making this up; he told me this.) Of the acceptable candidates, he looked for a lawyer with experience in medical devices used in spinal surgery.

Get lucky.

Third: I stayed generally in touch with a college buddy for many years. He ultimately went in-house. We arranged to speak together on panels occasionally (largely as an excuse to meet in New York periodically for good dinners). When his company ran a beauty contest to select counsel to defend a set of pharmaceutical product liability cases, he decided to send an invitation to me. My firm responded and ultimately won the business, which both resulted in some fascinating legal business and kept my buddy and me meeting for dinners regularly.

Stay in touch; get lucky.

But now I'm in-house, and what's the view from here?

First, know—and impress—the people who work here. Relationships, and recommendations from colleagues, are awfully important.

Second, stay gently in touch. To retain you, I must think of you on the day I'm picking counsel. If I've forgotten that you exist, then I won't think of you and won't retain you. Don't be a pest, but don't let me forget about you.

Right. But what if you don't know either my colleagues or me, so no one will recommend you and there's no one to pester?

One trick that I missed in private practice, but that seems like a great idea from my new in-house perspective, is to offer a relevant, high-quality CLE program for a small group of in-house lawyers at their workplace.

Many in-house lawyers are pleased to attend free CLE courses offered on-site at the corporation. Throw in a free sandwich and a cookie, and the whole legal department will show up.

That puts you alone in a conference room with a small group of people who can become clients.

But then comes the hard part: You must create a relevant, high-quality CLE program.

Relevance is a pretty easy target to hit. A ton of subjects matter to in-house counsel. But high-quality is much trickier.

If you offer a CLE program about the attorney-client privilege, and then spend a half hour telling us that there are people called attorneys, and people called clients, and communications between them are sometimes protected from disclosure, you're going nowhere.

Worse than nowhere. We've met you, and we've affirmatively decided that we don't care to hire you.

But if the CLE program is tailored to the occasion, thoughtful, and well-presented, you can win us over in a heartbeat. How about addressing, for example, how the attorney-client privilege applies to in-house counsel when lawyers in the United States send e-mails to their corporate clients in (1) common law countries, (2) civil law countries, and (3) formerly communist countries? Does the privilege remain intact?

And what about other collisions between national laws? Some civil law countries recognize only a limited attorney-client privilege, but permit no discovery in litigation. Confidentiality is maintained not by the privilege, but because your opponents cannot request the evidence. When those same attorney-client communications, which would not have been disclosed in their home countries, are sought in a case pending in the United States, there's a real conflict of laws. What happens? How, if at all, can one maintain the privilege?

Offering that program requires doing hard work. You won't create a great program by spending fifteen minutes the night before your talk jotting down stray thoughts on a legal pad. But it's surely worth your time to create a good program, and you could probably amortize the cost of preparation by presenting the same program to many corporate clients.

One final twist: Instead of simply offering an in-house CLE program, ask someone at the corporation what subjects the in-house folks are currently wrestling with. And then customize a program that deals directly with one of those subjects. You're likely to draw a larger audience to that talk, and you're likely to have more a more attentive audience.

My general point is obvious: To develop business, you must meet people. You must impress them. You must stay in touch with them. You must raise your profile. And you must get lucky.

But my particular point may be more useful: Figure out a way to put yourself in a conference room talking to a small group of in-house lawyers about an issue that matters to them. And then knock their socks off.

Good luck with it.

COMMENTS

GUEST: This was a really good article and made me think about client development issues. I'm only a third year, but I'm really glad to have come across this article. Thanks!

CONCERNED PASTAFARIAN: Boring ATL day, or the boringest ATL day?

GUEST: Speaking as a former Big Law type now in-house and in charge of selecting counsel from time to time, I think a lot of what's said here is spot on. But one key that will win me over every time is when a firm has overt confidence in its associates, since the reality is that's almost always who I'll be dealing with and whose work I'll be relying upon. If I go to a meeting and there are no associates there, then you lose. I don't want to hear about your firm's storied history or how so and so partner is chairperson of who gives a crap. Talk to me about your associates and who you will have staffed on my matters.

Another thing that will make a positive impression on me is if your firm finds me and sends me either an electronic or snail mail publication with news relevant to my field. Sure, I get the same info from the ACC daily e-mail feed, but if a firm can put together a good, topical, substantive quarterly mailer then I will look at it and I will think of you when I need legal services.

SAMIAM: Speaking as someone who is in-house and active in the ACC, we host programs given by outside firms all the time. In-house counsel take time out of their busy days to attend our programs, and the last thing they want to do is hear a sales pitch thinly disguised as a CLE. Likewise, while learning about the various statutes and rules, they actually WANT to hear war stories, but only as they relate to specific problems faced by in-house counsel under those statutes and rules. In other words, how do they solve a problem before it requires the full-blown assistance of outside counsel? Being proactive is the job of in-house counsel, so anything that makes that job easier is very, very useful.

A BUSINESS DEVELOPMENT TIP

This post is a two-fer: It both suggests a way for outside lawyers to develop business more effectively and offers a tip to in-house counsel to protect their legal departments. (I bet you can hardly wait.)

First, the business development tip.

Outside lawyers often ask whether in-house lawyers are annoyed or impressed by the brochures that firms mail (or e-mail) to clients and prospective clients. I, at least, am not annoyed to receive those things. It's awfully easy to delete things unread, so they don't exactly impose a burden on me.

But am I impressed by the brochures? Obviously not; that's why I now typically delete them unread.

What's unimpressive about the brochures? Let me count the things....

First, the content. A typical brochure tells me that a case recently came down; the case said X; and therefore a case came down. It's gotta be a mighty fascinating case for a purely descriptive brochure to interest me, but most law firms write purely descriptive brochures.

(It's really no surprise that typical brochures are unimpressive. How, after all, do they get written? Senior partner hears that an important new case came down and says that the firm must quickly crank out a brochure to beat the competition. Senior partner asks more junior partner to write up something. Junior partner enlists associate who promptly types away that in the case of *Smith v. Jones*, someone sued somebody for something. The trial court held something. And the appellate court held something. So everyone should know that the appellate court just handed down that decision. Junior partner says the firm should print it up and send it out. There's no quality control, but the senior partner is satisfied that the firm acted. The resulting brochure hits my computer screen, and I'm delighted to delete it unread.)

Even brochures that are not purely descriptive often do their best to hide the ball. The cover e-mail says, for example, that the Trial Practice department of Big Law Firm is pleased to present another of its periodic publications analyzing issues of importance to corporations. To read more, I should click below.

The only thing I'm clicking on is the "delete" button.

But if I accidentally hit the wrong key, the brochure opens with an introduction saying that an important case recently came down. The bulk of the brochure then describes the case and only at the very end does the author provide a paragraph or two of analysis. That's better, but still not good.

What would be more effective?

Think about what may actually matter to the recipient of the brochure. Assemble a cover e-mail that identifies—in a short sentence or two—the key point of the brochure. And invite the recipient to read more, if the topic is of interest. That way, if your point (and your short sentences) are relevant and good, I'll keep reading. If your point is irrelevant to me, I'll delete the brochure unread. You'll both have given your-self a chance and done me a service.

Here's a concrete example of what I mean, and it contains the second part of this blog post—a tip for in-house counsel.

Earlier this year, the federal court in New York handed down a discovery order in *Gucci America, Inc. v. Guess?, Inc.*, 09 Civ. 4373 (SAS) (JLC), slip op. (S.D.N.Y. June 29, 2010). During discovery, it turned out that an in-house lawyer monitoring a trademark case was only an "inactive" member of a state bar. The magistrate judge held that no attorney-client privilege applied to communications with this person, because he wasn't properly licensed. And the corporation itself could not claim the privilege because the corporation had not made "any effort to ascertain [the in-house lawyer's] qualifications as an attorney" during the eight years he had been employed.

This is a good issue. (It may be a bad result, at least for certain corporations, but it's a good issue for client development.) This issue matters to corporations, and it's therefore opportunity knocking for outside counsel. Indeed, law firms seem to have realized this: I must have received a half-dozen law firm brochures addressing the *Gucci* case in the weeks after it came down. But only one outside lawyer did the effective thing—and it didn't even require the effort of writing a brochure.

One lawyer sent me an e-mail that said, basically, "The S.D.N.Y. just handed down an opinion that says that in-house lawyers with bar licenses on 'inactive' status are not attorneys within the meaning of the attorney-client privilege. And the court held that the corporation itself could not claim the privilege because it had made no effort to learn the lawyer's bar status. Consider doing this to protect yourself from that result: (1) send an e-mail to all of your in-house lawyers asking them to confirm their bar numbers, the state (or country) in which they're licensed to practice, and that their license is on 'active' status, (2) show an administrative assistant (or paralegal) how to find the state bar (or national) websites showing bar status of each lawyer, and have the administrative assistant confirm that each lawyer is active, and (3) put a reminder on the assistant's calendar to check the bar status of each lawyer annually."

The e-mail continued, "That's really all you need to know about the case, but, if you'd like to learn more, I've attached a link to the decision below."

Perfect! He told me what mattered, suggested an easy way to avoid a possible problem, and invited me to read more only if I cared to.

Don't tell me that the problem the lawyer identified was obvious and the solution just common sense. That may be true, but most law firms missed this trick. Most law firms sent me brochures about "an important case that may matter to you," and I de-leted most unread. When I later went back and looked at a couple of those brochures, they tended to describe the case and note the danger, but not to suggest any solution at all—even the obvious one.

Worse yet, several brochures analyzed the things that mattered to law firms, but missed the preventive steps that a corporation could take. Thus, some firms concluded from the *Gucci* case that lawyers should (1) always do informal discovery to check the bar status of in-house lawyers working for their opponent, and (2) be wary of listing e-mails to and from an "inactive" lawyer on privilege logs, because the privilege won't hold up. Those are perfectly good conclusions, but the author is looking at the case from the perspective of an outside litigator, not an in-house lawyer. The in-house lawyer will be most interested in the immediate preventive steps his corporation should take, and only then interested in future litigation tactics.

So this blog post is a two-fer: First, for law firms, send short e-mails that briefly describe a problem and a solution, and then invite in-house counsel to read more, if she cares to. When you're drafting your e-mail and brochure, put yourself in the shoes of in-house counsel, so you'll say something that matters to your reader. That e-mail may actually be read by, and interest, the target audience.

Second, for in-house lawyers: Six months ago, you deleted unread a bunch of brochures about the *Gucci* case. Those brochures actually raised an issue that matters to you. But there's no need to go back and read those silly brochures now. Just implement a process that regularly checks the bar status of all of your in-house colleagues.

COMMENTS

GUEST: I work in-house and this describes perfectly how I approach these notices—I read a little to see if something useful catches my attention and push delete if I don't see immediate relevance to what I am working on. It would be great if I had time to read all of the news items that come across my desk, but I don't, so these promotional materials will be more effective if they get right to the point (practical solutions).

GUEST: But, is the point to get you to read it, or is the point just to get you to remember that Jeff is the guy who is always sending you updates on a certain practice area, so you think to call him when you have an issue in that practice area?

GUEST: What's ironic is you say that firms should cut to the chase and tell you what matters, yet your post rambles on needlessly. Plus, did you stop for a moment to consider that your readers might be dealing with GCs or other in-house types who might actually prefer the approach that you seem to despise? I've read all your posts and they seem to basically say the same thing–know what your in-house audience wants and you'll have an edge. Gee, thanks for the earth shattering insight.

GUEST: I am an in-house lawyer. Nobody prefers the approach Mark despises.

BLOGGING AS BUSINESS DEVELOPMENT

Is blogging a useful business development tool?

The folks who sell blogging platforms to lawyers say that blogging is the route to riches. But bloggers themselves are far less certain whether blogging actually generates business. What's the truth?

Let me start with my personal experience; I'll conclude with a thesis. The personal experience is just the facts—what I did as a blogger, how successful the blog was, and how, if at all, I profited from the experience. (I've previously recited parts of this story in both the print media and elsewhere. I'll try to add a few new thoughts here.)

What did I do as a blogger? For three years—from October 2006 through December 2009—while I was a partner at Jones Day, I co-hosted the Drug and Device Law blog with Jim Beck, of Dechert. We wrote almost exclusively about the defense of pharmaceutical and medical device product liability cases. We affirmatively chose to have the blog co-hosted by partners at two different firms, for two reasons....

The first reason was mutual respect: Jim and I had both practiced in the field for a long time, had worked together in the past, and had published a fair amount in traditional media on related topics. We trusted each other to produce the volume of stuff needed to fuel a blog.

The second reason for having two competing firms co-host the blog was to maintain plausible deniability. We figured that, if we typed enough words, we'd eventually say something that would come back to haunt one of us (or our firms). If the blog was co-hosted by people at different firms, each blogger had plausible deniability—"I didn't write the crazy stuff! That clown Beck did!"

We originally planned to publish only two posts per week (one apiece). We soon realized, however, that we would attract more readers if we added new content to the blog daily. Thus, for nearly three years, I wrote three or four blog posts per week, and Jim wrote one or two. (This arrangement was actually more equitable than it sounds: He wrote the long, smart posts that required legal research; I did the easy stuff.)

How successful was the blog? By the time I left the Drug and Device Law Blog (and the private practice of law) in December 2009, the blog's readership had grown to something north of 30,000 pageviews in a typical month. (That's quite good by "niche blog" standards, but abysmal for a blog aimed at a more general audience. Above the Law, for example, can get 30,000 pageviews in a single business **hour** on a typical weekday.) Drug and Device Law's readership, so far as we could tell, consisted of (1) other lawyers at large firms who defended pharmaceutical product liability cases, (2) plaintiffs' lawyers who labored on the opposite side of that "v.," (3) in-house lawyers at drug and device companies, (4) government officials interested in our field (we received, for example, occasional hits from the FDA and Congressional offices), and (5) people from other publications, including folks who wrote both at blogs and in traditional media.

We received a fair amount of attention for a niche blog. The *ABA Journal* repeatedly recognized us as one of the "Top 100" legal blogs. Other blogs linked to us regularly. We were mentioned in the mainstream media occasionally, including most notably one day when *The New York Times* did not simply quote us, but actually published our url in the print edition. For a little blog, we did okay.

How, if at all, did I profit from the blogging experience? Let me start with a disclaimer and then count the ways. First, the disclaimer: It's awfully hard work to fuel a good blog. If you publish one post a week, announcing "truck accident on I-95! Hire me!," your experience may not resemble ours. That's it for the disclaimer; now let me count the ways in which we profited from blogging:

1. I became a better lawyer. To fuel the blog, I had to analyze new decisions (and, heaven help me, law review articles) as they were published. I had to think about those subjects and then write articles commenting on them. This is more professional reading than a sane person would choose to undertake, but it does make you a better lawyer.

2. We influenced the law. Most prominently, we proposed an idea for a new FDA regulation in our blog and saw that regulation enacted within two years. We later heard an FDA official mention in a speech that the idea for the regulation had come from our blog. We also influenced the public debate on legal issues in our little sandbox, as other blogs, law review articles, and the popular media addressed issues that we raised. And we may well have improved the quality of advocacy in our specialized field of law, because we freely shared with other defense lawyers new ideas, arguments, and best practices for defending pharmaceutical products cases.

3. We became unbelievably plugged-in to events in our area of law. As our readership grew, people came to view us as an important presence in the drug and device field. Our readers would send us, for example, new decisions within minutes after they were handed down, briefs that made interesting arguments, information about grants of *certiorari* and other breaking news in the field, and so on. Our blog, by its mere existence, suggested that we were near the center of the drug and device universe, and over time that became a self-fulfilling prophecy.

4. We dramatically raised both our personal profiles and our firms' collective profiles in this particular field of law. Within our niche, we became startlingly well-known. When we attended conferences, strangers would say, "You do the blog?! I'm delighted to meet you." The General Counsel of Merck actually asked a mutual acquaintance to introduce the GC to me. If you're trolling for business in the drug and device field, that's a triple. (It would be a home run if the guy actually retained you.) And the mainstream media noticed the blog, too. As a result of our blogging,

we appeared on CNBC and Bloomberg TV. We were quoted in *The New York Times*, *The Wall Street Journal*, and countless regional publications across the country.

5. We received invitations that further raised our profiles in the field. People who sponsored conferences about drug and device issues were keen to have us participate—in part because we might know something about the subject, but more because, if we were speaking at a conference, we could be counted on to mention the conference on the blog and link to the conference registration materials. There's nothing like providing free advertising to make you a popular speaker. We were also solicited to write articles for publications large and small. The most notable invitations that came my way resulted in my publishing bylined articles in *The Wall Street Journal* and the *Chicago Tribune*.

6. We got our book deal. Oxford University Press contacted us about writing a treatise on defending drug and device cases. Beck had already written a book in that field, so he declined. But I accepted, recruited a co-author, and then wrote my chapters. The co-author is now finishing his piece, and we expect the treatise to be published in 2011. (That would have been a coup, I think, if I were still in private practice. Fat lot of good it does me now—from a business development perspective, anyway—given that I'm in-house.)

7. We had fun. Blogging is terribly hard work, but it's very rewarding, in a weird sort of way. That's worth something.

But now the grand finale: dollars and cents. Did the blog bring in business?

Here's the bottom-line truth: As a result of the blog, I was retained to write one *amicus curiae* brief in an appeal, which we agreed to do for a flat fee. I agreed to write another *amicus curiae* brief in a different appellate case free of charge, in part because the party that asked for help was a drug company, and the assignment offered a chance to create a new relationship. And I was contacted about endless other stuff—such as representing plaintiffs (not my business), writing other *pro bono* briefs, and so on— that didn't come to anything.

So, is blogging worthwhile?

It depends on what you want. A law firm will pay a lot of money to run advertisements to raise awareness of a firm's name. Our blog resulted in "earned media" exposure—newspapers voluntarily choosing to quote us—that would have cost a ton if you had been forced to buy the same exposure with advertising dollars. We also "touched" clients and potential clients regularly, because those folks read our posts (and heard our on-line voices) regularly. Ultimately, that exposure and those touches are worth something—maybe a great deal—but you may not be able to tie a particular retention to your blogging work.

Ultimately, however, our (or at least my—I don't know about Jim's) actual, dollars and cents, return on investment was pretty thin: One flat-fee appellate brief was the monetary payoff for maybe ten hours of work every week for three years. I shoulda flipped burgers at McDonalds.

Finally, my thesis: Whether blogging makes sense as a business development tool depends on your particular situation. Firms specializing in personal bankruptcy buy advertising space on billboards and time on television. Maybe a good personal bankruptcy blog would be a business magnet. So, too, for plaintiffs' personal injury work, which seems analogous from a business development perspective. Eric Turkewitz, for example, writes a solid blog in the personal injury field; maybe he can tell us if it's landed him any business.

Criminal defense work? Scott Greenfield, over at Simple Justice, blogs awfully well in the criminal defense field, and he insists that the blog hasn't been worth a dime in actual business.

For other fields? It depends. I didn't land any pharmaceutical mass torts from my blogging, but who would pick a mass tort defense lawyer based on blog posts anyway? And Jones Day is probably sufficiently high-profile in the mass tort field that its successes in that area wouldn't be affected by my "poor power to add or detract." I similarly suspect that a hot-shot international M&A lawyer at Cravath wouldn't cause the phone to start ringing off the hook if she started blogging about international M&A deals. If you work at a big firm that's already prominent in some field of law, then your firm already has the connections, and the blog just won't tip the scales.

(In that regard, I'd be curious to hear from Russell Jackson, at Skadden. He writes the very nice Consumer Class Actions & Mass Torts blog. If a big firm blog can bring in business, that one oughtta do the trick. I know that Russell thinks his blog makes him a better lawyer, raises his profile, and is a hoot to write. He's surely correct on those scores. But what about bucks, Russell? Is your experience the same as Beck's and mine? I suspect that it is—essentially no new business—although of course I don't know for sure.)

What about other firms or other situations? I can only guess. But it wouldn't surprise me if a medium-sized firm in Wilmington could attract a retention or two as local counsel if it blogged about some aspect of Delaware corporate law. Both corporate clients and lawyers at other firms might follow that blog, and they might think of you for a lawsuit in Delaware. Similarly, you might build a perfectly nice niche practice if you staked out and dominated a particular field in the blogosphere. (So far as I can tell, "Escheat Audits in Colorado" is wide open, and that might be the sort of thing that works. Go for it!)

(I just realized that blogging yielded one other (arguable) benefit for me: I'm not sure that Lat and Mystal would have asked me to write this column if they hadn't been familiar with my previous work in the blogosphere. So blogging yields more opportunities to blog, just like first prize in the pie-eating contest.)

Think hard about what you want to achieve, and whether you have a chance of achieving it, before you start the long, terribly difficult project of fueling a blog many times each week. Blogging can be very rewarding in many different ways, but it will create only a very few (if any) serious rainmakers.

COMMENTS

TIPS: OK, Mark—I love giving you a hard time, but this was a solid post. And kudos for giving up the one-sentence-per-paragraph style.

NO U: Monetizing the value of a blog is more than simply tallying the number of dollars from work that you obtained as a direct referral. What about clients who were choosing between firms that decided to go with you, perhaps unconsciously so, because the blog helped them see you as an expert in your field? Given the notoriety and respect for your particular blog, I have a feeling you're not giving it credit for the largest chunk of revenue it has probably generated.

GUEST: You'll see major dividends down the road. Like any similar marketing outreach in the realm of the law, it can sometimes take many years before fruit ripens.

JM67: I started a niche blog just over two years ago. I can attribute several hundred thousand in fees to calls generated directly by the blog. And I only post maybe twice a month.

SUCKING UP BY WRITING DOWN

Few folks use proposals for co-authorship to advance their careers. More should.

What am I suggesting?

Come up with a thesis for an article. Call somebody who matters to you, and propose that you write the article together. Write a first draft of the article, send it to your co-author to solicit revisions, and then publish the piece.

For whom might this work? Anyone who's looking to curry favor.

For business development purposes, an outside lawyer might call a client or potential client and suggest co-authoring a piece in the client's field of expertise. For career development purposes, a law firm associate might do the same with a partner, or an in-house lawyer might do the same with a business colleague or a supervisor. Few people would be offended to be offered co-authorship credit for an article, and many would be delighted to be given the opportunity and later to take partial credit for a published piece.

Why is this tactic used so rarely?

First, it's hard. Everyone wants to do client development when it involves joining a client to enjoy a fine meal, play a round of golf, or watch a sporting event. But no one wants to do client development when it involves ginning up a thesis, doing some research, putting fingers to keyboard, and producing a noteworthy finished product.

You should view that as opportunity knocking: You'll face less competition when you use co-authorship as a business development technique.

Why else don't people co-author articles? Because it's dangerous. If you're writing an article with someone else, you can't be sure how involved your co-author will become. In my experience, many solicited co-authors in this situation do very little. Some never read your draft and simply tell you to publish it. (Purists would say this poses an ethical issue: Should someone receive authorship credit for an article that he never read, let alone wrote? I'm sensitive to this charge and have certainly seen it redound to the detriment of people in fields other than law. In the legal field, for whatever reason, no one seems to object to this practice. I'm not taking sides here; wrestle with your conscience and decide how you want to handle this.)

Other co-authors will take a run through your draft and propose a few small changes.

And yet other co-authors will take it seriously when they're appending their name to something that will appear in print. (Back in the 1980s, the *National Law Journal* refused to publish articles written by associates alone; this was presumably a form of two-bit quality control. The *National Law Journal* thus rejected an article that I'd submitted unless I found a partner willing to serve as co-author. I went back to a senior partner at my firm—who had previously reviewed my draft article and commented on it—and asked him if he'd like to sign on as my co-author. He agreed, and asked me to send him the current draft of the piece. I asked why: "You've already revised it." "Yes," he said, "But before this was going to be your article, and now it's going to be mine, too." *See* Neil E. Falconer & Mark Herrmann, "Legislation Enacted in November Alters Law Governing Removal," *Nat'l L.J.* 18 (Mar. 13, 1989). (That puppy was not exactly a client magnet.)

If your co-author actually cares about the quality of your draft, then this project will present both risk and opportunity. The opportunity arises because you'll be working together with someone who will observe closely your facility with ideas and words. That's an awfully good way to impress a client or colleague. The risk arises because you'll be working together with someone who will observe closely your facility with ideas and words. If you're going to walk this path, walk carefully.

There's another risk for associates who choose this path to try to find a senior mentor or advocate within a law firm. Some partners are fair; others are not. When you propose to some partners that you write an article together, they'll like the idea and give you full co-authorship credit. Other partners will decide that it's unseemly to co-author an article with an associate and will relegate your effort (and your name) to a footnote, thanking you for your "research help" on the article that you in fact wrote from start to finish. When you choose a co-author, choose carefully.

What's my own experience with this?

In the partner-associate setting, I never voluntarily chose to enlist a more senior co-author to write an article with me. (I worked with a senior co-author only once, when the *NLJ* insisted.) But it seems to me that this idea could work, and people more politic than I was might well put this concept to good use.

In the business development setting, I co-authored several pieces with clients or potential clients. Their input ran the spectrum that I described above, from just barely being involved in the writing process to participating fully. The payoff varied, too, from never hearing a business-related peep from an in-house co-author to being given the chance to compete for substantial business.

And now, sitting in the client's chair, I haven't yet been approached by anyone about co-authoring anything.

One last thing: This column focuses exclusively on the self-interest involved when you co-author an article. That's obviously not the only reason to write, or to co-author, publications. Co-authors typically add real value to publications, although that may be more true when you pick co-authors based on their substantive knowledge, rather than what they can do for your career. Moreover, it often makes sense to publish your thoughts simply to share an idea with the public or to participate in an on-going debate. Please don't put me too firmly in the Samuel Johnson camp: "No man but a blockhead ever wrote, except for money."

COMMENTS

GUEST: Another absolute PIECE OF GARBAGE post. Well done, you CLOWNS are sinking to new lows of ineptitude.

MG1: What are you talking about? This was really useful advice for me.

GUEST: This article actually was a little helpful. Mark made some rather obvious points, but as noted in the article, associates aren't following his advice, so it's still worth mentioning. If you expected more from ATL, then the best place for you to be looking for ineptitude is in the mirror.

GUEST: This is good advice for associates (to get them to work on an article with a partner). That could develop into a working relationship and mentorship. I don't believe that this is such a fantastic idea for client development. I would have to already have a good working relationship with outside counsel before I wanted to co-author an article with them.

BENEDICK: I'm in-house and was approached by a law firm partner I hardly know about co-authoring an article. He offered right up front to do all the work (read: have one of his associates do all the work). I turned him down on precisely the grounds that I felt I'd have to vet it at my company, and the internal red tape would have been as much work as writing the thing.

IN DA HOUSE: From an in-house view this is probably one of the best posts yet (I'm not really a fan). Yes, it would be great to co-author articles on issues where the Company has a clear, consistent legal stance. And if the Company has already been "out there" with their position (on their web site, in litigation, etc.) then stating it would not necessarily give rise to any extra exposure.

Clearly, it depends on the particulars—but this kind of indirect business solicitation would (to me) be more welcome than yet another somewhat awkward dinner or event hearing how a firm specializes in "complex" litigation and can be a one-stop-shop for all of our legal needs. (I'm not putting down the need to market firm services; I'm just saying it gets old from the in-house side as well, unless you just love being wined and dined.)

GETTING BUSINESS BY INVENTING BUSINESS

I recently had lunch with a guy who had worked at a law firm, gone in-house, and later returned to a law firm. (It's actually more than that. This guy's bio is: assistant U.S. attorney; associate at K&E; partner at Bartlit Beck; deputy general counsel at Bank One; and now at his own small firm. That's called either "done it all" or "can't hold a job." Because this post will share with the world an idea that he proposed, I'll credit him publicly: He's Lenny Gail of Massey & Gail, a small shop based in Chicago and D.C.)

Lenny asked at lunch, as folks frequently do, what I'd learned about business development by having gone in-house. I answered honestly, as I occasionally do: When I was outside counsel, I always thought that business development was a game of chance. You tried a hundred different things, with no clue what might pay off, and then random chance struck and business arrived inexplicably, out of the blue.

As in-house counsel, my view hasn't really changed: If you're on our list of preferred counsel and we use you regularly, we're likely to hire you again. If you're a newcomer, there's not much you can do or say to draw that first retention. Everything you say at our introductory meeting simply repeats what some other guy told us about his firm last week, and virtually nothing you've done is so breathtaking as to make you irresistible.

Lenny nodded, and we drifted back into our iced teas.

The real problem with getting retained is the first nibble. As outside counsel, once a client retained us for one case, it was a lock that the client would retain us for another. The client would come to know our people, our firm, the quality of our work, and the results we obtained. Parlaying one opportunity into many was easy; the hard part is getting the first chance. As in-house counsel, that continues to strike me as true for many (but not all) firms.

How do you get the first nibble?

Offer to do the first case (or the first six months of a case) at a deep discount or for free? Maybe, but law firm management won't like that idea. And it might not work anyway. Maybe law is a Giffen good, and you'll sell less of it if you lower the price. The client might think, "You'll do a case for free? You're retained!" But the client might also think, "You're offering to do a case for free? You must be a truly awful lawyer!" Who's to know?

Lenny nodded again, speared a Tater Tot, said that his view was about the same, and then posed a question: "Suppose I researched your business and a legal theory, and I called you up and asked for an hour of your time. I wanted to talk to you about a lawsuit that your company could file that would do your business some good. The lawsuit might recover money damages, or it might obtain a useful injunction against a competitor, or it might create some other business advantage. Would you talk to me about that and, if my idea made sense, would you hire me to pursue the case?"

This is a great idea. Having heard it, it strikes me as obvious, and I can't believe I'd never thought of it before. I have only one excuse: I spent my career as outside counsel primarily as a defense lawyer, so I wasn't in the business of thinking up lawsuits for the plaintiffs' side. As in-house counsel, I would surely spend an hour listening to a lawyer who sounded rational by phone and told me that he saw some legal advantage that my client was overlooking. And, if the idea made sense, I'd almost surely hire the law firm that had ginned up the idea. After all, that firm had the creativity to unearth the concept, and the firm put in the time and effort to research the law and investigate our business. Come to me with that proposal, convince me, and I suspect I'll hire you.

I asked Lenny what his experience was with this form of business development.

He said first that it's a tough row to hoe. You have to learn an awful lot about a business, research the law, and generate an idea that a sophisticated business hasn't independently considered. That's a lot of groundwork for a speculative shot at new business.

And, Lenny said, the two times he'd tried this so far had both failed. Each of the two clients agreed to listen to his proposal. But the first client said it didn't want to be that bellicose, and the second identified a subtle aspect of its business that made the proposed lawsuit untenable.

That's 0 for 2, but I still think it's a good idea for business development. It's mighty tough for new outside counsel to land that first retention, and one way to get in the door would be to identify and research an opportunity that we'd overlooked. If you have any experience with this approach, please share in the comments. I'll be all eyes.

COMMENTS

TROLLFACE: I liked this column, but I see a number of reasons why this approach is probably more trouble than it's worth. First, it just seems too ambulance chaser-ish. I don't necessarily have a problem with that, but I imagine that the people doing the hiring do. They're risk averse and want to stay out of court, not get into court. Second, litigation—even if it is at first seen as advantageous to your company—can buy trouble, often unforeseen trouble. So I come up with a novel theory to bring a case against a competitor that might give me an advantage. What does the competitor do? He files counterclaims against me. Maybe they're frivolous, maybe they're not, but all of a sudden I have to disclose to partners, shareholders, auditors, regulators, whoever, that we're being sued for millions of dollars. That said, with less sophisticated clients, there are certainly times you can point out that they have rights that they're not exercising, e.g., your employer's doing what to you? He's not allowed to do that. Your commercial landlord's erected scaffolding that's covering the sign for your business and it's hurting you? Let's take a look at your lease.

GUEST: A luxury good where demand goes up with price is not a Giffen good.

  GUEST: It would be a Veblen good, no?

GUEST: This mentality is what's wrong with the legal system and what gives lawyers a bad name. Filing manufactured lawsuits against your competitors instead of besting them in the marketplace has got to be one of the lowest strategies out there (not that some large companies don't use it). If someone pitched that to me, I would ask them to get the hell out of my office.

CLOSER'S COFFEE: I think this is my favorite Inside Straight post. I am particularly interested in Mark's discussion about getting the first nibble. I don't think we should get too hung up on the problems of some of the ideas he's kicking around on how to get the GC's attention. It's easy to knock holes in this approach or that. The question (How can I get a GC to give me a shot?) is one that deserves our serious consideration, and lots of experimentation.

    MARK'S OTHER ALIAS: Well said, Lenny.

SOCK-RATES: This is idiotic. It may work in the insurance industry, and may seem like a good idea if you're in-house insurance litigation counsel, but in the real world we'd view the guy as a bottom-feeding unethical punk, no better than a patent troll, and tell him to be on his way. Inside the Fortune 100, that pitch may work with a type-A junior exec, who will then try to run with it only to be shut down by legal. Outside the Fortune 500, sure I'll bet there are plenty of machine shops and insurance sales companies that would love the idea.

Mark Herrmann, you embarrass me as an in-house attorney.

OUTRAGEOUS: Disagree. As the post acknowledges, this is a hard thing to do; however, it can be really effective and is not akin to a "patent troll." Sticking with the intellectual property area, it is not wrong to explain to a company how to assert its patent rights. That is why those rights exist.

ISAACLQUEDEM: Translate the idea out of litigation and into business law: Think up a tax strategy (maybe involving state income taxes), and offer to discuss it with the GC. If it's a reasonable idea that the company isn't already doing, the GC will likely engage the lawyer who thought of the idea.

GUEST: Honestly, firms (even the most "prestigious" ones) do this all the time, they're just not that blatant about it. Where I work in-house, firms will come in, give a presentation on a topic and then suggest how they've helped similarly situated companies. We usually don't bite, but if it sounded like a particularly good idea I suppose we would.

A TALE OF TWO PITCHES

As an in-house lawyer who occasionally influences our selection of outside counsel, I hear an awful lot of law firm pitches. And I must admit that I'm often entertained by them. I spent better than 25 years in the private practice of law, where attracting new business was an important part of the game. I was never sure which pitches had a chance and which didn't, so it's pretty amusing to sit on the other side of the table to see how other folks approach this.

I recently saw one good pitch and one bad one, and I just have to share.

First, the bad one. Several lawyers from a firm visited us for a chance to explain their firm's capabilities. I don't remember why we were meeting with them—we actually had a need for them; someone recommended them; someone important asked us to meet with them as a favor; whatever. I used to think that getting in the door to meet with potential clients was a big achievement; I now realize that it meant less than I thought.

Anyway, these guys started the pitch the usual way: The firm has lots of great lawyers who've done lots of great things in their lives. The firm is divided into several departments, and those divisions should for some reason matter to me. A couple of magazines had bestowed some awards on the firm or its lawyers. Yadda, yadda, yadda.

And then the associate speaks….

I actually thought there was a chance for something interesting here. Law firms don't often bring associates to this type of generic pitch. (If a firm is proposing a team of lawyers to work on one specific case, it's common for us to meet the senior partner proposed for the matter and some of the junior lawyers who will staff the case. But when we're meeting a firm to learn generally about the firm's capabilities, it's typically three or four very senior folks; the associates stay home.) What would the associate say?

Ha! He used the pitch that he must have used last week to try to recruit a second-year law student to spend a summer at the firm: "I worked for several years at a large, prestigious law firm. I didn't have the chance to do any real work; I reviewed documents, answered discovery, and wrote deposition outlines. I decided to move to this mid-size firm because I wanted some real experience. And I was absolutely right to make the move! In the two years that I've been at this firm, I've taken a bunch of depositions and even got to second-chair a trial!"

Nice pitch; wrong situation. That story might well convince a law student or lateral recruit to come to work for your firm. But it doesn't say much to a person who's trying to figure out if he should hire you. I'm delighted that your new firm has improved your life, but I'm trying to identify lawyers with substantive knowledge of our business and top-notch skills to represent us. I hate to be mean about this, but whether you've gotten to take a couple of depositions just doesn't weigh in my calculus.

Happily, there's the other side of the coin.

I had lunch with a highly-credentialed guy (fancy schools; Review; Coif; clerkship; federal prosecutor; blah, blah, blah) who had recently left a government job to join a large firm. This guy cast his pitch basically this way: "This pitch is only going to work for a year or two, so I figure I should make the most of it: I had the choice of joining the partnership at a fair number of prestigious firms when I left government service a few months ago. I thought about those offers, and I decided that this firm was the best. You're now making the same choice: You're deciding which law firm would be best for you. So let me tell you a couple of reasons why I decided to join this firm . . . ."

Sadly, he's right that his pitch will work for only a short time. But it was an interesting change of pace, and I'm always glad to hear things that are slightly unusual. (I can't yet say whether the pitch will work. I'm just saying that it was, at a minimum, slightly off the beaten path. I guess I don't set the bar too high for these things.)

COMMENTS

PELE_404A: Aren't the two pitches exactly the same? The associate and the highly-credentialed guy both talked about why they joined their firms. I agree that the highly-credentialed guy was in a much better position to make it work, but it hardly means the pitch was "off the beaten path."

> **VALERIE:** At the risk of feeding the trolls, I will respond. The new partner has the right perspective, the associate does not. An associate looking at joining a firm is not looking for the same things that a partner joining a firm looks for. An associate looks for opportunities, a chance to get experience, to move up, for great exit opportunities.
>
> A partner who is looking at offers to join multiple firms is probably looking for what each firm can offer as far as helping him take care of his clients: Do the attorneys have experience in complementary practice areas? Do the people there do good work? Does the firm have offices in places where my clients need me? Will the firm have a rate structure that is appropriate for my clients? Etc. The partner is thinking "which firm is for my clients?" and the associate is thinking "which firm is for me?"

GUEST: Didn't you already write a column not too long ago about (un)successful law firm pitches? Why do you sit through so many pitches? Sure, I understand that firms want your business, but it seems clear that you often have no intention whatsoever to use most of these firms, so why make them take the time and effort to do their song and dance? Kinda douchy if you ask me.

> **GUEST:** To answer your second question, we in-house guys let the firms do their song and dance even when we don't intend on using them because they won't leave us alone until we do. It's just as much a waste of my time as it is theirs, but at least at the end I will have bought a few months before I get hit up again to 'meet for lunch' or a request to 'let us parade our overpriced but impressive partner before you.'

UNBELIEVABLE! A SMART, NEW IDEA!

In 25 years working at law firms, I never offered this to a client. In two years working in-house, no outside law firm ever before offered this to me. But I heard it moments ago, and I couldn't believe how foolish I've been. I smiled, shook my head, hung up the phone, and popped open the blogging software for your benefit.

"When we're handling a major case that is so terribly expensive to defend," says my outside counsel, "we like to have an 'all-hands' meeting with the client once a quarter. Our entire team will fly to your headquarters for the event. We'd like you to invite not just any appropriate in-house lawyers, but also relevant people from the business unit and any senior managers who might either be concerned about the cost of the litigation or have ideas to offer. We find that people who aren't directly involved in the litigation often suggest great ideas.

"We won't charge you anything for these quarterly meetings. We'll write off our time, and our firm will pay the travel expenses. We just think it's a good idea to have these meetings regularly in cases as important as this one."

Brilliant!

I personally had nibbled around the edges of this idea when I was in private practice: "We'd like you to schedule a two-day educational conference about the product involved in the litigation," I had said in the past. "Have each of your folks who helped to design the product, know its regulatory history, and so on, speak for an hour. We want to educate our entire team and to meet the key players in person. Naturally, we won't charge you for our time or travel expense."

That's okay. It's a nice offer; it serves an important function; and it causes a bunch of your lawyers to meet a bunch of client representatives. But the offer I just heard is much better. It achieves so much more. Why?

Offering free quarterly meetings achieves everything a law firm is pursuing (except for an immediate cash payment, but don't be short-sighted here).

Offering free quarterly meetings shows concern for the client's cause. It shows a slight willingness to incur costs for the client's benefit. That's nice.

The meetings let in-house lawyers not involved in a case on a daily basis get a relatively quick update on what's happening. That's helpful.

The meetings let in-house lawyers responsible for supervising the litigation, who may be being beaten about the head and shoulders about defense costs, invite interested senior managers to learn about the case and ask for themselves any questions they may have about defense costs or possibilities for early settlement. That's not bad.

But that's just from the client's point of view. These meetings also give the outside lawyers a great platform to meet folks who matter at the company—in-house lawyers not involved in the case, key people in the business unit, and senior managers worried about expense (who may be very senior indeed). And these meetings aren't a cocktail party or a meet-and-greet, where outside counsel can do no more than hope to impress clients with their charm; this is a serious discussion that will let smart lawyers with good communications skills talk to an interested group of people about substantive matters. (That's why this idea is so much better than having your team fly out to sit and listen. From a business development perspective, the outside law firm wants to be the teachers, not the students.) If the outside lawyers are any good at all, they should be able to impress the assembled business folks and have those people ask, the next time they're involved in a similar case, why we don't retain those impressive lawyers who flew in to see us at our headquarters.

But there's more! My silly idea of flying folks out to learn about the product is a one-time event. That's good, but repetitive meetings are better. If the lawsuit goes on for any length of time—and the big ones almost always do—outside counsel will have spent some chunk of a day working with our lawyers and business folks on a quarterly basis for a year or two or three. Over that period of time, the outside lawyers will start to feel like old friends—or, at a minimum, like trusted advisors and counselors, which is plenty.

Maybe I was unusually foolish during the twenty years when I worked at a huge firm and the five years before that when I worked at a small one. But I never offered free quarterly meetings to my clients, I never heard any of my colleagues suggest doing this, and I never heard rumors that any of us were doing this.

Similarly, for the two years that I've been in-house (working with some of the finest law firms in the world), none of our outside lawyers suggested this before the guy on the phone today. (We've occasionally insisted that our firms come in and give presentations, of course, but outside counsel never affirmatively suggested it, proposed to hold the meetings regularly, encouraged us to expand the list of invitees, and offered to write off the associated time and expense. Those are new, and clever, wrinkles.)

If a lot of firms are doing this, then I'm just out of touch. But if, as I suspect, very few firms are doing this, then law firms are missing a trick. Holding free quarterly meetings helps clients to defend their litigation, is a great client relations tool, and creates the perfect business development opportunity. As between having regular meetings like this and participating in most other business development events that I've inflicted on others or had inflicted on me, this one wins, hands down.

Now you've heard about it. Don't be silly: Go forth and prosper.

COMMENTS

GUEST: Everything appears to be an epiphany for this fool. This has been going on for more than a few years in many companies and by many law firms.

SUPEDUPE: Mark: With excellent articles like this, you have no business writing at ATL. Now, I'll step aside for the obligatory lashing you'll experience from the rest of the comments.

MARKETING => NOT ENOUGH WORK: The opportunity cost of spending the time that Mark describes is low when lawyers are not very busy. Otherwise, it's not just the time given up, but the time not taken to build relationships with other clients. Rule of thumb: marketing efforts bear an inverse relationship to how busy lawyers are. More time on your hands, more time to market.

GUEST: It's a great way to deepen your relationship with a client and become their "go to" lawyer (or to completely screw up and have them pull all your files). Those of you who bash Mark forget what he does for a living—he hires and manages outside lawyers. I don't agree with everything he says, and I wouldn't do this for many of my clients or most of my matters, but it is a creative idea and worthy of discussion. Over the long term you don't make money by billing the hell out of every assignment, you make it by being the person they trust and want for the tough cases where they won't nickel and dime you. Grow up.

SHOWING, NOT TELLING, THAT YOU'RE COMPETENT

When we write briefs, we show—we don't tell—the reader that we win. Thus, we do not tell the reader: "This case is barred by the statute of limitations," which is mere assertion. Instead, we show the reader why we win: "The accident in which plaintiff was hurt occurred on June 1, 2008. The two-year statute of limitations therefore expired on June 1, 2010. Plaintiff did not file his complaint, however, until August 15, 2011. This lawsuit is time-barred."

At trial, it's the same routine: We do not simply assert in an opening statement or closing argument: "My client should win." (Nor do we beg: "Please, please. My client should win.") Instead, we present the facts, and we let the jury conclude from the facts that our client should win. Show; don't tell. It's more persuasive.

What's the equivalent for demonstrating legal expertise? What should law firms write (and say) on résumés and in responses to RFPs to show, not tell, their competence? And, as in-house counsel, what questions should we ask to investigate whether a firm is blowing hot air (which is what "telling" permits) or may actually be competent (which is what "showing" may suggest)?

Let's do an easy one first: Many lawyers include on their résumés the assertion that they're "widely published" or "have published many articles in leading journals." That's "telling." If, as outside counsel, you have published three articles in journals that no one has ever heard of, then you're probably better off asserting in your résumé that you're "widely published" and hoping that no one asks decent follow-up questions. In your response to RFPs, you should do the same thing: Assert that you're widely published, and hope that no one pursues the issue.

But suppose that an outside lawyer is in fact not bluffing about publications. Then show, don't tell. Perhaps: "Mr. Smith has published 57 articles in the legal and popular press. In the popular press, his articles have appeared in *The Wall Street Journal*, the *Chicago Tribune*, and other journals around the world. On the legal side, he has published law review articles in the *Tulane Law Review* and the *Arizona State Law Journal*, as well as shorter pieces in *Litigation*, *The National Law Journal*, and BNA's *Class Action Reporter*, among others."

This description shows—it does not tell—the reader that you're widely published. It permits the reader to assess your accomplishments intelligently. If your competition for a piece of business turns on the quality of your publications, then you're likely to win the work against run-of-the-mill competitors; if Alan Dershowitz or Scott Turow strolls into the room for the interview after yours, then you'll lose. But at least it's not all bluster; the cards are on the table.

As in-house counsel, what do you do? When the outside lawyer says that he's "widely published," you ask for the bibliography. If the outside lawyer is bluffing, you've exposed him as a fraud. If he's not bluffing, you'll get a list of publications and you can intelligently compare that candidate to the other candidates for the work.

What's the equivalent for trial experience? In that context, "telling" about credentials sounds like this in a law firm brochure: "We have vast trial experience in complex, multijurisdictional disputes." During a beauty contest, you'll hear variations on the "telling" theme. The oral rendition goes like this: "My partner, Smith, has tried more cases than you can count, and I personally believe my partner is the finest product liability trial lawyer in the country."

Very nice, but possibly pure bluster. What should outside counsel do if he in fact is not bluffing, and what questions should inside counsel ask to pierce the possible smoke and mirrors?

Outside counsel who isn't bluffing should list her trials on her résumé. There might be two categories: "Jury trials taken to verdict" and "Other proceedings." The first category would contain what it says. The second category might contain an amalgam of bench trials, arbitrations, preliminary injunction hearings, and other evidentiary hearings that are not the equivalent of jury trials. (Why do so few people actually do this on their résumés? Because the average lawyer is bluffing.)

As inside counsel, it's your job to call the bluff. When someone says that he's tried to verdict "more cases than you can count," ask for a list of jury trials taken to verdict. Perhaps counsel didn't appreciate that you can count to two. Ask the lawyer to include the result of each of those trials, so you can calculate the lawyer's batting average. Perhaps ask the lawyer to identify opposing counsel (or the amount in dispute), so you can see whether the candidate is trying cases in the major league or the minors. Ask for a couple of references: One from a client for whom the lawyer won a trial and one from a client for whom the lawyer lost a trial. (The second reference may actually result in the more interesting conversation. The client may be terribly disappointed in counsel's performance, or the client may say that counsel did a spectacularly good job with some horribly bad facts, and the loss was plainly not counsel's fault.)

What are the rules? As outside counsel, if you've really got the goods, then show—don't tell—that you've got them. Be completely transparent, provide full details, and annihilate the competition. On the other hand, if you don't really have the goods, don't be silly. Be less transparent. Don't lie, of course, but say little, and pray that no one thinks to follow up.

As inside counsel, don't settle for the usual pablum about folks being "widely published" and having "vast trial experience." Demand specifics, and follow up as necessary, to learn what you're actually buying. By imposing that rigor, you'll expose an awful lot of puffery, and you'll enable yourself to make more intelligent hiring decisions.

COMMENTS

JOE PESCI: A long time ago I worked for a consultant who had an interesting way of presenting his qualifications. He would use "case studies." Since he didn't want everybody to know the companies he invested in, sometimes he would call a company "A California technology company with 60mm sales." The case studies were not just lists of deals, but would highlight something of value that he did for the company that made it successful. Not naming the company allowed him to get into more details about what exactly he did for the client. After reading the case studies, you really got the point that he was a problem solver. Just giving a list of deals doesn't differentiate you from the competition.

I'VE WRITTEN A BROCHURE FOR YOU!

In this column, I'm presenting you with a gift: I'm ghost-writing for you a law firm brochure. I hereby grant all copyright interest in my brochure to you. Feel free to reproduce the following brochure, print it up, attach your firm's logo, mail or e-mail the brochure to clients and potential clients, and wait for business to beat a path to your door.

It's yours, free of charge, courtesy of Above the Law and yours truly. Don't say we've never done anything for you....

URGENT CLIENT ALERT!

On [fill in date], Congress passed a bill. The President signed the bill into law on [fill in different, later date]. The law becomes effective on [fill in yet a third date. Sorry: I realize this is more work than you'd anticipated. What can I say? Business development is hard work.]

The new law dramatically changes the old law. Indeed, the new law contains certain provisions: [fill in bullet points listing main topics covered by new law]. We're pleased to announce that we at the law firm of Bigg & Mediocre have created a "New Law Rapid Response Team" to answer all of your questions about the new law.

Our Rapid Response Team has carefully analyzed the new law. Here's the Team's advice about how your corporation should proceed:

1. Be sure to obey the new law. Appendices A and B to this brochure contain, respectively, the text of the new law and our Bigg & Mediocre summary of the law for quick reference. [Note: Actually creating Appendix B is optional. Don't strain yourself.]

2. There are penalties for failing to comply with the new law. Those penalties include, among other things, the possibility that someone will sue you—for damages! or fines! or something!—for violating the law. This makes it vitally important that you obey the new law.

3. Bigg & Mediocre strongly recommends that you train your employees to comply with the new law. By taking this critically important step, your firm will increase the likelihood that it actually obeys the new law, thereby minimizing your risk of being penalized for having violated the law.

4. Train your managers about the new law and how to implement it. This will enable your managers to answer questions that lower-level employees ask about the new law.

5. Take complaints relating to the subject matter of the new law seri-

ously. Implement a system for reporting complaints and addressing them. This will enhance your compliance with the new law and help to establish that your corporation acted in good faith to try to heed the new law's terms.

6. Review all of your existing policies to be sure that they comply with the new law. If your existing policies do not comply with the new law, revise your policies.

7. The new law may be amended from time to time in the future. Be sure to watch for amendments to the new law, and periodically review your corporate policies to be sure they account for any future amendments.

8. This new law creates a treacherous landscape, which can be navigated only by truly experienced outside lawyers, such as us. This is not a field for novices or morons, such as you and everyone else who works at your company. Accordingly, we recommend that you retain experienced counsel to assist you—counsel who have not merely read the law, but who have studied it and taken the time to think carefully about its implications, as this brochure demonstrates we have. Indeed, we at Bigg & Mediocre have one of the world's leading practices in advising companies about all kinds of laws. It's what we do—all day, every day. The Bigg & Mediocre Rapid Response Team stands ready to put that experience to work for you.

In the unlikely event that this is not self-evident, please note: The foregoing brochure does not constitute legal advice. Indeed, we're hard-pressed to call this "advice" at all. For legal advice, please contact members of the Bigg & Mediocre Rapid Response Team, whose names and contact information we list below.

[List names here. Don't forget to include the name and phone number of the relevant practice leader at your firm, even though he hasn't yet read the law and probably never will. You'll never hear the end of it if you leave him out.]

* * *

I've obviously tucked a hidden message into the preceding parody (or is it sarcasm? or perhaps vitriol?): When a new law becomes effective, it does make sense to alert clients to the development. Clients appreciate it, and those clients may in fact need advice. But you're not exactly impressing your readers when you send out a brochure (written by a dozen "authors") that resembles what I just cranked out in a half hour on a Saturday morning, showing my keen understanding of a "law" that's both generic and non-existent.

If you include even a whisper that there's a sentient human being at the helm of your brochure, you'll stand out from the crowd. Say something—anything—that isn't the usual pablum. Perhaps: "The new law may have an unintended consequence"—and identify it. Or: "This law may interact with another law in an important way." Or: "An industry association has announced that it will be filing a constitutional challenge to certain provisions in the law. If your corporation is interested in supporting that effort, call X." Or, for the truly industrious: "Bigg & Mediocre is launching a blog to monitor developments relating to this new law. If you'd like to subscribe to our blog, and thus to receive periodic updates about how the new law is being implemented, click here." But, unless you enjoy being perceived as one of the crowd, please don't tell us only that "a law was passed; you should obey it; we can help." Been there; heard that; not impressed.

COMMENTS

GUEST: While I agree with your approach for the most part, I got a chuckle out of this since I have written a number of client alerts and they do have their place. In fact, if written well they are often picked up for publication.

GUEST: Mark is Yadda Yaddaing the real work and value of this type of alert, which is reading hundreds of pages of Congressional hearings, pulling the important crap into an executive summary, and ideally trying to do this and send it out on the same day the legislation passes (which is impressive!) given that this Congress loves to play hide the ball and it can be difficult to track down a copy of the bill.

BUILDING A PRACTICE—A CASE STUDY

How do you build a practice for a law firm?

Everyone has a theory; I'll provide a case study.

In 1997, Congress was about to pass a law that would have been great for America, but horrific for business at the law firm at which I then worked. The firm thus (intelligently) created several committees to try to create new practices that could keep lawyers busy if the promised bill became law. I was asked to chair the "drug and device product liability business development committee."

At the time, my firm did essentially no pharmaceutical product liability work. I'd helped to defend a set of medical device cases, which was about as close as anyone had come to actual experience in the pharmaceutical products field, so I was the natural choice to lead this effort. When given that assignment, what do you do? How do you build a practice essentially from scratch?

Get famous. Make contact. Repeat. That's all there is, and all there ever will be. But how do you do it?

First, how do you get famous?

My little committee started a campaign of (1) writing articles, (2) giving talks, and (3) meeting folks in the drug products field. Publishing articles is easy: Journals are desperate for material, and if you have anything that resembles an idea, you can write it up and find a place for it in print. (Some lawyers set the bar even lower, self-publishing stuff in their law firm newsletters. I always preferred publishing articles in the real press first, and reproducing those articles in our firm's vanity materials later, to show the world that our thoughts had originally passed some editorial review process.) After an article has appeared in print, send copies to clients and potential clients, so the world knows that you exist.

I figure details matter here, so you can decide whether you personally care to undertake this type of business development effort. I went back through a collection of old reprints, and these are the numbers: I wrote or co-authored three articles in 1998, seven in 1999, four in 2000, one in 2001, two in 2002, and five in 2003. I also co-authored a book, *Statewide Coordinated Proceedings: State Court Analogues to the Federal MDL Process*, in 2003, and then worked on the revised edition that came out in 2004. (I didn't say this was easy. I said this was one way to develop a practice.)

When you write articles, don't do it alone. Contact in-house lawyers, and explain that you'd like to co-author articles with them. That gives you a chance to impress an in-house person with the quality of your mind and written work, and it lets the two of you work together. That's a good way to convince a potential client that you're competent. So that's a start on getting famous: Write articles.

Giving talks is also easy. If you write articles, people who sponsor seminars are likely to find your name and ask you to speak. Even if they don't, CLE providers are always searching for people willing to assemble course materials and give a talk, so it's easy to find a lectern and an audience. (Some law firms set the bar for talks lower, arranging in-house CLE programs, perhaps over lunch. That's nice if it works, because that gives a bunch of your lawyers a chance to chat up potential clients in a small group setting. But in-house CLE is also a dicey proposition: It's embarrassing to run a CLE class and have only a very few—two or three—clients attend. And in-house programs are relatively expensive to arrange and run. I generally preferred the other format: a CLE provider (or trade group, or whoever) would attract the audience and rent the space, and we'd then speak to the audience that the sponsor provided.)

Can I provide details here, as I did for the publications? I can't reconstruct precisely how many talks I gave as part of the business development initiative, so I'll estimate: I was probably giving four to six talks each year to fuel this effort.

When you speak, don't give your talks alone. If you're invited to participate on a panel, tell the sponsor that you'll find an in-house person to sit on the panel with you. Start making calls to find an in-house person interested in the opportunity. (Even if people decline the opportunity, they'll be flattered that you asked, and you'll have made contact.) Tell the in-house person that you'll prepare all the course materials and you'll distribute an outline of the presentation a week before the date of the talk. That makes the in-house person's life easy, and it again gives you a chance to impress a potential client with your competence. That's the second piece of getting famous: Give talks.

That covers getting famous. What about making contact?

Meeting potential clients is a hard part of this effort. Ask your colleagues at your firm to do some cross-selling (or, at a minimum, cross-introducing) for you. Have your partners who do transactional, intellectual property, or tax work for drug clients introduce you to the in-house product liability folks. Depending on your firm, this type of cross-selling may or may not be possible. If your partners hoard clients, they may not want to introduce you to their client contacts. On the other hand, if your firm manages to convince its lawyers to work for the common good, cross-selling should be relatively easy.

The members of my little drug and device committee were not uniformly industrious. Some folks refused ever to write an article or give a talk, preferring instead to bill time and, they thought, be rewarded for what counts. (That's not a crazy choice in many law firms. Firms seem to under-appreciate business development efforts and over-appreciate business development successes, not realizing that one often leads to the other.) Other members of the committee played along for a while, giving a talk or writing an article here or there. By the time three years had passed and our efforts had come to naught, however, everyone on the committee had basically given up. We stopped meeting regularly, and I alone continued writing, speaking, and meeting through the years.

I wasn't actually doing any legal work in this field, mind you. I was doing other types of product liability cases and mass torts, but I wasn't representing anyone in the pharmaceutical industry. I was just talking the talk. In a sense, my prolonged bluff was remarkable. Folks attending various conferences told me that I must have "a huge pharmaceutical product liability practice, because I see you speaking at all these conferences, and your name is everywhere." The sad truth was that, despite our massive efforts, we still had essentially no business in this area.

Our first nibble came in late 2004. (If you haven't done the mental arithmetic, that's seven full years—seven years!—of effort, with no payoff whatsoever, before we finally managed to convince a client to retain us in this field.) That first retention was plainly tied to the business development initiative, because a person who I'd (1) known for years, (2) spoken with on panels, and (3) co-authored articles with called to say that we'd be invited to participate in an RFP. We landed that RFP—"we'll take a chance on you guys, even though you don't seem to have much experience in the pharmaceutical world"—and finally started laboring in our chosen field.

In 2007, our pharmaceutical product liability practice was worth eight figures to the firm. The publications that rank law firms proclaimed us to have one of the country's leading pharmaceutical product liability practices (which may have in fact been true by then). What should my reaction have been—"Eureka!" or "Thank God"?

Where do you go from there?

Push harder, of course. Rather than mail reprints of articles to potential clients, I decided to invite potential clients to visit my writings. I figured this would avoid burdening uninterested recipients with unnecessary stuff, and I could establish an on-going relationship with more readers. I teamed up with a lawyer at Dechert and launched the Drug and Device Law Blog.

Why did I reach outside my own firm for a co-blogger? First, I knew from personal experience how hard it was to convince lawyers to write even one article per year as part of a business development initiative. I was about to ask (and rely on) someone to write one or two articles per week. This takes a very special brand of insanity, and I knew (from having worked with him in the past) that Jim Beck was my kind of lunatic. Second, Jim's firm had a longstanding drug products practice, and Jim had many contacts in the field, so Jim would be well-placed to let the world know that the blog existed. Finally, I anticipated that Jim and I would be writing many words, and we were thus likely to inadvertently write something that we later regretted. If the blog was hosted by two different people at two different firms, each firm had plausible deniability: It was always possible that the other guy was responsible for any post that came back to bite us.

We published one (real, substantive) post on the blog every weekday. When we started the blog, in late 2006, we were writing largely for ourselves, our parents, and a couple of other readers. But perseverance pays off. Within three years, we were drawing 30,000 to 40,000 pageviews per month. (I've posted previously about the costs and benefits of blogging. It was hard to trace any substantial business directly to the blog alone, but the blog did dramatically raise the profiles of the two of us who were feeding that unforgiving beast.) We had finally gotten "famous," in the sense of being relatively well-known to the people who retain lawyers in our specialized field.

In 2009, Oxford University Press contacted my co-blogger and me about writing a book on the defense of drug and device cases. Jim declined (because he'd already written a book on the subject); I accepted. My plan at the time was to use that book as yet another selling point, sending free copies to clients and potential clients and leveraging the book into opportunities to give CLE presentations in-house at drug companies and thus to make more contacts.

Sadly, there's many a slip 'twixt the cup and the lip. At year-end 2009, I went in-house, leaving behind the defense of drug and device cases and getting no compensation (other than a feeling of pride) when I finally held the book in my hands two years later.

I'm now out of the business of promoting a law practice. Because I'm no longer playing the game, however, I can be (and have been, in this post) brutally honest about the costs and benefits. The costs? A ton of time and effort, spanning many years, which many (silly) law firms will view as nonproductive. And the firm may ultimately be proven correct. For all your efforts, your business development initiative may not work.

The benefits? If you keep at it for longer than you'd care to admit, and if you get lucky, you can build, largely out of whole cloth, the practice that you'd like to have. Although I've discussed in this column only my own personal case study, the fundamentals of building a practice in any field are the same: Get famous; make contact; repeat.

Am I proud of what I did? Sure. (I've now re-read the column I just typed, and I fear that I haven't concealed my pride particularly well. So be it: I worked awfully hard, for an awfully long time, at fairly significant personal and professional sacrifice, to try to achieve something. And it worked. What can I say? I'm proud.)

Why did I choose to give it up and move in-house? Once every 25 years, you should try something completely new. It's good for the soul. Life can surprise you.

I'm not sure whether this column will encourage or discourage people from trying to build a practice. The process for building a practice (if your firm doesn't have one or is unwilling to bequeath one to you) is obvious: Get famous; make contact. The main question is whether, for you personally, the game is worth the candle. On that score, I'm afraid I have no insight.

COMMENTS

SAMIAM: The effort you describe is something that a 1st year associate should endeavor to do, even at the expense of billable hours. The associate shouldn't tackle the hard stuff right out of the gate—overview articles on the current landscape of the law are fine. If the associate tries to jump right into predicting the effect a new Supreme

Court decision or law will have on the industry, the associate will be blown out by those who really know the score.

DISGRUNTLED SENIOR ASSOCIATE: Key insight is "little bit of luck" comment. The same set of facts will, more often than not, result in a burned-out associate with no book of business spending 1/2 his money on his kids and ex-wife and the other half on alcohol and drugs to ease the pain of his miserable existence. Glad you got lucky.

CLOSER'S COFFEE: Mark Herrmann has an excellent case study here. It's encouraging to see that with planning, pluck and persistence good things can result. He is also a super positive guy, which is why he had the ability not to fall prey to deadly cynicism as the years wore on. What he accomplished is still being enjoyed by his erstwhile former partners.

GUESTY: This was very informative. However, unless you have a lot of clout at a law firm, most attorneys do not have 7 years to build up a practice. But it's good to know that hard work pays off in the long run (sometimes).

DETOUR

TALES FROM THE INTERVIEW CRYPT

I wish I could name names; I really do. But I work at the world's leading insurance broker for law firms, and I can't go around offending the clients (or potential clients). You'll just have to guess.

All of these interviews actually took place. I swear it.

First, there was the senior partner at a major New York firm, interviewing me at the start of my second year of law school: "You know, a lot of students want to make excuses for not having perfect grades. Sometimes, those excuses are pretty good: You hear from the single mothers. You hear from people who are working full-time and going to law school at night. The excuses aren't bad.

"But I have to tell you something: If you have to give me an excuse, I don't want to hear it. We have too many people who are perfect looking for jobs here. If you're perfect, we'll hire you. If you have to make an excuse, don't even bother telling me. If you have to make an excuse, we're not making you an offer."

I didn't say these stories were uplifting. I said only that they were true.

The next one's at my expense:

I had pretty good grades at the end of my first year in law school, so I naturally plastered my GPA on my résumé, so that no one would miss the point. One on-campus interviewer, from a leading San Francisco firm, glanced at my résumé and cleverly asked: "3.91, huh? What did you mess up?"

Now, I'm thinking: "I'm sitting in the top two percent at one of the great law schools in America, and the first thing you decide to ask me about is . . . grades? Why are you permitted to conduct interviews?" But I resisted temptation; I didn't snarl at the guy. No, not me. Instead, I said, completely straight-faced: "I'm the perfect candidate for you. All As and a B+ in Ethics."

I interviewed on campus with six firms that fall, and I got callbacks and offers from five of the six. I guess he didn't have a sense of humor.

The other side of the coin: I'm an associate at a small firm in San Francisco, and I trot over to Hastings to do our on-campus interviewing in 1986. The Hastings student tells me that she did research at the American Enterprise Institute one summer when she was in college. "Really," I ask, "What issue did you think about?"

"I wrote a paper on youth unemployment."

"Youth unemployment at the AEI," I pondered aloud. "Were you for or against?"

She wrote a letter to the managing partner of my firm, complaining about the "high-stress interview technique" to which I had subjected her.

(Why do you suppose I occasionally write "Inside Straight" columns about interview techniques? I plainly have a lot to learn.)

My last example isn't a personal one. One of my law school classmates interviewed at a big New York firm, known mainly for its expertise in bond work. My classmate asked one of his interviewers: "Your firm seems to do mainly bond work. Isn't that a pretty narrow area of law?"

"Oh, no!" thundered the partner. "We do all aspects of bond work. We represent issuers. We represent underwriters. We do corporate bonds. We do municipal bonds. We have a hugely varied practice."

I'm sure they do.

But that's unlikely to seem true to law students, no matter how loudly you insist. Perhaps that's why the story has stuck with me for these many decades.

COMMENTS

MARK: During an interview with a California firm, one interviewer indicated I was there because he was a huge fan of SEC football and was thrilled to see someone from Ole Miss Law apply to his firm. At that point, I had to decide whether to admit that Mississippi College wasn't The University of Mississippi. I did, and it was quickly clear I wasn't getting the job. We ended up talking about football for an hour.

GUEST123: Him: How are you?
Me: I'm doing very well. How about yourself?
Him: I'm good. Do you remember the 4 requirements for Rule 23 certification?
Me: No.
Him: Well, thanks for coming in.

DARTHLAWYER: [Scene: Me lying in bed, about 10 AM after a night of "celebrating" the last final exam of 1L year.]

Phone rings...

Me [From under the covers, still with the clothes (with sneakers) on from the previous day]: Hello.

Voice: Hey, Tom, how you doing today?

Me [Believing I had recognized the voice as someone I was out with the night before]: I'm hungover like a big friggin' dog.

Voice: This is _____, the partner at ___ & ____ who you'll be working for this summer.

Me: Uh...

Voice: That's the BEST answer you could have given. What were you drinking?

CORPORATE POLICIES; CORPORATE POLITICS

THE SINS OF INSIDE COUNSEL

It's time for the other side of the coin.

Sitting here in the catbird's seat, it's easy to criticize things that outside counsel do. (It's not just easy; my hope is that it's also worthwhile. When I was in private practice, I paid close attention when I learned about things that annoyed clients.) But we're equal opportunity critics here at ATL. It's time to turn my sights on myself: What do inside counsel do that works to our own detriment?

I haven't heard much from my outside counsel on this score, perhaps because I'm the client, and outside counsel are reluctant to criticize me (to my face). And I don't innately sense all the things that I'm doing that are grossly stupid. But I do remember a fair number of silly things that inside counsel inflicted on me when I was at a law firm, and I can work backwards from there.

What are the sins of inside counsel?

First: Be wary of your influence. When I was in private practice, we'd sometimes send a brief to the client for review, and the client would suggest six idiotic changes. We'd struggle with this: "Making any of these changes will make the brief worse. But we can't just tell our client that she's nuts and refuse to make any of the changes;

she'll be offended. We probably have to make revisions to reflect three of her suggestions, and we'll reject the other three. Which three of the client's suggestions do the
least harm, and how can we make changes that nod in the direction of the suggestions
without screwing up the brief too badly?"

Clients sometimes forget that they're clients. When they speak, intelligent outside
counsel listen and act accordingly. So inside counsel should be careful when they
speak. If you're unsure of something, seek advice. If you're going to require action,
be sure that the action serves a helpful purpose and is worth the cost. If you speak
without thinking, you're likely to trigger a flurry of activity, or responses to your requests, and that costs money and can be affirmatively harmful. Think first; then speak.

Second: Remember where you stand in the hierarchy of clients. If you're a big
client—you're buying every waking minute of my month—then you get full control
over my time. You want me in Seattle on Wednesday? I'm in Seattle. You change your
mind and route me to Denver? I'm in Denver. You know what I'm doing, and I'm doing it all for you. If you want to change my priorities, have at it. I'm all yours.

But if you're not buying every waking minute of the month, you have to permit
me to tend to my practice.

When I was in private practice, I fired only one client, and it was because he (or
she, but I'll use the masculine for convenience only) didn't understand how he fit into
my life. (Over time, my secretary and I came to refer to this in-house lawyer as "the
creature from Hell," which we later shortened to "Creech." So that's what I'll call him
here.) Creech retained me to handle a couple of small breach of contract cases. Those
cases occupied perhaps ten hours per month of my time.

I was, at the time, largely pinned down representing a defendant in a mass tort that
involved multiple allegations of wrongful death caused by an industrial chemical. The
mass tort kept me at the office nights and weekends. The contract cases did not.

Creech just didn't get it. I treated Creech with the utmost respect, as I did all of
my clients. (Well, okay. Maybe giving this guy the nickname "Creech" wasn't exactly showing the proper respect. But we never called him that to his face.) Although
I treated Creech with respect, Creech showed no respect in return. For example, I
was once at a meeting with senior executives of the multiple-wrongful-death client
and got an urgent e-mail from my secretary: "You must talk to Creech immediately.
Creech asks that you break out of your meeting and speak to him now."

I obediently excused myself from the multiple-wrongful-death meeting and ended
up chatting with Creech about how we'd handle reviewing some documents that we
wouldn't be producing for several weeks yet.

Sorry, Creech. That message should be left on my voicemail, with a request that I
call you back when I have a minute. That's not the stuff of "drag me out of a meeting
with another client, insulting them at your behest." How would you feel if another
client pulled me out of a meeting with you?

I didn't fire Creech for that alone. He did plenty of other crazy stuff, too. He insisted that we do unnecessary work and then refused to pay the resulting bills. When we tried to talk to fact witnesses to assemble discovery responses, Creech was slow to return calls and would run us up against deadlines. I suffered for a while, but ultimately I put the two pending contract cases to rest, and then referred Creech to other firms when he called for help in the future.

Third: Understand the realities of how a firm is handling your case. If yours is a huge matter, the senior partner who's working on the case may in fact be giving the case personal attention. But if your matter is smaller, the senior partner may have only a passing familiarity with what's going on.

This has implications: If you want to know what's happening on the case, call the person who knows, which may not be the senior guy. If you call the senior guy, he'll bluff his way through the first call with you, and then he'll check with his underlings and call you back later with the actual answer. That's unnecessarily expensive.

If you schedule a meeting with outside counsel and insist that the senior guy attend, realize that your outside law firm will be scrambling for 48 hours before the meeting, because the senior guy will realize that he's dumb as a stone and is about to embarrass himself in front of a client. The senior guy will ask junior people to run around crazy for two days pinning down irrelevant tangents, so the senior guy feels comfortable despite the depth of his ignorance. You can schedule this meeting if you really want to, but consider the activity it will trigger on the firm's part.

(If you're not happy with the senior person's lack of concern for your case, hire a different lawyer or a different firm. If you pair projects and lawyers carefully, you may be able to get the level of attention you prefer.)

Finally: If you ask for something (and the task is performed responsibly and intelligently), be prepared to pay for it. You can set up a meeting with the senior lawyer for next Tuesday, but don't be outraged by the time entries for the Sunday and Monday that precede the meeting. You can insist that partners personally review all documents that are being produced in a case, but you can't later cut the bill because the cost of document review was too high.

As I'm typing, I realize that I'm working up a head of steam here. I left private practice more than a year ago, and my blood pressure still rises just thinking back on these things. Give me a while to calm down. I may return to this topic in the future, if my heart can take it.

COMMENTS

GUEST: Mark, I was critical of a couple of your prior posts, but this is a good one. I hope for more like it in the future.

LATINTHUNDER: It seems like you could summarize two and three as "if you're a small client, realize that the firm doesn't really care about you and almost all of the work is being done by midlevel/senior associates."

SR ASSOCIATE: Not exactly. I care about my small clients, but I can't have something by end of day just because the small client asked for it. Yes, that may be 8 hours, but that client has no idea if I've been up for 36 hours straight on another deal or if I have something that has my day slammed. So, it's important for all clients to set reasonable timelines. Another way of saying what Mark says (and it's one of my chief complaints about clients) is that many clients behave as if you are just sitting in the bullpen waiting to be called. It doesn't work that way, unless (as Mark said), you've bought all of my time. Then, your stuff takes priority during that period. When it's your turn, and your matter truly is hot, then all of my time will be yours.

And as for work by midlevel and senior associates, while there are a number of knowledgeable partners out there, typically those partners are managing the project, taking only the highest level meetings, and advising on the business issues (but usually making the principals feel better), but they aren't researching the minutiae of the applicable facts, rules and recent best practices and digesting all of the specifics of the client's situation. Or drafting any provisions, no matter how complex. That is a poor use of partner time and billing rate.

G: Outside counsel should remember that inside counsel are lawyers, and if you send a brief to a lawyer for review, there will be changes. Just like when you send it to the partner in the firm for review. And you will consider many of the partner's changes idiotic. And you will make most of them anyway.

IHATEDISQUS: Best just to file a bunch of stuff on your own, without talking to inside counsel. Right?

GUEST: I think the point is that in-house counsel should realize they retained outside counsel for a reason; the outside guys know this stuff better than the client. In-house counsel shouldn't get miffed if outside counsel pushes back on the client's suggested changes; after all, they were hired to be the experts. Let them do their jobs.

KNOWITALL: No. I don't always hire outside counsel because I think they know better than I do. I hire them because I'm not licensed in the jurisdiction in which the lawsuit is filed, and even if I were I can't drop everything else I'm doing and work on a brief or a motion or discovery, etc. For the most part, I don't question outside counsel's conclusions, but when they get something dead wrong I don't hesitate to speak up. And I certainly will correct grammar and word choice when necessary—you don't have to be an expert in a particular field of law to edit a brief.

LEGAL VIKING: Though in fairness, in every Creech lies an opportunity for a more junior attorney. I was handed my office's Creech in my fifth year, when the senior partner got fed up with the nonsense. I stuck with him though the good and the bad (the bad included all of the above and then some); primarily, it was just about the only client I could put my name to.

A few years later Creech has grown his company, and is sending me some $250k worth of work every year. We have also been able to work out a reasonable way of dealing with his (real or perceived) emergencies, to the point where my wife no longer puts needles through his effigy.

GUEST: I once had a talk with the Assistant GC in charge of litigation for a Fortune 500. He freely acknowledged that: (1) he expected all calls and e-mails to be immediately returned, even if there was no real urgency; and (2) he expected my complete attention whenever I was working on his matters or in a meeting with him. When I asked him how I was supposed to do both of these things for more than one client, he told me that if I wanted him as a client I would have to make him feel like he was my only client, even if he wasn't paying bills to support that.

When I heard this, I discovered something that I have carried with me to this day. It isn't overly aggressive opposing counsel, complex and conflicting laws, or out of touch or biased judges that make this profession terrible—it's the clients. They screw up, and they want me to clean up their mess, which is fine because that's my job. But they also want perfection when they are unwilling to pay me to spend the time required to achieve it. They want my undivided attention, but only budget for 40 hours of my time a month. They want certainty, but they insist on walking as closely as possible to the line between lawful and unlawful conduct, even if that means knowingly strolling through legal gray area.

> **ETHICS NERD:** It's not the clients; it's the lawyers who put up with that stuff, creating a race to the bottom of sorts.

> **BOSTON PATENT LAWYER:** It's one thing to have the GC of a Fortune 500 company request such nonsense; it is another when a silly little client demands the same. At least with the Fortune 500 guy, you have a chance to bring in some big bucks. I had a client that spent maybe $5000 a year scream at me over e-mail that I had to call him immediately after he received my out-of-office response that I was on paternity leave starting that day (i.e., my kid was born that day). His exact words–"Your unavailability doesn't work for me. Call me immediately." Oh, and the biggest insult was the partner who actually got all the origination didn't back me, but rather chimed in that I needed to call this client back. I was so happy when I came in-house a year ago, and that e-mail has stuck with me: I will NEVER act that way to my outside counsel. I expect good work, I expect prompt attention, and I expect things done by real deadlines; but I also expect my outside counsel to enjoy time off with their families and deal with their other clients.

T.H. CRITIC:

1. I would bet dollars to donuts that Mr. Herrmann has been granted a nickname or two far cooler than "Creech" by former and current colleagues. I invite you all to guess at a few of them.

2. Outside Counsel often fail to remember that Inside Counsel know the business and facts much better than outside counsel, and often know the areas of law involved just as well. We don't, however, want to waste time drafting briefs, worrying about filing deadlines, and dealing with all the headaches of litigation–especially when it's hard to predict the resource needs in advance. Let's get this straight–unless we're talking about some highly specialized legal issues (which mass torts certainly don't qualify as), your client is fully qualified to tell you what about your brief sucks, and how to fix it. The quality of outside counsel never ceases to amaze me (how bad it is).

3. Any client treated as "second rate" is at the wrong law firm. If the client isn't big enough to get good treatment, he should go to a mid-size firm where he'll get people just as smart (if not smarter than the associate nincompoops handling his matters at the large firm) who want his business.

4. I disagree with everyone else and think this is another lousy installment. Hermie.

GUEST: In-house counsel need to know when to fire the outhouse when the "senior" person staffed on the deal doesn't know the case. You are just throwing money away by continuing to work with such a crap firm. MH may be speaking from experience at his old firm, but the ignorant should not assume other firms operate this way. The senior person staffed on your matter should be the expert on it.

BENEDICK: If a senior partner is "the expert" on the contents of a million-page document production, scores of non-party deposition transcripts, and all of the case law governing discovery disputes in the state—not his own—where the mass-tort case is pending, then his firm is doing it wrong and his client is overpaying.

OVERSEEING INTERNATIONAL LITIGATION

I've spent my whole life watching my ignorance be exposed.

When I worked at a small firm in California, I thought the whole litigation world was my oyster: We handled all civil cases (other than immigration or family law matters) in all state and federal courts in California.

I moved to a huge firm in Cleveland and lost my bearings: I now held myself out as being able to handle any civil case filed in any court in the United States. (This was a big change. When I worked in California, at least I knew what advance sheets to read. Cleveland set me adrift at sea.) Now, surely, the world was my oyster.

Wrong again. Now I've gone in-house, and I'm ultimately responsible for all litigation filed against my company anywhere in the world. The world is my oyster.

You'll be pleased to read that I actually have a point here, other than regaling you with fascinating details about my personal life. In fact, I have two points.

Both points expose my ignorance....

First, there's the lesson I'm learning in comparative civil procedure. When I talk to outside counsel about a lawsuit pending in the United States, I have a reasonably good sense of what's going on. My mind is in gear.

But when I talk to outside counsel overseas, I'm clueless. I now have a standard litany before I start one of these conversations:

"Before we talk about my particular case, I have to ask you a few questions. First, do you have juries in your country for a case such as mine? Second, in your country, does the losing party pay the winning party's legal fees? Third, in your country, is it possible to learn before trial what evidence the other side is likely to present in court? If so, is that procedure restricted to learning in advance what documents the other side will offer, or are we allowed to put the other side's witnesses under oath and learn before trial what the oral trial testimony is likely to be? In your country, is it possible to get out of a lawsuit before a trial is held? If so, when will we have those opportunities, and what standards will the court apply?" Finally, in a few (but by no means all) countries, "Can we trust the judicial system, or are the judges typically corrupt?"

Then we can talk.

This has been fascinating (to me, at least, but I realize I'm a little odd) in several ways. I never before focused on what a U.S.-centric litigation life I had been living. There's a brave new world out there, and I'd never given it a moment's thought. Once I gave it thought, I was surprised by how few questions it actually takes to get one's mind in gear. My standard litany hardly turns me into an expert in, say, Sudanese civil procedure, but my few questions are enough to elicit the general lay of the land. It's also surprising to see that, so long as the judiciary is honest, it's possible to participate in basically any type of judicial proceeding and be generally comfortable with the process. The rules of procedure vary wildly, but you can basically live with 'em all.

The second spot where I was ignorant involves a dicier issue. In the United States, the ethical rules forbid lawyers from threatening to initiate criminal proceedings to obtain an advantage in a civil case. So we don't do that.

But the rules in, say, Sudan may not be so clear. (I'm picking on Sudan because it's on the so-called OFAC list, which forbids U.S. companies from doing business there. So my employer is pretty unlikely to find itself before some Sudanese judge who's ticked off because I made fun of his country in a post at Above the Law. You can't be too careful, you know.)

(By the way, did I mention that I hold the Sudanese judiciary in the highest regard?)

Anyway, suppose opposing counsel in Sudan threatens my client (or my local counsel) with criminal proceedings to try to coerce settlement of a civil case. If that's the way people litigate in Sudan, can I tell my local counsel to retaliate by threatening to initiate criminal proceedings of our own? Or am I constrained by American rules of propriety even when I'm playing in a Sudanese sandbox?

It would probably violate attorney-client privilege to reveal whether I've yet confronted this issue in my in-house job. And I must say that my initial reaction is to play by the American rules of ethics (for a host of reasons, including self-preservation). But I worry that while I'm playing by the Marquess of Queensberry Rules, the other side will be playing by the Marquis de Sade's, and my client will suffer from my failure to be a sufficiently zealous advocate.

Here's the beauty of having been invited to write for Above the Law: Now that I've posed this question publicly, it's likely that some knowledgeable person will be able to provide an answer.

If so, I'm all ears. I've been ignorant for long enough.

COMMENTS

DIPLOPHOBE: Litigation abroad, particularly in the developing world, can be expensive and nightmarish. This is especially true when dealing with a country that has no litigation bilateral agreement with the U.S. International arbitration clauses are the way to go, assuming that the government or foreign party you're doing business with is a signatory to the New York Convention (the major international arbitration treaty which assures enforcement of awards and offers certain due process rights to the parties involved in the dispute).

> **FLUX CAPACITOR:** While you are probably correct that "international arbitration clauses are the way to go," I imagine our guest columnist is dealing with several scenarios in which there is already litigation pending abroad and that he possesses no time machine with which to go back and urge the parties to agree to international arbitration in the relevant agreement.

FROZT: On the one hand, I'm sure a state Bar would disapprove if you bribed a Sudanese judge, even if they were hopelessly corrupt, so I'm disinclined to think that all bets are off so long as the matter is in a foreign jurisdiction. On the other hand, the Bar wouldn't bat an eye if you withheld evidence that you would be required to turn over under U.S. law but not Sudanese.

With absolutely nothing to back me up, I'm going to guess the Bar would discipline you for threatening to bring a criminal suit overseas to help with litigation. The reason is that the decision to bring charges is not simply a procedural, administrative aspect that's likely to vary from jurisdiction to jurisdiction. It's substantive—it's the whole kit and caboodle (did anyone else think it was "kitten caboodle" when they were growing up?) and I think the Bar would frown on raising the whole case for corrupt reasons, even if not barred in that jurisdiction.

Of course, that's based on the idealized, Professional Ethics conception of the Bar, so cynics will certainly have their own opinion about what would influence them.

THE GOLDEN RULE: #1–Foreign Corrupt Practices Act.
#2—Frozt is an idiot.

NOOB QUESTION: Does FCPA apply to non-publicly traded corporations?

THE GOLDEN RULE: From DOJ website:
Since 1977, the anti-bribery provisions of the FCPA have applied to all U.S. persons and certain foreign issuers of securities.

FROZT: It does, and Golden Rule seems to misunderstand the issue, which is whether Herrmann could ethically raise criminal charges. Yes, the U.S. attorney could prosecute him or his corporation under FCPA for bribing a judge, but it could not for threatening to bring criminal charges to aid in litigation. But regardless of the U.S. attorney's decision to prosecute criminally, the question is 1) whether it would be ethical for Herrmann to do so, and 2) whether a state Bar could bring charges.

GUEST: Of course, the following is just speculation and not legal advice . . .
The rules of professional conduct apply whether or not you are involved in a legal matter. For example, you are subject to discipline if you engaged in dishonest non-legal activities, like running a Ponzi scheme. If the rules apply to non-law-related conduct, then they should also apply to extra-territorial law-related conduct.

Of course, the above is just begging the question. The issue boils down to whether an action, which if committed in the US would clearly be unethical, is still unethical when committed in a country where such action is routine. An above commenter made an analogy to bribes, but I don't know if that is entirely helpful, because bribery usually doesn't include "grease payments." Is threatening the other side with criminal charges more like a bribe or more like a grease payment?

One thing you might consider is whether the given extra-territorial action is prohibited, but not enforced; expressly allowed; or merely condoned without any official position one way or the other. If it is expressly allowed, you probably have a good argument for it also being ethical to take such action in that country. If it is expressly disallowed, but not enforced, then there is a good argument for it being unethical. And, of course, if there is no clear rule one way or the other, you're back where you started. Of course, a pattern & practice of such behavior occurring without any official denouncement could probably be taken as a tacit approval, leaning towards such behavior being ethical.

In this scenario, the best course of action is probably to get an opinion letter from an ethics attorney stating that taking such action is not barred by the rules of professional conduct so you can CYA if a complaint is ever filed against you.

GUEST: First, I suggest doing some quick spot research before you go into unfamiliar lands (most paid search services have some overview on the country). Having the initial knowledge will also help you assess the foreign counsel you are dealing with.

Second, the CYA comment above was on point but misguided. You are NOT practicing law in foreign countries and you must rely on the advice of foreign counsel. If foreign counsel suggest a way of advocacy that they are comfortable with, then you should entrust them with that decision. However, it will be different if you are actually participating in the act and, of course, you cannot commit criminal acts nor condone those committed by your legal representatives. So if threatening criminal actions in conjunction with civil actions is fine, then let the foreign counsel do it. If you really want to do the threatening, then it might be better to CYA with a legal memo.

From a practical point of view, your role changed when you moved in-house. You no longer have a firm to insulate your liability nor do you have malpractice insurance. While you want to give your client good representation, it is not in your self-interest to always seek the best possible representation when it could result in sanctions against you personally. I've met many different types of GCs—some care a great deal about this and some set the line at illegal (or barely legal) and pay little attention to US legal ethics when doing business overseas.

For the bribery example, this is way off base. Not only would it likely violate the law in Sudan, it would also violate the law in the US. Nothing to win here and NEVER, EVER be involved in bribery or "greasing." Not worth it and it is ridiculous to think bribery even merits discussion.

I WANT TO HIRE ... ME!

I've never met Steve Susman, but he cracked me up recently.

Susman clerked at the Supreme Court, and the word on the street is that he's a pretty theatrical guy. He was recently interviewed about the ideal candidate to work at his law firm, Susman Godfrey, and here's what he had to say:

"Someone who's clerked at the Supreme Court, is brilliant, and has theatrical presence. There's a theatrical aspect to trial work."

Ha! Susman wants to hire . . . Susman!

Isn't this true all too often?

Years ago, when I worked at a small law firm, two partners played big roles in the hiring process. One of the partners had gone to Yale Law School, although my guess is that he hadn't been a superstar there. The other partner had attended UC Davis, worked on the law review, and later served as a judicial clerk. Whenever we were making hiring decisions, I'd always hear from the first guy that "what matters is the school you attended, and not so much how well you did there." The second guy would simultaneously be saying that "the top students at all law schools are basically the same; what matters is where you finished in your class." In short, the best person to hire is . . . the person who looks just like me!

I now hear the same thing when I talk to folks about in-house hiring. The person who just barely graduated from a law school you've never heard of, but has worked in one industry for a couple of decades, insists that the key factor in hiring new people "is industry expertise; we need people with real knowledge of our business."

On the other hand, the person who went in-house with great credentials, but no knowledge at all of the industry that he or she was entering, says that industry experience is terribly overrated. "We want the best athlete available. Any smart person can learn about an industry. Just give 'em six months. We need to hire people with raw intelligence who are great lawyers."

(If you're wondering where unintentional discrimination breeds, I suspect one place is the subconscious mind. If many people subconsciously prefer to hire people who resemble them, it's then an awfully short step to creating glass ceilings and a lack of diversity in the workforce.)

Personally, I'm still on the fence about this. We haven't yet hired too many folks on my watch, so I'm not quite sure where I come down on the need for industry expertise. When the time comes, I'll try to overcome my likely bias against requiring industry expertise that results from my having had none when I took my current job. (That bias may well be reinforced by my having spent my life in private practice as a general litigator, where we always told potential clients that "litigation is a toolkit. Good litigators can handle any kind of case, no matter what the subject matter. Industry experience is irrelevant." Whether or not that's precisely true is another matter, but it's surely the mantra of the general litigator.)

I'll be curious to hear from people who have strong opinions, one way or the other, on the "industry experience" versus "best athlete available" debate. If you choose to join that discussion in the comments, however, please disclose your bias: Based on your academic and professional background, would you be better described as a "best athlete available" or a "person with industry experience"? Armed with that information, we'll be able to judge what you say.

I do know that, when we have our next opening in our law department, I'll probably be looking for someone who did reasonably well in college and law school, clerked for a federal appellate judge, worked at one small law firm and one large one, and stands about 5'11", maybe 175 pounds. If you fit the bill, give me a call. You sound just about perfect.

COMMENTS

GUEST: This is true of all professions, where people want to hire someone who took the exact same road, seeing it as the best way possible.

GUEST: Hire the Best Athlete Available, without question. We work on the legal side, not on the business side.

Sometimes we need to say "no" to the business people. It is better to be more independent of them.

> **HENRY:** Good strategy for CYA–horrible strategy for getting good peer reviews when it comes time for performance evaluation. Really, really horrible strategy when it comes to dealing with your board, who are inclined to find business solutions and simply want you to note the legal issues and give them "probabilities" (yes, percentage odds of various outcomes!). If you just say "no," you won't go far and won't last long. You need to find ways to make the business solution happen and mitigate legal risks to the degree possible and document that you advised of the legal risks at the time and a business decision was made to accept those risks (so when things blow up, you're covered).

THE RESISTANCE: If you work in an industry with any technical base, hiring people with a background in it makes a HUGE difference. The more technical lawyers in my group catch things that others miss constantly, and very few of the non-technical ones ever fully catch up IMHO.

STRANGERINTHEDAY: I lean to "best athlete available." But I am always asking myself whether a potential hire is looking for a job or looking for a career. Someone who has been in the industry has proven his commitment to the industry at least. A best athlete available who is looking for a job will probably just get up to speed when he leaves. But I am a person from a top school who thinks that great people go to various schools for a variety of reasons: money, scholarship, significant other, staying close to family, a parent went there. That does not make people from these non-elite schools anything less than top notch.

But I do like a journal or law review. It shows that the person is willing to work long hours for free.

LITIGATIONTOCORPORATE: I actually made a shift from commercial litigation to in-house corporate work. I agree with the 'toolkit' theory, and from my perspective I'd like to add the 'anatomy' theory. Medical students study the body and how it works by studying cadavers. Why do we believe lawyers can only gain contract experience through drafting and not picking apart every detail of a contract in litigation? If I had to do it over again, I would not have gone into litigation out of law school, because it is hard to change tracks down the line. (Is it really surprising that I went into litigation when we study everything in law school, even corporate law, through appellate decisions?) I could not get in the door at any company until I took a quasi-legal contract position which eventually led to me becoming one of 2 in-house attorneys at a company that never had an in-house legal team before. I think my experience as a litigator (quick thinking, knowing how to find an answer fast, explaining legal concepts to clients) helped me succeed, and in the 2 years I was there I probably crammed in more corporate work than any associate at a larger law firm. Bottom line, I go for the best athlete, although I want to at least see an interest in the industry (I was a bit of a tech geek, which helped a lot).

OY, LIBYA!

The Libyan rebels have it easy. All they have to do is overthrow a megalomaniacal dictator who has mustard gas.

But in-house lawyers? Now, they have it tough.

(I write these columns several days before they appear on-line. If Qaddafi is still in power as of Monday, March 7, 2011, then read this column as providing advice for the future. If, on the other hand, Qaddafi's already out of power, then view this as a remarkably quick historical case study.)

On February 25, President Obama signed an Executive Order prohibiting certain transactions relating to Libya. Australia, Canada, and the United Nations Security Council promptly imposed sanctions of their own. Other countries will surely follow suit.

The rules governing trade with Libya will evolve in the United States as, among other things, the Treasury Department's Office of Foreign Assets Control identifies entities linked to the targeted regime or that engage in targeted behaviors. The rules will also change in the rest of the world, as other countries create and implement sanctions regimes. Large multinational companies will be doing business in countries that will impose differing economic sanctions on Libya.

What will smart outside lawyers do?

They'll monitor this situation closely, assemble multinational teams of lawyers who can answer questions that arise in any country, and dispense sage advice. The advice will often be accurate and precise: "Don't do business with any person or entity that has materially assisted the commission of human rights abuses related to political repression in Libya." With luck, as the guidelines become a tad more specific, the legal advice will follow in turn.

But think about the poor in-house lawyer. Even when the rules become clear, it will be awfully tough to heed them. A big company may have 100,000 employees working in 100 or more countries around the world. You can't exactly send out an e-mail asking, "Yo! Any of you guys do any work in Libya?" (Well, I suppose you can. But that's only a short-term fix.)

So the outside lawyer recites what the rules say, and the poor in-house schlub has to figure out how to operationalize the rules. Do we have service contracts with any Libyan companies? (Those contracts may have been legal yesterday and become illegal today.) To whom do we sell products in Libya? In the insurance space, have we placed any insurance policies that cover Libyan risks? If someone makes a claim on one of those policies tomorrow, what, if any, claims handling is permitted? And what about reinsurance contracts? Are there any insurance policies covering Libyan risks for which we've placed reinsurance that must now be treated delicately?

It's not exactly like you can answer those questions by making a couple of phone calls.

Once you identify your company's relationship with Libyan entities, you must then draft and implement policies to avoid missteps. Is there a way to cause the Finance Department not to pay bills to certain Libyan companies or that relate to Libyan issues? And how do you update those policies, country by country and day by day, to stay current?

The mergers and acquisitions team may not have it any easier. If you're thinking of buying a company that does business on a global scale, you must now conduct due diligence to determine whether the target does any prohibited business. If no one's been tracking the Libyan business, how do you unearth it in due diligence?

Finally, after the rules are in place, unsophisticated outside advisors will continue to punt the tough issues to inside counsel. (Please don't take what I'm writing here as implicit criticism of the outside compliance advice that my company receives. We're lucky to work with some of the very best.)

Eventually, the sanctions rules may well specify new categories of people or entities with whom you can't do business. But the rules will be amorphous. They may, for example, provide that you can't do business with a "government-owned entity." (In fact, the rules governing Libya may already say that. I'm not exactly a compliance jock. You want legal advice? Consult your lawyer.) Outside counsel will say, "Don't do business with government-owned entities." And inside counsel will be stuck with the hard job—advising the business folks whether or not they can do a deal with a company that is, say, only 30 percent owned by the Libyan government, but over which the government has management control.

Or the U.S. rules will ultimately say that U.S. companies can't "facilitate" forbidden transactions, but the Swedish rules will be more forgiving. Will our U.S. employees be allowed to hand off business to our colleagues in Stockholm who can take over the deal? Or is that forbidden? When our customers are about to be left in the lurch because we can no longer assist them, is it legal to place those customers in the hands of competent third parties (in other countries) who could help?

The best outside lawyers will distinguish themselves in two ways. First, they will help inside lawyers to operationalize policies. Counsel will tell us that Company A did this to operationalize a new compliance policy, and Company B did this, and we might try an amalgam of those approaches, coupled with a few new tweaks, to comply with the new sanctions regime.

Second, sophisticated counsel will not shy away from the tough issues. Don't tell us that we can't do business with "government-owned entities" or "facilitate" forbidden transactions and then leave us to our own devices. Rather, use your specialized knowledge, substantial resources, and the luxury of time to think through the hard issues and provide compelling (and reassuring) advice. And don't shy away from putting your neck on the line. The in-house lawyer ultimately puts his or her neck on the line by making the tough judgment call. Come along with us for the beheading; we love the companionship.

COMMENTS

IN-HOUSE BEHEADING: "Come along with us for the beheading; we love the companionship."

As an in-house counsel who has a senior position at a multi-billion dollar company, that line made me laugh. It is so true. Awesome. I will use that with our outside counsel.

GRIZZLED VETERAN: Relax–unless you're a bank doing major banking for Libya or Oxy Pete or another major doing petroleum business with Libya, nobody will ever know. The DOJ has better things to do, like surf the web all day and avoid bringing suit against the Black Panthers.

If Aon writes a policy for a company that is 30 percent owned by the Libyan government, nobody is going to know or care except Aon.

Quit worrying about non-issues. Unless you're an oil major or oil service company doing biz in Libya or a bank with significant Libyan accounts, this is a complete non-issue that a seasoned in-house counsel would not lose sleep over.

Don't sweat the stuff that is never going to come up and is de minimis if it does. No DOJ attorney is going to waste any time pursuing such a non-issue.

BRIAN: Excuse me, but I think a whistle-blower would make everyone know.

TOP: And there is no Central Scrutinizer checking businesses for whether they are doing business with Libya or not. It's not like the DOJ just assigned 300,000 lawyers to audit every business contract in every US or multinational company with a US presence.

In these situations, ignorance is a fine defense. It is stirring up memos and e-mails that raise these non-issues that will give rise to liability, if any, if ever.

What are the penalties–tops is maybe a small fine. Big deal. Best to quit worrying about trivial, non-core business issues.

JOEY_33: To the extent our jobs are irrelevant and our clients can break the law with impunity, you have a point. To the extent that some clients want to follow the law–for a variety of reasons–and occasionally a company gets creamed for its willful ignorance, I don't think this advice should be too heartily embraced.

IN-HOUSE COMPENSATION

I really don't care much about compensation.

Let the abuse begin.

If you hate your job, then no one can pay you enough to make going to work every day worthwhile. And if you love your job, you won't be sitting around fretting about your pay. I understand that this is America and all that, but within very broad limits, you're nuts to accept one job over another because of a small difference in compensation.

(I understand that you may be trapped in a job, because of student loans, or kids in college, or the like. I understand; trapped is trapped. And I understand that I personally have been awfully lucky, because I've never had to worry about finding money to pay next month's rent, so I speak from a particular point of view. Despite all that, I stand by what I said—if job A and job B are meaningfully different from each other in ways that matter to you, and you're not trapped, you're nuts to take one job over the other just to earn a few extra grand each year. Period.)

Naturally, since I'm not interested in the subject, you can guess the question I've been asked most often since Above the Law anointed me an in-house counsel guru:

How does in-house compensation work, and what questions should I ask about compensation if I'm interviewing for an in-house job?

I was clueless. So I cobbled together a recent post (from links elsewhere on the web) about bonuses paid to in-house counsel. And now I've talked to a co-worker who deals with compensation issues and has an office nearby, and I reached out to folks at other corporations. Here's what I learned.

First, several industry-wide compensation surveys exist. They include the Hildebrandt Law Department Benchmarking Survey, Inside Counsel's annual compensation survey, and Altman Weil's Law Department Compensation Benchmarking Survey. If you look there, you'll get a general sense of what to expect.

Second, compensation for companies tends to track company sales. Companies with more revenue tend to pay more compensation for similar jobs.

Third, extra incentives such as bonuses and stock are an important part of in-house compensation packages. (I actually knew that before the guy down the hall told me so.) Your compensation will probably consist of a base salary, a bonus, and (depending on your position in the company) an award of stock or options.

Fourth, at many law firms, you receive a certain amount of compensation and then pay for many other things on your own nickel. Depending on the firm, that may include some items that are pretty significant (such as paying for some or all of your health insurance) and others that are less important (such as paying for your BlackBerry, continuing education programs, certain business development expenses, and so on). Corporations vary in this regard, but some will provide a basic compensation package and also pick up some of the extras, which raises your overall remuneration.

Fifth, compensation will naturally be affected by your level of experience and area of legal expertise.

Finally, many corporations are today making increased use of discretionary (rather than fixed) compensation. You may thus have a base salary that more or less tracks the rate of inflation, coupled with discretionary bonuses that reward you for individual or corporate performance.

In addition to pestering folks for that general information about in-house compensation, I also asked for suggestions about questions one might pose to potential employers. (I must say that I asked none of the following questions before I accepted my in-house job, and you'd have to have much better interpersonal skills than I do to get away with asking some of these puppies during a job interview. But this is what people suggested to me, and who am I to censor?)

- How are incentives calculated? Are they based on company revenue, department performance, individual performance, or a combination of all three? How is individual performance measured?
- Are there midyear reviews that allow you to track your performance against specified goals?
- What will your career path be within the law department? Are there career paths that will let you develop your skills and move up in the ranks?
- What has been the corporate culture about cost cutting? Have there recently been cuts in the company's shared services functions (such as the law department)? If so, what has the effect been on salary increases, career progression, and bonus payouts during the last few years?
- What is the range of bonus targets for employees at different levels within the law department, and how are those ranges determined?
- When you receive a bonus, are you allowed to take the full bonus in cash or are you required to defer some of your bonus in the form of a stock award? If a stock award, what is the vesting period?
- What type of market analysis does the company do to set lawyer compensation, and how often does the company adjust compensation to the market?

Frankly, and apparently unlike many folks who visit Above the Law, I don't find compensation to be a fascinating topic. But you asked, and I've done what I can to help. I hope that serves a purpose.

But I didn't take much joy in it. Please don't expect me to return to this subject for a good long time.

COMMENTS

GUEST: Would you seriously feel insecure or uneasy about asking questions about incentives, performance reviews, and career advancement opportunities? Wow.

DAVID LAT: My general advice is to get the job offer first. Then, once you have the offer, you can kick the tires a little and ask more probing questions about pay, performance reviews, etc.

Of course, the line separating these two states—pre-offer and post-offer—isn't always perfectly clear. Sometimes the offer is contingent upon the employee being willing to accept certain terms, and the potential employer explores this in the interview process. E.g., "This job involves [X]—can you accept that?"

BITTER IN-HOUSE: Corporations also lie through their teeth about this stuff in recruiting, and, unlike with a firm, there is little public market for the info.

In interviewing for my new in-house gig before leaving firm life a few years ago, I was informed that I should expect bonuses to be around 15-20% over my base, and that the company was in the process of adjusting its base comp structure upward significantly as well. The latter smelled like smoke and mirrors, but the former seemed market and I had no reason to think my future boss would lie straight to my face, so I took him at his word.

I've now been here, at a Fortune 500 company, for a few years, and received only one bonus—of less than 6% of annual comp—and one raise—of less than 2% of annual comp—despite the company making very good profits and issuing dividends regularly since then. I've gotten well-priced options that make up for some of this so far (though that could easily dissolve overnight if the market turns), but they of course vest over years, so this is all something to keep in mind.

If your offer does not include a set bonus value on a set timetable tied to a set and easily measurable goal that they can't screw with, in writing, in the offer (e.g., annual bonuses of not less than X% as long as the company is profitable, and even that latter one has been used to screw countless employees when the CEO and other exec staff take big bonuses and push the company into the red, esp. with smaller family-type businesses), you will likely get screwed, and you should in any event assume your salary will be fixed in perpetuity at whatever your initial offer is.

ELIE'S COMING BACK: Most corporate law departments outsource litigation to external counsel and only need maybe one or two in-house litigation people (and maybe one of those is a paralegal) to coordinate issue-spotting, handle document transfer for production, translate business issues and relevant institutional knowledge, and mediate interviews and depo prep with internal personnel.

Litigation associates are a dime a dozen, so expect around $130-180K depending upon level of experience, plus some modest stock options and a bonus that depends on meeting both your personal and the corporate goals (the latter of which you have little to no control over). Without prior significant corporate and securities experience and connections into I-bankers, you'll likely go no higher than at most assistant GC or associate GC–ever.

BG: Commenter gives more useful info than supposed expert. Thanks. I'm not really interested in going in-house, but it's good to be informed.

GUEST: Mr. Herrmann, since you don't care about compensation, walk down the hall to your boss's office and announce that, to improve your company's bottom line, you will take a voluntary pay cut to $25,000 per year and will accept no perks. That will improve profitability, and you will enjoy your job just the same. Saying you don't care about compensation is just about the biggest lie I've ever read in print. It's absurd, smug, drivel that is very out of touch with your readership. You may not care about compensation now because you make enough so that you don't HAVE to care about it. But, at some level you better care about compensation or you'll end up homeless. You complained in an earlier column that outside counsel need to provide meaningful insight when communicating with in-house counsel. You, sir, are no different when communicating with your readers. And, you just lost one.

NO COMPLAINTS: I worked for 6 years as an associate in the investment management group within the Corporate department of a major NY law firm. At the firm, I was making $250K plus a market hours-based bonus at the time I accepted an in-house offer in December '07. I left to work as a VP in the legal department covering the asset management business in the NY office of a top European investment bank. My offer for '08 was $160K base with a guaranteed cash bonus of $150K (my first year guaranteed cash comp was $310K). Obviously the financial markets tanked and comp at the bank was frozen for '09 (i.e., same base and bonus), but I was happy to keep my job. For 2010 my base was raised to $200K and I received a cash bonus of $140K for total cash comp of $340K. The Bank also provides matching 401k and some stock. However, the stock vests over time based on a complicated formula where you forfeit the stock if you ever leave (5+ years to get anything). So the stock only has real value if you stay for the long haul. Comp in the in-house market is all over the place based on industry, however, I believe what I have received is typical for legal within an investment bank across practice areas (litigation, capital markets, IP, asset management, etc.). Hope this is helpful.

IN-HOUSE GUEST: I am also an in-house attorney (and have been for 4+ years–before that I logged 4+ years of top tier Big Law litigation). I work at a very well-performing Fortune 50 company. My experience has been exactly the same as the commenter Bitter in House. I receive excellent reviews. Compensation is crap. When you are recruited they don't tell you how bad it really is compensation-wise. Starting salaries are between 100 and 115K for top tier candidates with 4 or more years of experience. Bonuses are completely discretionary and you're lucky to get 6% of your base as a bonus (12K average). I've received virtually the SAME bonus each year despite taking on more work (with less employees to spread the work out between due to continuing layoffs). And raises, yeah right. Raises were frozen for the last 24 months companywide, but on average you can expect a 2% yearly raise of your base compensation (and that's for a well-performing employee). Oh, and promotions—those don't happen either very often. Average of 5-7 years for exemplary employees between each promotion and even longer now that the economy crashed.

Think twice before jumping ship from a big firm...for this is your future.

BEMUSED: First time I have read this blog, but my attention is drawn more to the silly comments. General observations: 1) wayyyyyyy too much time on your hands; and 2) while posting these attack comments may somehow be "therapeutic" for you, perhaps only a licensed therapist can help you find the root causes of your feelings and neuroses. Just saying.

THE TRUTH BEHIND E-BILLING

I'm an idiot. I really am.

When I was in private practice, clients said that they instituted e-billing for reasons of efficiency: "We can process bills and pay you faster if you submit bills electronically. E-billing speeds the process for both of us."

I knew that bills that we submitted electronically underwent some kind of review. It always felt as though it was review by chimpanzee, as clients seemingly whacked hours randomly, leaving us with the hard choice whether to remain silent or quibble about a few bucks here and a few bucks there. But fundamentally I accepted the basic proposition that e-billing improved efficiency.

Now I know better....

(Actually, I don't really know much better. I added a provocative sentence followed by an ellipsis so that Lat would know precisely where to put the break for the "continue reading" icon when he loads this post into the ATL blogging software.)

Where was I?

Oh, yeah: It's true that e-billing solves many administrative burdens for corporate clients, and e-billing can in fact speed the payment of bills. But e-billing does several other things that I never really considered until I moved in-house.

First, e-billing makes it easier for clients to eliminate charges that appear to be improper (such as a firm having taken too many hours to perform a task or having assigned too many lawyers to a case). When corporate clients made those adjustments in the world of paper bills, the adjustments required an exchange of correspondence and a series of conversations to sort things out. When clients make those adjustments in the world of e-bills, the law firms are typically able to press a button and print a report of the disallowed charges. The firms thus see what was disallowed (and a short-form description of the reason for the adjustment) without the need for exchanges of paper and phone calls simply to set the stage for a conversation.

Second, e-billing makes it much easier for clients to track the fees that they've disallowed. In the days of paper bills, clients could track the hacked fees only by manually entering dollar values into a database. E-billing tracks the disallowed fees automatically. Needless to say, in-house folks are better able to take credit for saving a company money if they're able to track the amounts that they've saved.

Third, the e-billing system can automate parts of the process for reviewing bills. If someone is manually reviewing paper bills, that person must remember all of the applicable rules: Is it a quarter, a dime, or a nickel for photocopies? What's the rule for charges for computerized research? Who pays for cab fare home after a lawyer's late night at the office? And on and on.

E-billing permits corporations to load their pre-set rules into the database, and the computer will apply those rules uniformly and accurately to all incoming bills, eliminating some of the tedium and many of the errors caused by manual review.

Am I pleased with this?

In one sense, sure. If we can speed a process and make it more predictable and measurable, that's probably a good thing. And if the computerized process can reduce the amount of time that lawyers and clients must spend discussing billing issues, both sides would surely be pleased.

On the other hand, automated systems that unthinkingly cut bills can lead to unintended consequences. For example, some corporate clients refuse to pay for more than ten hours of a single lawyer's time billed in one day unless the lawyer is physically at a trial site. On its face, that seems like an innocuous rule; after all, most lawyers become inefficient after billing more than ten hours in a day, and restricting payment may be a two-bit safeguard against lawyers padding their bills.

But, if a client absolutely refuses to pay for more than ten billed hours in a day, you can bet that outside counsel will be aware of that rule. Suppose a lawyer could schedule a jam-packed day, leaving the house at 6 in the morning, studying key documents on the plane, spending most of a day with a witness, and flying back on the 8 p.m. outbound, to arrive home, exhausted, just before midnight. Impose a no-more-than-ten-hours-a-day rule, and only the most devoted lawyer will schedule that trip, even if it might make sense to run that gauntlet for a particular client in a particular matter. Instead of working hard and not getting paid, the lawyer may well choose to leave home at a more civilized hour, work fewer hours with the witness, enjoy a leisurely dinner (courtesy of the client) on the road, stay overnight at a hotel, work with the witness for an hour or two the next morning, and then fly home mid-day. The computerized e-billing software will approve those charges, even though the client may well have incurred extra cost as a result of the conduct the rules encouraged.

I'm not taking sides here. I was outside counsel for a long time and I understand the billing process from that perspective. Now I'm in-house counsel, and I'm looking at the other side of the coin. Law firms should produce quality work for their clients at a fair price, and clients should not nickel-and-dime their firms over every time entry or expense that's subject to quibble.

On the other hand, it's probably worthwhile for lawyers and clients to think for a moment about how their e-billing process can help or hinder creating an effective working relationship.

COMMENTS

CHINGGIS KHAAN: As an outside lawyer, I never understood the nickel and diming aspect of legal bill review. Outside lawyers learn quickly how to game these processes. It seems that in-house counsel should have a good grasp of what a transaction or litigation matter should cost and ensure that outside counsel doesn't exceed that cost without good cause. In-house counsel can also save more money by hiring the appropriate outside counsel for the job. Why hire top billing firms for routine corporate or litigation work (which happens all the time)? The nickel and diming is a waste of time. Great, I reduced that $100,000 bill to $95,000, when in reality the bill should have only been $60,000. Not being an in-house lawyer, I can only wonder.

IN HOUSER: A good method for controlling external legal costs I've used in the past is to obtain an estimate from outside counsel of the range of hours/costs it will take to complete a particular assignment, draft a letter/response, get us through the next stage of litigation, etc., and ask outside counsel to notify you prior to exceeding the estimate.

IHATEDISQUS: The "no more than x hours in a day" rule is asinine. Most outside counsel work on multiple cases. There are some days where it is much more efficient to crank away on one matter, because you know work is coming up on other cases and you won't have time to spread it out over multiple days. All the "no more than x hours" rule does is build up a backlog of work that needs to be done at the last minute (often taking much more than x hours per day) because trial is coming up and it was not done earlier.

> **DEVIL IN DISGUISE:** I had the same reaction. Frankly, one wonders whether whomever thought such a rule would be a good idea ever practiced.

JTM: This post is a great demonstration of just how insane hourly billing is. Tracking time is such a misguided way of measuring value. Clients don't care how long it took you to do something. They care about the results and how much getting them costs. I do litigation and dispute resolution. When a client brings me a case, we agree on the price in the beginning. Works like a charm. I never have to worry whether the client will accept my hours. I never have to track those 0.1s. Even the clients are happy because they know they can just give me a call without adding to the bill.

If I were in-house, I would never ever pay anyone by the hour.

REPORTING ON DEPOSITIONS

When is a litigator thinking most keenly about a specific witness's testimony? There are two days: The day you're taking (or defending) the deposition of the witness, and the day—months or years later, if ever—when you're examining the witness at trial. So when should you be making notes about the witness's testimony and your reaction to it? That question answers itself: You should make quick notes of key points during the deposition, and you should write notes to yourself immediately after the deposition ends. "Immediately after": Not later in the week; not the next morning. Now, when your brain is fully engaged.

Those notes don't have to be comprehensive, but they have to memorialize the things that you noticed during the deposition that you're likely to forget by either the next morning or the day, a month later, when you're reviewing the transcript. The notes are quick and easy. Write an e-mail to yourself that says: "Today I took Smith's deposition. These were the highlights: (1) He admitted A; (2) He denied B; remember to create some other admissible evidence on that point; (3) He evaded on C; there's something fishy going on there; (4) Opposing counsel started interrupting when I got near D; we should press harder on that point; (5) His testimony opens up issue E; let's do some legal research." There might be a half dozen points; there might be a dozen. But the key is to record immediately the fleeting ideas that you had while your brain was most in gear.

During the deposition, you're as attentive as you'll ever be. Don't lose the moment; capture it.

What do you use those notes for?

Many things. First, as outside counsel, those notes force you to focus your attention on a key event at the very time that the event occurred. Before you get in a cab, sit down in a quiet room, think hard about what you just lived, and distill the key points. You're at your best then; use it.

Second, you use those notes as a memory aid. Three months from now, when you next think about Smith, you can look back at your notes and remember, "Oh, yeah. I forgot that. Opposing counsel did get antsy when I raised D. Let's look into it." (In the words of some great sage: "Everything has been thought of before. The difficulty is to think of it again.")

Third, you can use those notes to keep your colleagues abreast of what's happening in the case. You can, of course, wait to prepare notes until you have a transcript, and then choose from among the many bad choices: Have your six colleagues working on the case all read the transcript. Have a legal assistant prepare a long and unbearable deposition summary, which doesn't differentiate between the important stuff and the witness's job history. Read the transcript yourself to write a report, hoping you still remember the things that struck you on the day you were living the deposition. But all of those are second-best alternatives, and none of those are instantaneous.

The best, cheapest, and quickest way to share information is to write the bullet-point memo as soon as the deposition ends.

What does this mean for in-house lawyers?

If you agree that bullet-point memos are a valuable tool, then insist that all outside counsel prepare them. Ask outside counsel to copy you on that memo as soon as it's ready. By receiving the memo, you'll stay abreast of the case in real-time; you'll see how counsel is reacting to events; you'll have a chance to discuss new ideas that should (or should not) be explored as a result of the testimony.

You'll also be able to plug others into the loop. The hierarchical structure of most in-house legal departments means that more-senior lawyers are further removed from the facts of specific cases. It doesn't help the people who are supervising a case from a distance to hear the usual pablum from outside counsel: "The deposition went pretty well." Or: "I killed him." Or, when outside counsel defended a deposition and the witness gave away the ranch: "He was a terrible witness. I did everything I could, but he just wasn't educable."

(I'm starting to wonder why the good stuff always results from outside counsel's keen skills, and the bad stuff is always due to fate. It's never: "I really botched the witness preparation, so the witness performed poorly." And it's never: "We wrote a brief that was too long, so the judge didn't read it, and we weren't able to convince him orally." No, no: It's always a bad witness or a lazy judge. Remarkable.)

As an in-house lawyer, if you receive the bullet-point memo for every deposition, then you can easily let others gently monitor a case in real-time. You—the in-house lawyer responsible for the case on a daily basis—know everything. A supervisor can ask for the bullet-point memos in all cases, or select cases, or for select witnesses. For the monster cases, the supervisor's supervisor can read the bullet-point memos, keeping that person abreast of the litigation, keeping that person's mind gently in the case, and giving comfort that smart people are tending to important cases diligently.

If outside counsel need other ways to track testimony, they can of course do what's necessary to prepare a case for trial. But consider requiring instant bullet-point memos, to focus your outside counsel's mind at the right moment, and to give you real-time information in a format you can easily share with others.

COMMENTS

POINT WELL TAKEN: This is really, really good advice. Seriously.

BEST GUEST: I'm sure that the client's in-house counsel will not object at all and definitely will not try to negotiate a write-off of the extra billable hour that the first-year associate spends drafting a memo to himself containing bullet points of his version of what happened at a meaningless third party deposition....

GUEST: Those who don't appreciate Mark's advice were never in charge of a litigation.

Only the lead trial lawyer whose reputation is at stake would pay so much attention. Go ahead and make snide remarks and you will never go anywhere close to making partner or a lead trial counsel. All you associates are just trying to make the hours and hoping/praying for a bonus. However, if you can't do the work efficiently, why do you even deserve a job? Pay attention to the teaching Mark gave you. It's free and perhaps you can use it on the job—and get to keep your job.

PLAINTIFF LAWYER: Taking notes, writing memos, etc. are a waste of time. I HATE watching other people in the room take detailed notes during the depo. I like reading the 4-page-per-page (condensed) version and highlighting the good parts (as soon as I get the transcript). You're going to need these quotes anyway—so why write useless notes about them (then, you just have two sets of things to look at)? The notes aren't going to tell you which page number, what the quotes are, etc. So why have all that extra useless paper floating around?

> **GUEST:** Because YOU don't answer to a client who wants a summary of how the deposition went the next day.
>
> I've also found you do lose valuable impressions about nuances of testimony that don't come through on the transcript and can assist you later.

PROJECTING DEFEAT

During my 25 years litigating at law firms, I fretted about two words: "winning" and "losing." (As one old-timer put it: "They don't pay you twelve dollars a minute to lose.")

Now I'm in-house, and I'm still fretting about two words: "probable" and "estimable."

What happened?

The accounting rules require corporations to take a reserve (which causes an immediate hit to the P&L) when a "loss contingency" (which is accountant-speak for lawsuits, among other things) becomes probable and estimable. If it's likely that you're going to lose, and if you can estimate the amount (or, at least, the lower bound of the amount) of the loss, then it's time to take a reserve.

This can make in-house life odd….

Suppose your mistaken judgment causes you to take a $3 million reserve for a case. You then try the case and lose only $2 million. Foolish people—like outside counsel fretting about winning and losing—might be disappointed by having suffered a $2 million loss. But, if you reserved the case for $3 million and lost only 2, you're an in-house hero: You just brought a million bucks back into income! (It's like Eddie Murphy breaking the expensive vase in the movie "Trading Places" and being told that his clumsiness would yield a huge insurance recovery: "You want me to break something else?")

But enough of that. As an in-house litigator, you have (among others) two jobs: One is minimizing the costs of defense and judgment. The other is predicting when costs will be incurred, so that the folks in finance don't receive nasty surprises at inopportune times. That second task is harder than it seems, and it's made harder still by the words "probable and estimable." It's often possible to predict when you'll win or lose, which tends to occur (in the United States) as a trial ends. It can be much harder to predict when a loss contingency may become probable and estimable.

Think about it: Plaintiff files a product liability case against you. The case is defensible; you figure you have a 60 percent chance of winning. That's not a "probable" loss; that's a "probable" win, so you don't take a reserve. At trial, the jury hits you for $5 million. Presto—instant probability and estimability!

Or the other side of the coin: You make a blatant arithmetic error that indisputably causes a customer precisely $1 million in damages. On those facts, the customer doesn't necessarily have to file a complaint for the loss to become probable and estimable; the first nasty phone call may do the trick and prompt a reserve.

In that environment, how are in-house litigators to avoid inflicting nasty surprises on finance at inopportune times?

You can't, of course. You don't know who in your organization is screwing things up in ways that may cause immediately probable and estimable losses to pop up tomorrow. But you can do things to minimize the surprises, and you should think hard about that.

Consider creating reports that estimate when losses may become probable and estimable. Those reports won't be complete, because surprises happen. But those reports are surely better than nothing.

What would the reports say? They would provide dates (or date ranges) of events that may cause losses to become probable and estimable. Some of those events are obvious: If we have a $0 reserve on a case, and the case is set for a two-week trial in November, then there's a chance that a loss will become probable and estimable during the fourth quarter. Let finance know.

Arbitrations are akin to trials; they may cause loss contingencies to become probable and estimable. Let finance know when arbitrations will occur.

Mediations are similar. You can't "lose" at a mediation, in the sense of being ordered to pay a judgment. But mediations are meant to, and occasionally do, prompt settlements. Thus, a mediation might prompt you to offer money to settle even a case that you have a 70 percent chance of winning. The loss would not be "probable" before the mediation, but would become probable no later than the instant the case settled for a sum certain. Alert finance to upcoming mediations.

What else goes on the calendar? Anything that may crystallize the amount of a payment. Will you take a stab at settlement while your motion for summary judgment is pending? If so, that may be an event (or a time period) that concerns finance. Has the plaintiff filed a motion for partial summary judgment on liability? If that motion is granted, improbable liability may turn probable pretty darned quick. Let finance know when the argument will occur and when the judge may issue a decision.

And so on.

You can't guarantee victory in all pending cases, and you can't predict with any precision when losses may become probable and estimable. But you can think hard about upcoming events that may affect the "probable" and "estimable" calculus, and you can let finance know when those events may occur.

That's not fun; it's not fun to project when you may suffer a defeat or choose to settle a case. But it's often possible, and it's part of your job. You owe it to the folks in finance to make those projections regularly.

INTERVIEWING TO RETAIN OUTSIDE COUNSEL

Your company was just named in a new complaint, and there's no obvious choice of counsel to defend you. What do you do?

You ask around internally to see whether any of our lawyers has worked with good counsel in the jurisdiction. Perhaps you ask a trusted outside lawyer or two for recommendations. You narrow the choices down to two or three candidates, and you decide to interview the top three firms.

This brings us to the subject of this post: What do you ask at the interviews?

There are two ways to approach this: You can set up a meeting with the proposed lead lawyer, and maybe a colleague or two who will serve on the case team, and chat generally about credentials and experience. Or you can send the lead lawyer a copy of the complaint a day or two in advance, and then schedule a meeting to get counsel's first thoughts on how to defend the case.

I had a strong preference for one type of interview when I was in private practice, and my preference hasn't changed now that I'm in-house.

When I was in private practice, I strongly preferred receiving a copy of the complaint in advance and then spending the interview talking about the merits of the lawsuit. I figured that if I were really the best candidate to defend the lawsuit (and, for the right cases, I naturally believed that I was), then a substantive interview gave me the best chance of landing the case. If we received the complaint a day or two before the interview, we'd spend the available time beating the living daylights out of the complaint. We'd think about potential motions to dismiss, analyze ways to defeat class certification, and start doing some basic legal research. We'd outline areas for factual investigation. We'd think about staffing in appropriate cases: Was this a matter where the race or gender of lawyers (or experts) in the courtroom might favorably (or unfavorably) influence a jury?

We would then use the interview to prove that we were smarter and better prepared to defend the case than the competition was. We'd present the potential client not just with our résumés, but also with an intelligent outline of the issues and concepts, copies of a key case or two, and other proof that we'd thought through this case harder than the other guys. If we did that, we'd be more likely to win the business. That made the interview easy: You start with introductions, but you then quickly turn to a substantive conversation with the potential client, making yourself the client's working partner before you'd even been retained.

Did that always work? Did we always land the business? Of course not. Sometimes the potential client hired one of our competitors, and we'd wasted 36 hours of research and thought. We always suspected that the client would share our ideas with the lawyer who was actually retained, but that was only a slight injustice. After all, we'd had the opportunity to compete for the business, and our thoughts in the first 36 hours almost surely wouldn't be sufficiently well developed to lead straight to victory.

I also preferred substantive interviews for personal reasons. If we didn't receive a copy of the complaint before the interview, then the interview would consist of an hour of my colleagues and me sitting around a table bragging: "We've handled many of these cases before. We've won some of those on summary judgment. We also have vast experience in related areas of law, and we know the local judges better than anyone else. We're awfully nice guys. You'd love to have a beer with us. Blah, blah, blah." While you were blathering on, you knew full well that the client would be meeting tomorrow morning with some other clown who'd be bragging in exactly the same way. I personally preferred being given an opportunity to distinguish myself.

Now I'm on the other side of the table, and my opinion hasn't changed. If we're interviewing counsel for a particular, recently-filed case, then I really don't want to hear about where potential counsel went to law school, how well he did, and why counsel thinks he's God's gift to our generation of lawyers.

Instead, show me—don't tell me—why we should retain you. If you're smart, prove it. We'll send you a copy of the complaint, and you do a better job analyzing our position than your competitors do. If you win that competition, and you don't otherwise disqualify yourself from handling our case, you get the business.

As in-house counsel, why should you conduct substantive interviews?

First, it's better for a good outside lawyer. It gives the lawyer a chance to distinguish herself, rather than to make idle chat about how great she is.

Second, it gives you more insight into the quality of the lawyers that you're assessing. Any clown can brag about how great she is; only a competent lawyer can generate creative ideas about actually defending a case. And you'll have the benefit of three competing lawyers all trying to outdo each other, so you'll have a real basis for comparing your candidates.

Finally, this process educates you about how to defend your case. You'll receive ideas from each of the three firms competing for the business, and some of those ideas might be pretty clever. You can use ideas generated by one firm to prod the thinking of either other firms during the interview process or the counsel you ultimately retain. (Right: You may be taking ideas that you didn't pay for from the two losing firms. That didn't offend me when I was outside counsel, and I don't think that should offend me now. We gave you a fair chance to compete; that was the payoff for your work. Maybe, next time, you'll win the business.) Early brainstorming about a case with multiple firms may accelerate your learning and give you a better understanding of your position. In any event, that's surely more helpful than hearing during an interview about who went to which law school and clerked for what judge.

You naturally can't conduct substantive interviews unless you have something substantive to discuss. If you're interviewing candidates for your panel of preferred counsel, you may have no choice other than to listen to a parade of folks tell you about their vast experience in complex cases. But, if you have a choice, consider conducting substantive interviews. They're more valuable, more revealing, and a whole lot more interesting to attend.

COMMENTS

GUEST: Herrmann: Why do you keep enticing us with "how to get business" posts without actually telling us THE REAL way to get business? We all know substantive discussions of law are worth nothing because all lawyers can do that. How do you REALLY choose the lawyers you hire?

> **GUEST:** Because there is no "magic bullet." His previous posts had told you things that you "can" do to lose your chances of getting the business, i.e., acting like a jerk, etc. Now he is telling you how to impress the potential in-house client. Perhaps the proactive way is to find any newly filed cases, study them, then write unsolicited letters/e-mails to in-house counsel and ask for an interview. Sure it takes time, but if you landed one case in 10 tries, it's worth the effort.

AVOIDING E-MAIL STUPIDITY

There's one guy in your outfit who understands the need not to write stupid e-mails: That's the guy who just spent all day in deposition being tortured with the stupid e-mails that he wrote three years ago.

That guy will control himself. He'll write fewer and more carefully phrased e-mails for the next couple of weeks. Then he'll go back to writing stupid stuff again, just like everyone else.

You can't win this game; no matter what you say, people will revert to informality and write troublesome e-mails. But you're not allowed to give up. What's an in-house lawyer to do?

I propose three things.

First, prepare a program about responsible business communications. Deliver that presentation either in-person or over the web. And insist, to the extent that it's within your power, that all employees participate.

During that program, scare the bejesus out of your colleagues. Show (or describe) examples of horrifying e-mails to illustrate precisely how careless e-mails can come back to haunt you. To make your point, use examples of bad e-mails drawn from either the public domain or your company's own closed case files.

If you decide to use examples from the public domain, you might rely on a couple of old classics. Don't overlook the employee of a pharmaceutical company, under siege for selling a diet drug that allegedly caused heart and lung problems, who wrote in an e-mail: "Can I look forward to my waning years signing checks for fat people who are a little afraid of a silly lung problem?"

Or use the example of the large software company accused under the antitrust laws of using its dominance in operating systems to influence the personal computer market. The CEO was presumably not pleased to be shown at deposition the e-mail he received from one of his colleagues: I "strongly believe we need a WW [worldwide] hit team to attack [a personal computer company] as a large account, whereby the relationship should be used to apply some pressure."

If you'd like to personalize your presentation a little more, cull stupid e-mails from your own company's closed cases. Employees may be shocked when they see that their own co-workers have written remarkably silly things in the context of your own business. (If you choose to do this, remember that you may some day have a fight over whether the slides used in your "responsible business communications" program are discoverable. Be sensitive to this.)

Either way, the idea is to scare your people straight: Show them examples of bad e-mails, and hope that the message will sink in.

It won't.

So repeat the message in writing. That's my second suggestion: A month or two after each employee attends the program about responsible business communications, send an e-mail reminding people what they learned. Among other things, you might note:

1. E-mails and instant messages are documents. They may be discoverable in litigation. And even if they're deleted, it's likely that they can be recovered.

2. E-mails are great for communicating factual information. But they're terrible for discussing sensitive or highly charged issues. That's why God created telephones. Avoid informality in e-mails, and remember that the things that you think are funny today may not seem funny to a jury five years from now.

3. Remember the *New York Times* rule: Assume that any e-mail you send will appear tomorrow on the front page of the *Times*. If you would be embarrassed to see your e-mail published in the *Times*, don't press "send."

4. If true, remind employees that they have no privacy rights in e-mails sent on corporate computers. Remind people (if true) that employees have been terminated for improper use of corporate e-mail systems. (I'm not trying to be draconian here, but saying these things may spook people into thinking that Big Brother really is watching them, which might prompt more responsible communications.)

Finally, my third suggestion: Re-send the written reminder about responsible communications at regular intervals. It's hard to cause people to heed advice about e-mail communications, but you can take all reasonable steps to try. Although most folks will delete your routine reminders without reading them, at least you did your best.

Two closing thoughts:

First, if you work in an international business, have a conversation with your colleagues who work in the law department outside of the United States. Remind them that the status of the attorney-client privilege is uncertain in many other countries, so lawyers working abroad should assume that their e-mail communications with you will be discoverable. If something is truly sensitive, don't discuss it in an e-mail, even between lawyers.

Finally, lawyers working at law firms shouldn't sit there feeling so smug. Lawyers at firms are surely sending stupid e-mails at roughly the same rate as non-lawyer corporate employees. But those lawyers are not taken to task unless the law firm is sued in a case that makes the silly e-mail relevant and discoverable. As litigators, we spend our days wallowing in other folks' silly e-mails, and even then we can't resist writing boneheaded things ourselves.

You can't win the fight against stupid e-mails. You can't tie. And you can't get out of the game. All you can do is your level best to try to minimize the number of unhelpful e-mails circulated within your business.

COMMENTS

CONCERNED_PASTAFARIAN: Pick up the phone.

TW4491: Placing aside the fact that even a newly minted lawyer would know all this, most people in companies already know not to write dumb things via e-mail, and the ones who choose to do so anyway either don't get it, think it doesn't apply to them, or simply don't care.

THE ON-BOARDING PROCESS

Two comments from folks who recently moved in-house prompt this post.

The first comment came from a guy who spent more than ten years with an AmLaw 100 firm before moving in-house: "When I was reading the newspaper on Sunday, I realized something. Before I moved in-house, I never truly understood 'Dilbert' and the cubicle culture. Now, I do."

The second comment came from a guy who spent more than 20 years with two different AmLaw 100 firms before moving in-house: "When I moved laterally between law firms, my new firm understood that my time had value. I arrived at 9 on the first day and was working on client matters before noon. My office was ready to go, and we held the bureaucratic stuff to a minimum.

"I moved in-house, and it took days before I could start working. I screwed around with immigration forms and health insurance; I needed computer passwords; when I arrived, my office didn't have even a pen and pad of paper, let alone a telephone or a computer in it. You realize pretty quickly that you're in a nonbillable world, and no one seems to care very much whether or not you actually do anything. I figure that, if they don't care, why should I?"

In the words of Mr. Kurtz: "The horror! The horror!"

If you work in a supervisory position in-house, you really can't let this happen.

If you hire enough people, you'll hire some bad ones: People who arrive at 9 in the morning primarily focused on leaving at 5.

But if you're lucky enough to have hired good people, you can't dishearten them on the first day. New hires can't arrive at the office ready to be productive and then be prevented from doing anything because the company wasn't prepared to receive them.

Good lawyers at law firms don't spend days at the office marking time. Good lawyers arrive in the morning as early as necessary to start getting things done, and they leave when the tasks have been accomplished. Sitting in the office killing time isn't on the agenda.

When a good lawyer moves in-house, don't let your bureaucracy kill the industrious spirit. You simply cannot project to a solid employee the sense that work doesn't matter, and no one really minds if you spend your first week doing nothing. It's easy to kill a good attitude, and that will do it.

If your company doesn't automatically have a decent on-boarding process, then take things into your own hands. The night before the new hire arrives, be sure that the person's office (or cubicle) is fully equipped. It needs a computer. It needs a phone. It needs a BlackBerry that can send and receive messages on the corporate system. The desk should have a pad of paper, some pens, and the other essentials.

On the new employee's first day, you obviously must follow the protocol. Do the things that HR requires. Introduce the new employee around. Explain the basics of the company and the job. Set up a lunch date to introduce the new employee to some of the old-timers. And then put the new employee in an environment where it's possible to do some work. The corporate attitude must be that we need you up and running as quickly as possible, because we actually do things in this department.

Corporations, and law departments, that don't tend to the on-boarding process are making a terribly—perhaps irreparably—bad first impression.

You don't want your new lawyers going home after their first week on the job, popping open the Sunday paper, and realizing that now, for the first time, they truly understand "Dilbert."

COMMENTS

FOOL: If you think anyone reads your column, YOU DEAD WRONG.

> **NPEART:** You have nothing better to do, Fool? Really?
> This was a good article that hit on some salient points regarding on-boarding.

GUEST: Sir, the reason people go in-house is so they can leave at 5. When you start paying Big Law salaries, you will get Big Law productivity.

GUEST: This got a good laugh around the office. Because we've seen it happen!

PACKAGING FLOTSAM AND JETSAM

Admit it: Your corporation has a lot of legal flotsam and jetsam.

This is probably true no matter what business you're in. On the corporate side, you have routine business transactions, and you may well handle those in-house. On the litigation side, you have a bunch of routine cases that pose little risk to the company but represent a recurring, and predictable, expense.

I propose that you package up that flotsam and jetsam and sell it off.

What am I thinking?

Look at your litigation caseload. You truly care about some fraction of the cases you're defending. There are cases that pose material risks to the company, and you disclose those in securities filings. Other cases don't reach the threshold of materiality, but are nonetheless financially significant. Yet other cases involve fewer dollars, but pose business or reputational risks to the company. Let's set those cases aside for today.

What about the rest of the stuff? There's some percentage of disputes—maybe half of your cases; maybe more—that are routine. Perhaps you're in the fire protection business and you face a predictable flow of product liability cases alleging that your product failed to prevent a fire that caused a relatively small amount of property damage. Look at those cases and decide how to define them: In the preceding sentence, I carved out personal injury cases (which may pose a more serious financial or reputational risk to your company), and I've suggested that you carve out high-dollar property damage cases (because you may care deeply if your gadget failed and contributed, along with Mrs. O'Leary's cow, to the Great Chicago Fire of 1871). But there's some definable category of routine cases that pose little risk to the company.

No matter what business you're in, you probably have a predictable stream of individual wrongful discharge and discrimination cases. Identify which of those cases are truly routine. You may, for example, want to give serious individual thought to a wrongful discharge case filed by a high-ranking corporate officer. If so, exclude those significant cases from the collection we're talking about here. We're going on a flotsam-and-jetsam hunt.

Once you've identified the flotsam and jetsam, bundle it up and send it out for bid. To do that, you'll have to cull a little bit of historical data: How many cases of this type have you faced in the last, say, three years? In what states (or cities)? How long did the matters last? How much did you pay (individually and in the aggregate) to defend and settle the cases?

Put together the relevant charts. Identify a half dozen law firms that you trust and that have the capacity to handle these cases for you. And send out a request for proposal that asks the firms to handle these matters on an annual (or longer) flat-fee basis.

See what the firms say. All of the contenders will likely bid less than what you're currently spending, because the firms will build in discounts based on the volume of cases you're offering, the likelihood that the firm will over time develop more efficient ways to handle the cases, and the opportunity to do more work for you in the future (among other reasons). So long as you're working with lawyers you trust (and that's the only kind you should hire anyway), you can create a win-win situation by packaging up your flotsam and jetsam and putting it out to bid.

Do remember when sending out a proposal of this type that the volume of new cases is likely to start slowly and ramp up over time. You'll probably stick with existing counsel to handle pending cases and assign only new cases, as they come in, to the firm that wins the RFP. Your billing arrangement should account for the likelihood that your new flotsam-and-jetsam firm will be handling few cases for you on day one, more cases for you on day 90, and perhaps something resembling the entire caseload after a year or 18 months. Price things accordingly.

This leaves three questions:

First, is my proposal new news?

Not at all. Some companies have been doing this for years. But a fair number have not yet caught on, and those companies are missing a trick.

Second, does the brave new world of RFPs put pricing pressure on law firms?

Maybe. This surely forces firms to think hard about their internal procedures and to develop ways to handle sets of similar cases more efficiently. Some firms will choose not to play in this sandbox, confident that they can survive while disdaining "commodity" work and holding out for premium matters. Of firms interested in the lower-value business, intelligent firms will figure out how to compete, and less creative firms will suffer, which is probably how it should be.

Finally, what the heck are flotsam and jetsam, anyway?

That's why God created Wikipedia.

From an in-house perspective, the rule is easy: Flotsam and jetsam are terrible things to waste.

COMMENTS

KILROY: Flotsam is the result of a shipwreck. Jetsam is the stuff that is thrown overboard or lost overboard off a ship. I think you mean to outsource the jetsam, but you really need to worry about the flotsam.

GUEST: Might be more impressive if the link to the definition weren't in the article.

PLAINTIFF LAWYER: Isn't this all common sense? Also, in this economy, if companies have not been constantly beating down attorneys' fees, they are stupid. This includes the "high risk" or "non-routine" work. I'm still not clear on why any company is paying more than $100 an hour for ANY kind of outside hourly representation. If the lawsuit is really high-stakes, then there should be plenty of hours to defend it, so even at $100 an hour, the defense firm would be raking in a lot of money.

THE LAND OF THE BOBBLEHEADS

We recently had to hire a new lawyer to help with our litigation in the United States. Not surprisingly, that got me to thinking: What are we actually looking for in lawyers that we hire?

Some companies litigate their own cases in-house, writing their own briefs, taking depositions, and trying cases. If that's your company's model, then you'll need to hire lawyers with a certain skill set.

My joint operated that way at times in the past, but now uses in-house lawyers to manage litigation. We hire outside counsel to represent us, and the in-house lawyers typically supervise the work being done by outside lawyers. In that environment, who's the right person to hire?

Even in that more restricted world, the answer isn't immediately clear....

Among corporations that don't litigate cases in-house, there are at least two possible roles for in-house lawyers. Your in-house lawyers could basically be conduits for information and keepers of records. To prove that I can be as snarky as the next guy, I'll call that the "bobblehead" model of litigation management: Outside counsel makes requests and speaks words; we obediently nod in agreement and do as we're told. Thus: "Outside counsel must interview Witness A; I'll set up a meeting with Witness A. Outside counsel says that we'll spend $50,000 over the next six months defending the Smith case; I'll budget a $50,000 expense. Outside counsel filed the attached brief for us last week; I'll calendar the hearing date. Outside counsel says the case is worth $100,000; I'll plan to spend $100,000 to resolve the case."

That's not a crazy model. If your litigation is routine and you trust your outside lawyers, you could hire some very inexpensive in-house lawyers (or legal assistants, or the kids down the block), and ask them to play this role. The job qualifications are easy: "The successful applicant will have an exceptional ability to take notes and to bob his or her head in agreement with words spoken by outside counsel." By using this model, you would reduce your in-house legal expense, and your litigation results might be just fine.

The alternative is the non-bobblehead model: You hire in-house lawyers who double-check the thinking of outside lawyers, suggest strategies, and think independently about the value of cases. That's a very different approach to case management, and it requires a different skill set in in-house lawyers.

If you've worked in a law firm for any length of time, you realize how terribly imperfect outside lawyers are. You've routinely seen lawyers of all kinds—partners and associates, at firms big and small, in all fields of law—overlook critical issues, do sloppy research, draft incomprehensible briefs, and make oral arguments that affirmatively hurt the client's cause. How can you be sure that your in-house lawyers will approach the ideas proposed by outside counsel with the appropriate degree of skepticism?

At the hiring stage, we've decided that we're looking for candidates who have spent a fair amount of time actually litigating cases in private practice. Someone who went from law school directly to an in-house position can be a very fine lawyer, but that person is unlikely to have a sense of how litigation actually works. A person who never took depositions, argued motions, and tried cases may inappropriately defer to outside lawyers who have spent their lives doing those things. Undue deference will turn an otherwise competent in-house lawyer into a bobblehead doll.

So, too, for very junior litigation associates. If you spent three years reviewing documents and carrying litigation bags at a large law firm, you might foolishly think that the partners at large law firms are competent folks, and you might be tempted to defer to their judgments. We need someone who knows to his very core that ideas are ideas, and we never assume that an idea is correct simply because of the identity of the person who spoke it.

Thus, when we're hiring, we need someone with a fair amount of actual litigation experience.

After we bring the new person on board, we must make sure the person remains vigilant over time. When we ask one of our in-house lawyers, "What's the value of that case?," the correct answer is not, "Outside counsel says the case is worth $100,000." We didn't ask how outside counsel valued the case; we asked for your independent judgment on the issue. If all you can do is repeat outside counsel's words, then we're back in the land of the bobbleheads.

When we receive draft briefs from outside counsel, we edit them. We edit them sensibly, recognizing that outside counsel is at the helm of the briefing effort, and the author of the brief may be closer to the facts than an inside lawyer who's supervising a large number of cases. If an editorial change is a close call, or purely a matter of style, then we don't make that change; we defer to the author. And we're awfully careful not to make briefs worse.

But we realize that outside counsel are imperfect creatures, and we suggest arguments that have seemingly been overlooked, shorten sentences that run on for half a page or more, and fix grammatical and typographical errors.

Naturally, in-house lawyers should also serve another function: Outside counsel have the advantage of seeing similar issues play out across a wide range of companies. But in-house lawyers should have deep knowledge of their company's particular industry (or industries) and unparalleled knowledge of the company itself. In-house lawyers should be able to identify both the closets that hold the corporate skeletons and the chests that hold the corporate treasure, and in-house lawyers must help the outsiders navigate appropriately.

We need a rallying cry for in-house lawyers who actually add value to the cases that they manage.

How about: "We are not bobbleheads!"

(Or does that maybe feel just a tad defensive?)

COMMENTS

GUEST: Yes, you could hire somebody who is a bobblehead and is "inexpensive." Getting what you are describing, however, is going to cost you. If you want attorneys who will take ownership of projects/cases, think critically, and throw a lot of energy into their job, then you are going to be paying higher salaries. I have observed in-house jobs where the expectation is more 9 to 5, and others where attorneys work nearly as much as they did at law firms. The only way you get competent attorneys to do the latter is to pay well and offer opportunities for promotion.

GUEST: Good article, Mark. Now, how about some advice on how to deal with moronic outside counsel who fight you every time you question their judgment?

LEARNING FROM MY 360-DEGREE REVIEW

Here's proof that I view my readers at ATL as family: In this post, I'm going to share with you the results of my recently concluded 360-degree performance review and tell you how I plan to improve my personal job performance. (That may not be quite as sexy as pictures of naked judges, but you must admit that I'm making terribly personal information awfully public.)

I'd never been through a 360-degree review before. As part of the process, I completed a self-evaluation, so we could see whether my self-perception matched how the world perceives me. In addition to my self-rating, I received anonymous feedback from (1) the person to whom I report (who was classified as a "peer," so that his responses would remain anonymous), (2) five other "peers," or people who hold jobs equivalent to mine in the company and who work with me occasionally, and (3) seven "direct reports," or folks who report up to me through the ranks. The human resources guy who discussed the review with me did a very nice job; he knows a fair amount about performance evaluations. (Aon is not just the world's leading provider of insurance and reinsurance brokerage, but also the leading provider of human capital consulting. This means that (1) at long last, Aon finally just got some free publicity out of my having written this column for almost a year, and (2) we have many colleagues at Aon who do human resources consulting for a living, so they're slightly better at delivering the results of reviews than the kid down the block or the head of your practice group at your law firm.)

What did I learn from the results of my 360-degree review?

First things first: I was told that 360-degree reviews often disclose multiple blind spots to folks in "executive leadership teams"—people who hold relatively senior jobs and are responsible for managing others. On a scale of one to five, executive leaders often view (and rate) themselves as fives across the board, and those executives are dumbstruck when everyone else in the neighborhood rates them as twos. I was pleased to learn that I didn't suffer from that problem. Although my self-ratings didn't always match up perfectly to the ratings that others gave me, the ratings were generally similar. Moreover, the mismatches ran in both directions: I occasionally rated myself slightly higher than others rated me, but I also occasionally rated myself lower than others did. (Thank God! There's one personality flaw that I don't suffer from.)

We then focused on what the HR guy said are the most interesting parts of a 360-degree review: "Hidden strengths" and "blind spots." "Hidden strengths" are areas in which you give yourself relatively low ratings, and your peers or direct reports rate you significantly higher; you're better in these areas than you perceive yourself to be. "Blind spots" are the opposite: You give yourself relatively high ratings in these areas, and your peers or direct reports rate you lower. (As I said, "executive leaders" apparently tend to be loaded up with "blind spots.")

What was my single biggest "hidden strength"? The category was: "Takes visible stands on issues that exemplify ethical behavior." I rated myself a 3 in this category, because I figure I'm about as ethical as the next guy, and I surely don't go around pounding my chest about my honesty. My "direct reports," however, rated me a combined 4.7 in this category—a full 1.7 higher than my self-rating.

That "strength" of mine, if it is one, was truly hidden from me; I can't explain this at all. Maybe the nature of my job—the global head of litigation—prompts the surprisingly high ratings. On the few occasions when folks at my firm are accused of errors (or lapses in judgment), I spearhead our defense, and I also work proactively to try to prevent errors (and lapses in judgment) from occurring. Perhaps that institutional role naturally causes me to be an enforcer of ethical standards, which makes me take "visible stands on issues that exemplify ethical behavior" more often than the next guy does. (If that's true, then I'd expect our global head of compliance to have received similarly high ratings in that category. I think I'll go down the hall and ask her.) In any event, I'm not quite sure what I learned from having this "hidden strength" revealed to me, apart from the obvious: Next year, I'm rating myself a 4 on ethics to show that I'm keenly self-aware.

And now the part you've been waiting for—and from which I learned the most during this review process: What was my single biggest "blind spot"? The category was: "Fosters a culture of recognition by celebrating individual and team accomplishments." My self-perception was that I'm pretty good at celebrating accomplishments: When we win something, I congratulate the person who had day-to-day responsibility for the accomplishment, and I send an e-mail to either senior management in the law department or senior management in the company (depending on the size of the victory). Although I send those e-mails, I studiously avoid taking personal credit for anything that we achieve. I never give myself credit for anything, and I always identify both the in-house lawyer who was directly responsible for the matter and the outside law firm that handled the case. When I rated myself in this area, I figured that many folks in my position would claim credit for accomplishments actually achieved by others in the department, and my studied unwillingness to do that was a supervisory strength. Call me crazy (as my direct reports did), but I gave myself a 5 for celebrating accomplishments.

Shame on me: My direct reports rated me, in the aggregate, 3.1—a whopping 1.9 points below my self-rating. That obviously was a blind spot of mine, and I'm going to fix it. In the future, I'll be doing much more to celebrate the accomplishments of folks on my team. These are the things I've thought of to date: First, I will send e-mails reporting our victories not just to senior management (which I foolishly thought was kudos enough), but also to everyone on our team, senior or not. When you accomplish something, you're probably looking not only for praise from above, but also for a shared sense of achievement with others in your group. How could I have been so blind?

Second, I can work harder to mention the accomplishments of others during departmental phone calls and meetings. When we have those calls, I can save a minute or two to mention that some of the folks in my area recently achieved some good results for us, and I can congratulate folks by name.

Third, I can convey congratulations more personally. An e-mail, or a phone call, or swinging by an office (or cubicle) to say congratulations is nice, but perhaps a congratulatory lunch (or at least a cup of coffee) feels more personal. (On the other hand, forcing folks to endure yet another cup of coffee or lunch with me may not exactly be perceived as improving our working environment.) I can—and will—celebrate our accomplishments more effectively.

But remember: This is my blind spot. Don't take advice from me on this subject; I'm lousy at this. In fact, if you have additional suggestions for things that I (or others situated similarly) could do to celebrate individual and team accomplishments in a corporate law department, please let me know. By next year at this time, I won't be so blind.

COMMENTS

GUEST: I'm sorry, I don't believe in HR. A person either takes the time to personally, and informally, learn sales and leadership skills, or he doesn't. A shocking number of lawyers don't; maybe because so few in firms actually make it to be in command or have to hustle business.

I don't believe in HR or "reviews," except to lay the foundation to fire (or not promote) an employee that the leadership doesn't like and have that decision papered by an "objective review."

Mark is usually a no-nonsense, tells-it-like-it-is litigator. I guess he had to pitch Aon's "human resources consulting" practice on this one.

TROLLFACE: You work too hard and you care too much.

GUEST: I'm glad the feedback you received seemed useful, and if it turns out to be helpful, that's great. But I remain quite suspect of reviews that attempt to quantify performance on qualities that are purely subjective. How are differences in perception of what is being ranked accounted for? How are statistical variations dealt with (especially since the number of reviews is usually too small to have any statistical meaning)? What systematic approaches are used to account for bias?

My understanding is that the answer to these and similar questions is "none," making the quantitative comparisons essentially useless.

GUEST: All of the questions essentially boil down to "how well do you like this person." This basic statement is just reworded into 70 different flavors of questions that sound quasi-objective.

DISGRUNTLED SENIOR ASSOCIATE: You can be the smartest, hardest worker at a place, but unless you suck up, you won't get ahead. The written review is just a formal way of stating "you do good work, but no one likes you."

ANKYLOSAURUS: Reviewing the management strengths and weaknesses of partners and associates is a great idea. So many "good lawyers" are terrible managers.

DUTCH: We're supposed to be constantly communicating directly with our superiors, peers, and subordinates to help them understand and improve their strengths and weaknesses. If you're not doing that, you're not doing your job.

Having HR pay consultants to conduct online and brief in-person data collection using amorphous metrics is a waste of time. HR should be focused on making the work environment a place where people are made comfortable providing and receiving continual feedback up and down the org chart. The IT helpdesk person should feel comfortable and know how to tactfully tell everyone up through the CEO that the problem is the user's unwillingness to take the time to learn a particular software package. The IT person should point them (again) to the training materials and assist them in learning as needed. Everyone should feel comfortable receiving this immediate direct feedback from the IT helpdesk person. HR needs to work to create this atmosphere where all levels can communicate immediate feedback to others regardless of level.

Absent that, a 360 review won't be specific enough to either catch or convey such specific problems or even the larger general problem of failures to communicate between and across levels and functions. Beyond that issue, the 360 review process doesn't suggest remedial measures or how to implement them.

I've gone through the 360 process and participated in 360 reviews of others, and I think the process is of no or very little value. In my opinion, HR departments use this as a checkoff item on their annual goals and objectives list because it sounds good and they don't have too much to do in the process. It's also a quick answer for HR to use when asked what the organization is doing to foster free, open communication between levels and functions.

THINKING ABOUT INTERVIEWS

People have occasionally asked me for advice about interview techniques.

My suggestion has always been short and pointed: "Say something smart. Say something funny. Ask a good question. And get the heck out of there."

What about on the other side of the table? I really don't trust interviews. I don't believe that it's possible to tell during a half hour or an hour conversation whether someone is truly competent or a great bluffer. I never thought I learned much from forcing people to talk about their résumés. So when I was interviewing candidates for jobs at a big law firm, I'd try to identify something that the applicant claimed to know—a practice area, a procedural issue, a case the person had defended—and engage the person on that subject. I figured that I was thus showing interest in something about the applicant while giving myself a chance to assess whether the applicant was sentient.

But now I work at a place that sells human resources consulting as part of its business. That requires folks to think a little harder about interviewing techniques. After all, if you're offering professional advice about conducting interviews, you ought to interview your own job applicants effectively. I've recently been educated on this subject and, as a dutiful blogger, I'll share with you what I've learned. What is behavioral interviewing, and why is it better than traditional interview techniques?

Think about the competency you want to assess. If you're interested in judging the applicant's flexibility, ask something like: "Give me an example of a time when a project you were involved with did not produce the outcome that you expected. What was your role? How did you handle the situation? Was it a successful approach?"

If you want to judge communications skills, you might ask: "Tell me about a time when you made a mistake that hurt a client or colleague. What was the situation? What approach did you take to telling the client or colleague about your error? What was the result?"

If you're thinking about teamwork, you might ask: "Give me an example of something you've done to motivate a team and how you measured any improvement."

What's the benefit of conducting behavioral interviews?

First, it'll put some spice in your life. Admit it: You've spent years doing traditional interviews. Break up your routine. Do something different. Live a little.

Second, spare the applicant the torture of explaining over and over again the thesis of some publication or why he left some earlier job. You're not just putting variety into your life; you're adding variety to the applicant's life, too. You're almost a hero.

Finally, empirical evidence suggests that behavioral interviews are better able to predict an applicant's job performance than traditional interviews are. I don't have a clue about the methodology here, but I'm looking at a piece of paper that reports that traditional interviews have a "mean predictive validity" of only .20 to .42, whereas behavioral interviews have a "mean predictive validity" of .50 to .58. (You have to love those social scientists. Lord knows how they generate those numbers or what the heck they mean, but I, for one, will not pass up a chance for a .30 to .16 improvement in the mean predictive validity of an interview I conduct. That would be like giving away free money, wouldn't it?)

Yeah, maybe I'm slightly skeptical. But I'm going to give this a shot and see whether behavioral interviews seem more meaningful than traditional ones. Maybe I'll be pleasantly surprised.

On the other side of the interview table, consider yourself forewarned. If the human resources consultants are telling employers to conduct interviews this way, then applicants had better be prepared for this type of questioning. There's no excuse now for being surprised.

COMMENTS

CURMUDGEON STRIKES AGAIN: "I'd try to identify something that the applicant claimed to know—a practice area, a procedural issue, a case the person had defended—and engage the person on that subject."

Thinly veiled effort to let us know he would comb the applicant's resume, find the most esoteric, unimportant piece of minutia and grill the person after thoroughly researching the topic, all to make himself feel superior and create a "gotcha" moment. Bravo. You're the man.

GUEST: Behavioral interviews are terrible. I would much prefer talking about what I can do than getting these "describe how you behaved in this specific type of situation questions." I often can't even remember an analogous situation. "What was your last failure and how did you mitigate. Please describe what team building approach you used and how you communicated to overcome." Just shoot me.

INFLATING YOUR OWN OUTSIDE LEGAL SPEND

Years ago, I handled a *pro bono* case for a client unable to afford legal services. (I actually handled a fair number of *pro bono* cases, but I'm choosing to describe just one here.) The client was a very nice guy, and he desperately needed legal services. But he had no idea how to use a lawyer cost-effectively and, because he wasn't paying for my services, he had no incentive to restrain himself. The guy called incessantly, asked endless questions, and was always trying to schedule meetings with me. I mentioned the situation to one of my senior colleagues, and the colleague's reaction was immediate: "What that client needs is a bill."

During the decades when I served as outside counsel representing clients, I noticed that some of my clients permitted me to do their work efficiently and others affirmatively obstructed that effort. Now that I'm an in-house lawyer, I'm thinking about the other side of that coin: What should I, in my role as client, do to permit outside counsel to represent me efficiently?

I'm not thinking here about the basics of retaining and supervising counsel. I'm thinking about other stuff. After you've picked a good lawyer, negotiated a good fee deal, arranged for appropriate staffing, and reviewed the budget, how can you still unnecessarily inflate your costs?

Let me count the ways.

First, you can insist on formal written memos where an informal phone call would suffice. Outside counsel will be honest with inside lawyers they trust. When I was at a firm, inside counsel would often ask me, for example: "Of these thirty cases that all resemble each other, which are the dangerous ones?" And I could answer in a heartbeat that cases A, G, M, and Y were keeping me up at night and the others not so much.

If that's enough, then outside counsel has efficiently answered your actual question. But go one step further, and you're inflating your legal bill: "Could you give that to me in writing?"

Outside counsel just got expensive. If outside counsel is preparing a document that's getting stored in a file, to be used against the firm when things go unpredictably badly, then outside counsel must (intelligently) play self-defense. It's not good enough to sit down at a keyboard and crank out in five minutes the advice about cases A, G, M, and Y that you just provided orally. Now you're forced to have people review each of the files, find the specific points of distinction between the cases, and do things up right. If, as a client, you need that effort, then by all means request it. But if an informal response will suffice, don't make things formal. Formality implies expense.

Second, as inside counsel, don't fret the small stuff. As lawyers, we're making endless decisions every day about how to handle particular matters. Some of those decisions really count: When we go to mediation, what will be our settlement authority?

That's the big stuff; fret it.

But we make innumerable decisions about things that really don't matter at all. Those things may simply be insignificant: Should the deposition occur on Tuesday or on Friday? Who cares? Just set the thing.

Or those matters may be very significant, but utterly unpredictable: We could file suit in either Jurisdiction A or Jurisdiction B. Everything is identical except for the pool of judges. There are two good judges and two bad judges in Jurisdiction A and two other good judges and two bad ones in Jurisdiction B. Where should we file the complaint?

We could discuss that forever, if you were so inclined, but the advice wouldn't change things. You'll file the complaint; you'll draw a judge randomly; you'll be either delighted or dismayed. But good lawyering can't change the odds, and long discussions won't change the situation. Don't fret about things when fretting can't help.

Third, as inside counsel, don't turn everything that's on your desk into an emergency. The outside lawyer is probably handling many separate tasks for you. If counsel happens to mention one—we're thinking about issue X—don't go nuts: "Issue X! Now that you mention it, that's a great issue! I should mention it to my boss, who should mention it to his boss! And we should do that immediately! Get me a memo on issue X by first thing tomorrow!"

Calm down. Some matters are urgent; some less so; some not at all. Let things proceed at appropriate paces. You'll just inflate your bills if you insist on getting everything done simultaneously. And you'll also learn less about your cases: If outside counsel realizes that anything that enters your line of sight will immediately become a crisis, then fewer things will enter your line of sight.

Fourth, distinguish between different forms of communication. Some events require in-person meetings. If we're doing jury research, a bunch of people will necessarily all fly to a single location to observe the exercise. Some things cannot be done by phone.

But other things can be handled perfectly well by phone (or video conference). There's a big difference in cost between flying a lawyer into town for a one-hour meeting (which will run you round trip airfare, a couple of meals, and a whole lot more than an hour of time) and conducting the same meeting by telephone. If a personal meeting is essential, then have it. But if a phone call will do the trick, then don't be silly.

Don't turn yourself into an expensive client. Your outside firms aren't representing you *pro bono*. They don't need your conduct to jolt them into realizing that "you need a bill." They'll send you one every month, and it may be partly your fault if the bill seems a little high.

COMMENTS

THE_HATERADE: "Because he wasn't paying for my services, he had no incentive to restrain himself. The guy called incessantly, asked endless questions, and was always trying to schedule meetings with me."

Isn't this the definition of a *pro bono* client? I am always amazed at how ungrateful people are when you are doing them a tremendous favor.

—Guy who used to think *pro bono* was the duty of every lawyer until he had multiple attorney friends get ridiculous bar complaints from *pro bono* clients.

BONOBO_BRO: Sounds like a pretty odd client, I've handled a few *pro bono* matters and found that after the initial meeting the clients rarely called or asked for any contact with me whatsoever beyond what was absolutely necessary.

GUEST: You are making a few good points. This is also one of the reasons why I don't like capped fee arrangements—because they invite clients to behave like tourists at an all-you-can-eat buffet. In a transactional context, treating everything as an emergency, not having a strategy for the transaction management, expecting that everything will be easy and quick, unrealistic prospective closing dates, tendency of some clients to negotiate agreements against their lawyers instead of the people they do business with and re-trades are unnecessary drivers of legal costs.

GUESTY: Asking for a formal memo—>translation—> I'm too dumb to remember what you told me, so I'm going to ask you to write it down. And doing *pro bono* is the most thankless, stressful thing ever. Why is it that indigent people tend to be CRAZY? It's probably because they are entitled prima donnas who think the rules don't apply to them and have nothing better to do than to call their lawyer. I couldn't take the stress caused by being nice to poor people anymore.

MARK: This is an excellent piece of advice. I manage eDiscovery matters and have seen this very clearly on two of my different cases. Both had a roughly equal volume of work, but one isn't going to be finished before the new year because in-house counsel, in an attempt to save money, keeps limiting how we can get our job done. They request endless estimates and projections for tiny populations, require separate custodian-level billing, and want to hold weekly meetings that require significant preparation time not only from my team, but also several external law firms. The other matter was completed a month ago, at a far lower cost than projected. Unfortunately, the cost-saving counsel can't be convinced that he is doing more harm than good, even by large invoices.

PLAINTIFF LAWYER: I wonder how many judges think about how local rules, etc. drive up litigation costs unnecessarily. For example, I'm amazed at how appeals courts keep piling on little requirements continually—as if everyone who files a brief with them is supposed to be an appellate lawyer who has nothing to do all day except work on appeals in their court.

And yes, the *pro bono* posts above are good. Why don't we have court reporters, judges, etc. doing things *pro bono*? Why are sucker lawyers expected to do things for free? Doctors, hospitals, etc. all have Medicaid and Medicare.

REVAMPING INTERVIEWS ENTIRELY

A couple of weeks ago, I posted about the difference between résumé-based interviews and behavioral interviews. (In a nutshell, résumé-based interviews ask applicants for opinions about their personal histories; behavioral interviews ask for factual descriptions of how applicants handled certain situations in their lives.)

I really didn't expect that to be a controversial topic, but I received messages by the e-mailbag full. Two folks recommended entirely revamping the way we interview candidates for legal jobs, and I'm sharing those two thoughts here—revealing the less controversial suggestion before the jump and the more controversial one after, just to leave you hanging.

My first correspondent, from a large West Coast law firm, said that he liked the idea of doing behavioral interviews, but he didn't think interviews should be a game of "gotcha." Thus, we should not surprise applicants at their interviews by asking an applicant to, say, identify a situation in which the applicant was forced to lead a group, what the applicant did, and how the applicant assessed the results. Instead, my correspondent suggested, firms should send to applicants in advance a set of behavioral interview questions that might be asked during the interviews, so the applicants would have a chance to think about their pasts, identify responsive situations, and give considered answers when later asked the questions.

I think that's a fine idea, but I don't think it's a novel one. I recently saw several business school applications, and many B-school essay questions read strikingly like behavioral interview questions: Identify a certain type of situation in your past, and explain how you dealt with it. If business schools think that carefully crafted written answers to those questions yield meaningful insight into whether to admit an applicant into school, then there's no reason why law firms shouldn't ask similar questions and give applicants plenty of time to frame their answers.

But my second correspondent was even more radical . . . .

The second person is a student enrolled in the JD/MBA program at Columbia. (He gave me permission to use his name in this post: He's Alessandro Presti.) Alessandro criticized the entire idea of behavioral interviews. In his words: "Most people who know they will face a behavioral interview can (and do) prepare three or four canned stories from their prior background that will address 90 percent of behavioral interview questions." The answers given at interviews thus don't, in Alessandro's view, adequately reveal an applicant's true skills.

Rather, Alessandro suggests, legal employers should follow the lead of management consultants. During management consulting interviews, the applicant is presented with a business case study and asked to devise a solution on the spot. It's much harder to game those interviews, and those interviews give some insight into how applicants structure problems, analyze issues, communicate their findings, and so on.

I'm not one to let students off easy, so I asked Alessandro to give me an example of what he had in mind for legal employers. He didn't disappoint me: He suggested giving an applicant a relatively non-technical contract and asking the applicant to interpret it or identify issues that the contract left open. This might give insights into the applicant's ability to identify issues and analyze them. Once the applicant identified the issues, you could explain that your client wants to launch a new product and ask whether the contract permits this. This would force the applicant to synthesize information and present it, thus demonstrating communications skills.

Why don't legal employers use these types of interviews? That's a little hard to understand. Since management consultants have been doing this for years, law firms surely know that the technique exists. Perhaps the legal world is just too mired in tradition (or precedent). We've been doing silly interviews for years, and the firm is still doing okay, so why should we change? Or maybe, as Alessandro also suggested in one of his e-mails, it's fear of backlash: If one law firm conducted interviews that were tough and meaningful, applicants would fear that firm. Perhaps firms fear a backlash from applicants and thus refuse to lead the pack in this area.

That seems to me both timid and silly: If simulation-interviews permitted firms to judge the quality of applicants more carefully, then firms using those interviews would improve both their associate retention rates and the quality of candidates ultimately considered for partnership. Over time, firms that moved to a better interview system would surely see better results.

What's my conclusion? I have only one that I'll say with confidence: Hey, Alessandro, send me a résumé! Our interviews may be a little tough, but I'm pretty sure we can find a spot for you.

COMMENTS

HAYDEN ARSE: The differences between applicants, and their respective experiences, are small enough that a more involved process is not likely to yield significantly different results. Additionally, time spent interviewing candidates is not billable to clients; the more involved the interview process, the more it costs the firm.

> **GUEST:** I agree with this, especially at law firms. Competence is basically presumed based on experience, and the few valuable minutes devoted to an interview are better spent trying to make quick judgments on whether the candidate is someone you can spend lots of time around and is presentable to clients.

GUEST: Mark: I'm sure you're familiar with law school exams. Your law student's proposal sounds a lot like giving law students another law exam instead of interviewing them. Perhaps law firms are comfortable relying on law schools to grade law school exams, and would prefer to get a more informal feel for the candidate during interviews. You know, they just want a general idea of whether they like the cut of someone's jib.

I agree with you though, that behavioral interviews test the candidate's ability either to come up with a good canned story or to bluff their way through answering the question on the fly.

IS OUR LAWYER AGGRESSIVE ENOUGH?

Why do so many people think that you must be a blowhard to be an effective litigator?

I've recently heard several tales of business folks (or in-house lawyers) worrying that outside counsel is not aggressive enough. What prompts the concern is the lawyer's performance during a conference call or at a meeting: The lawyer is civilized. The lawyer speaks quietly, asks probing questions, gives intelligent advice, and appears to be an effective advocate.

After the meeting, one of the participants says: "Are you sure we should use that guy? He doesn't seem very aggressive."

Remarkably (at least to me), I've heard the same thing at law firms. I've heard transactional lawyers wonder about litigators who are calm and intelligent at the lunch table: "He's such a nice guy. I'm not sure I'd trust him in court."

What's my reaction? On the one hand, we can't ignore perceptions. If a lawyer is so low-key that he doesn't inspire confidence, then that is a legitimate concern. If I don't trust the lawyer who'll represent me at trial to defend me during a vigorous cross-examination, then that's a real issue; we shouldn't hire that lawyer. Confidence matters.

On the other hand, if the concern is simply that the litigator is not a blowhard—the lawyer speaks quietly and intelligently during business meetings, where there's no need for bluster—then I have a very different reaction. In fact, I have three reactions:

First, having a larger-than-life personality does not mean that you're a good litigator. Loud is not necessarily bad; it just isn't a substitute for good. Some of the finest litigators I've known have been low-key people who would quietly and methodically unearth great legal theories and disembowel witnesses on cross. No muss, no fuss—just victory.

Second, people often have different personalities in different situations. The college professor who's so commanding in a classroom may be a very different person when he's pulled over for speeding at midnight on Friday night. The partner who berates associates in private may be charmingly smooth when he's chatting with the CEO of the big client. The person who's calm in a conference room may be entirely able to deliver a hot blast by telephone (or in front of a jury) when it's necessary. Don't judge people after you've observed only one of the many roles they play.

Third, being a blowhard can in fact undermine a lawyer's effectiveness. As a client, I really don't need to spend money on tangential discovery disputes caused by lawyers with too much testosterone being unable to get along. Being civilized can reduce costs and help speed a case to resolution.

Finally, because I'm an old, doddering fool who just can't resist, here's a story to illustrate my point:

It's 1996, and my then-partner, Rick Werder (then at Jones Day; now at Quinn Emanuel; then and now, a very fine lawyer) and I are defending a mass tort. Because it's a mass tort, there are 20 or 30 lawyers who found insurance companies to foot their bills who are traveling around the country watching Werder and me (and a few other lawyers at other firms) depose key witnesses. (Werder and I affectionately referred to that crowd as "the malingerers.") I'm finishing up the second day of deposing the plaintiffs' expert bioethicist in one conference room; Werder will be starting with the plaintiffs' expert orthopedic surgeon in the afternoon.

The bioethicist had opined that, because of a supposed technical glitch in the informed consent process, physicians who performed a certain state-of-the-art surgical procedure were engaged in conduct that was analogous to "the experimentation conducted at Nazi concentration camps during World War II." The expert and I spent part of the morning quietly and methodically reviewing the specifics of the "experiments" that Dr. Josef Mengele and others had conducted at Auschwitz and elsewhere, including amputating limbs without anesthesia, inducing hypothermia, and the like. I never raised my voice but, by the end of the morning, the expert had conceded that he had over-reached, withdrawn his opinion on informed consent, and acknowledged the possibility that he should perhaps apologize for having given his original opinion. (As I recall, plaintiffs' counsel objected when I tried to extract an actual apology on the record.)

When the deposition ended, I joined a bunch of the malingerers who were heading into the other conference room to watch Werder do his bit. (My plane didn't leave town for a couple of hours, so I had a little time.) Werder went after the orthopod quietly and methodically, hacking off testimonial body parts left and right. At the first break, one of the malingerers came over to tell me: "You and Werder are living proof that you don't have to raise your voice to badger a witness."

I was proud then; I remember it now. "Loud" is not necessarily "good." We should strive not to let people confuse the two.

COMMENTS

THOMASY: Sometimes clients want the lawyer willing to make a bad argument. I'm guessing Mark wasn't their choice for that. They needed someone aggressive in the legal sense—willing to let volume substitute for analysis, because there is no underlying analysis.

> **GUEST:** It's not just a "bad argument"— it's passion + a willingness to ignore the facts.
>
> Granted I work mainly on product liability cases so we face personal injury lawyers. Many plaintiff's lawyers are willing to tell what I'd consider a flat-out lie in front of a jury. We object of course, but the courts rarely, if ever, grant mistrials on things like that.

GUESTY: Sophisticated clients understand that successful lawyers don't have to be blowhards, but they can be very aggressive when it's to their tactical advantage to do so. That's why so many family lawyers, criminal lawyers, and plaintiffs' personal injury lawyers are full-time blowhards, because their less savvy clients demand it.

GUEST: Actually it is divorce lawyer clients who like it when their lawyers scream. Of course the divorce lawyers are usually friends with each other and take their clients to the cleaners while they pretend to scream at each other. Criminal clients like it when their lawyer is friends with the prosecutor; it helps get them a good deal. Personal injury clients just care about the money.

The most incivility that I've ever seen is from big firm non-trial-lawyer litigators. I've never been able to figure out why. Maybe it's because they spend their lives in front of a computer and think incivility is intimidating in a deposition or meeting. To opposing non-trial-lawyer litigators, maybe it is intimidating.

DON'T TELL OBVIOUS LIES!

Okay, I confess: I made the headline intentionally provocative. You shouldn't lie at all, and you should absolutely forbid witnesses from lying under oath. (If we, the lawyers, don't obey the law, who will?)

I'm thinking today about a person who is not under oath and will be sorely tempted to tell an obvious lie. Don't do that yourself, and advise others that it's not a great idea, too.

When are people tempted to tell obvious lies?

In the corporate context, a quarterly earnings announcement might boldly proclaim that the company earned $1 per share this quarter. The Street expected only 90 cents, so this appears to be great news. But there's something else tucked into the earnings report that disappoints the analysts: revenue declined; margins compressed; organic revenue growth stalled; whatever. Thus, despite the happy headline, the stock price drops two bucks on the day of the earnings announcement.

The next week, you, or the head of your department, or the head of a business unit, or whoever, has to brief an internal audience about the quarterly results. The speaker will be sorely tempted to tell an obvious lie: He'll pull excerpts from the slide deck used for the earnings announcement, emphasize that the company beat the Street's consensus estimate by ten cents a share, and tell the gang that we had a great quarter.

Meanwhile, everyone in the room is thinking: "If we had such a great quarter, why did the stock price crater on the news? Do you think I'm an idiot? Why are you lying to me, and do you lie often?"

I'm no expert in corporate communications, but it strikes me that it's a bad idea to tell obvious lies. How do you avoid telling obvious lies?

When you prepare a presentation, think for a minute about the elephants in the room: What are the topics that your audience will plainly expect you to discuss? Include those items in your talk. If it's necessary to admit to a failure of some type, admit it and explain what you'll do in the future to improve things. Thus, if your stock price dropped because margins compressed, be honest: "We beat the Street by a dime a share. Despite that, the stock price dropped on the news. I don't read minds, so I can't guess what investors were thinking, but the most likely explanation is that analysts were unhappy with the compression in our margins. I think that's shortsighted: Our margins were lower in Q2 because we made an investment that will improve our business over the next several years. I'd like to think the stock price dropped because we're looking further into the future than many big investors are." Or whatever—but don't ignore the elephant in the room, or your audience will simply dismiss you as a liar.

Here's another example of a tempting lie: Suppose that a corporation is moving some key business leaders (or a law firm moving practice group leaders) from San Francisco to New York. In that situation, the guys that run the joint will be sorely tempted to tell an obvious lie to the San Francisco employees: "We're not making any operational changes. Although we're moving a few people away, this won't affect you at all."

The speaker is thinking: "I'm duty-bound to calm the troops. I must tell them that nothing is changing."

The audience is thinking: "Does this clown think I'm an idiot? Things are about to change dramatically. This guy is lying to me."

What's a better way to handle this? Don't tell obvious lies. Recognize that your audience is not stupid; instead of denying the truth, explain how you'll deal with it: "It's true that there will be some changes, because Smith, Jones, and Doe will no longer be here on a daily basis. But, as you know, those guys are frequently traveling anyway, and each of them has committed to be in San Francisco X days in each of the next Y years even after the move. Not only that, but we're showering goodies on people who remain in the City by the Bay, bestowing opportunities on some people, prestige on others, fancy offices on yet others, blah, blah, blah." The words (and truth) will vary with the situation, but the concept remains: Discuss the elephant in the room.

My last example, because I just can't resist, is taken from the law firm environment. You see firms that are aggressively hiring lateral partners saying publicly: "We don't buy books of business. We hire laterals only to bring the very finest lawyers into the fold."

That's almost always an obvious lie, and everyone who hears the statement recognizes it as a lie. There are the partners at the firm (many of whom now cry along these lines on my in-house shoulder) saying: "The managing partner just de-equitized Smith and threw Jones out of the partnership entirely. The managing partner told Smith that he's a great lawyer, but he just doesn't bring in enough business to justify equity status. And now we're hiring laterals who are great lawyers, but don't have any business? I don't think so."

Or, in the words of another partner with whom I spoke recently: "We're hiring guys who don't have any business? I sure hope we're not that stupid!"

Don't tell obvious lies yourself. You're getting caught, whether you realize it or not, and you're undermining your own credibility.

And suggest that others not tell obvious lies. When you're advising someone who's in a situation that will tempt him to tell an obvious lie, talk him off the ledge. There are ways of handling tough issues, and lying is probably not the best approach.

COMMENTS

GUEST: You might think this is a lesson that lawyers don't need. Unfortunately, you would be wrong. Consistently telling the truth—to yourself, first and foremost—is one of the most difficult traits to embrace. Great post, Mark. I think more attorneys need to understand the long-term collateral benefits of being honest.

SHOWMETHEMONEY: Good post, Mark. This is a lesson we learn in kindergarten, but is all too often forgotten in the real world.

CREATING THE WRONG INCENTIVES

I won't say whether I actually heard these conversations or I just dreamt them.

First: The head of the business unit confronted with a new litigation matter:

"This is an outrage! How could they have accused us of this? We want to fight! Fight! Fight!"

"The defense costs will be charged to your business unit, which will reduce your bonus pool."

"Settle!"

Second: One partner at a law firm—who wants to visit a client, make a presentation, and take the client to dinner—to a second partner—who is the relationship lawyer for the client:

"There's no way our practice leader will authorize me to spend $1000 to fly out there, take Smith to dinner, and stay overnight at a hotel. I'll just bill the cost of this trip to the client, and you can then write off that expense at the end of the month, so the client doesn't actually pay for it. Can you give me a client and matter number for that charge?"

Third: A law firm and a corporation enter a flat-fee agreement, so the corporation will pay an annual fixed fee and the law firm will defend all litigation matters for that sum.

At the law firm, the partner: "Assign more first-year associates to those matters. We have to minimize the fees we record for that client, and we have to train the associates somewhere."

Meanwhile, the in-house lawyer at the corporation: "The plaintiff made a very reasonable settlement demand. Let's reject it. Under the flat-fee deal, it doesn't cost us anything to try the case, so we might as well put the plaintiff to the test. Besides, if we try some cases, we'll prove to other potential plaintiffs that we're tough."

Fourth: A corporation holds the law department responsible for a travel and expense budget, which includes all travel costs incurred by in-house lawyers. But the corporation does not hold the law department accountable for outside legal fees and settlements, because the law department should not be unfairly penalized if, say, negligence in the business units leads to a surge in litigation and increased defense and settlement costs. Year-end is approaching, and the law department is about to exhaust its travel and expense budget:

"We could send an in-house lawyer to L.A. to prepare the witness, stay overnight, and defend the deposition. That would cost us $1000, which would put us over-budget on travel and expense, reducing our bonuses. Or we could hire an outside lawyer to fly to L.A. and handle the deposition for us. That would cost us about $7500, but it wouldn't hit our budget. Which outside firm should we call?"

When we create rules, we want people to follow them. When we build incentives into rules, we want people to be motivated by those incentives. But the rule-makers cannot foresee all of the consequences of the rules they create. In the end, we're counting on people to act in good faith and use common sense.

That will work, won't it?

TANGENT

A PARTNER'S LAMENT

By virtue of writing this column, I've seemingly become the shoulder upon which the disaffected cry.

I hear from recent law school graduates who can't find jobs. (I can't help.) I hear from law firm associates looking to move to relatively junior in-house jobs. (I can't help.) And I hear from partners with decades of experience who'd like to replicate my relatively recent move and jump from a big-firm partnership to a relatively senior in-house job. (I can't help there, either.)

I'm devoting this column to thinking about the third of those three groups: disaffected partners.

The plight of the recent graduate is easy to understand: You're massively in debt, looking for work, and can't find a job. I get it. The plight of the associate is also easy to understand: You're working too hard, not enjoying much of what you do, and have only an uncertain future. I get it.

But the plight of the big firm partner is different: You succeeded at law school, succeeded at your law firm, have hot and cold running associates at your disposal, are being paid the riches of Croesus every year, and are perceived by the world as being wonderfully successful. What the heck are you complaining about?

Remarkably, it seems as though you're all complaining about essentially the same thing . . . .

I've recently spoken to three partners at three different law firms seeking advice about how they could jump ship. Each shared a résumé with me, so I have a sense of these folks' credentials. All of these people glitter on paper; they're highly perfumed. These three all graduated from top law schools—Harvard, Michigan, and Stanford—in the 1980s. They all served on their respective law reviews. They all clerked and ended up (directly or indirectly) at prestigious large firms as associates. They all ran the partnership gauntlet successfully. One of the three is an equity partner at his or her firm; I'm uncertain whether the other two are equity or non-equity partners. One I knew in passing from my days in private practice, where we'd occasionally speak on different panels during the course of a day-long seminar; that person, at least, maintains a relatively high public profile and seems to generate a fair amount of business (although perhaps from a single client). I don't know how successful the other two have been at generating business. Perhaps needless to say, none is part of the small leadership group—typically referred to as the "compensation committee" or "points committee"—that actually runs the joint at which he or she works.

And what is the partner's lament?

None of these people complains about having been mistreated as an associate. (It's possible they all were mistreated, of course, but none is complaining about it anymore; memory is such a fleeting thing.) Each had plenty of work to do as an associate and presumably did it well; each was, after all, elected to partnership. And none of these people complains about having been mistreated as a junior partner. Each still had plenty of work to do and felt as though he (or she) was being treated, and compensated, fairly. Indeed, each of these people, in separate conversations on separate days, noted that his (or her) law firm felt like an actual partnership for a fair number of years after the partnership decision. Senior partners were still relying on these junior partners for work, permitting the then-junior partners to feel engaged and productive.

But a funny thing happened on the way to retirement: As these folks aged in the partnership ranks, they felt increasingly disaffected. There were fewer senior people to bestow work on them, so these folks were forced to generate their own business. (As I said, I don't have a very good sense of how they fared in this regard.)

Each of these folks said that his (or her) firm was run by a small group of people who did two unfair things: People in the small group (1) arrogated to themselves institutional opportunities and (2) did little to advance the careers of their relatively senior peers. Thus, these partners lamented, when new clients approached the firm, the cabal chose one of the cabal's ranks to lead the pitch. When high-profile stuff happened in lawsuits or on deals, the member of the cabal stepped out of the shadows and into the limelight. And when my shoulder-crying acquaintances sought help to bolster their own practices, they received little assistance. One complained that he (or she) had recently published a scholarly article, but senior colleagues refused even to mail courtesy copies to other clients who might be interested in the subject matter. Another said when the press called for comments on deals in which the firm was not involved, the firm's public relations folks always routed the calls to the same member of the cabal, raising that person's profile, but not helping others.

As one person memorably (at least in my paraphrase) put it: "I always figured that I could earn my way into the inner sanctum. If I worked hard enough, achieved great results for clients, and brought in enough business, then eventually the powers that be would let me into the club. But it doesn't really work that way. And, once you realize that the guys who run the joint refuse to share opportunities with you, you realize that you'd be crazy to share opportunities with them. Instead of working in partnership with your law firm, you're working in parallel to it."

(When I heard those words, I flashed back to the time, more than a decade earlier, when a partner at yet another law firm told me over lunch: "We have three different categories of lawyers at my firm. We have the associates, the partners, and the owners.")

None of my three new acquaintances complained directly about compensation. But all three worried about how they might be treated in the future. "I see what's happening to my colleagues, and I know that I'm just a missed step away from being thrown under the bus with the rest of the crowd," said one. And all three complained about how the profession had changed out from under them: When they left law school, they entered a profession; now, they found themselves in a business. One of them said, in words I'd heard elsewhere before: "The opposite of love is not hate, but indifference." (Writing this column is so good for me: The miracle of the internet just taught me that Elie Wiesel is credited with having first spoken those words.) "I don't hate where I work. I just run on a parallel track to the place. The firm does nothing for me, so I do nothing for it. It's like a bad marriage; we survive, but there's no passion."

My three recent acquaintances are hardly the first big-firm partners to speak words such as these. Steven Harper (a 30-year veteran of Big Law) devotes his blog (and an undergraduate class) to discussing many of these issues. But it was odd for me, at least, to hear the same concerns expressed over and over again by people who are seemingly so successful.

I suspect that many readers of this column have no sympathy for these partners' lamentations: You chose the game; play it. If you have no business and can do no more than service the clients of others, then you're simply a senior associate who's outlived his usefulness; you never should have been made a partner. Life is tough; "America isn't easy . . . You've got to want it bad."

What about the partner who seems to have a fair amount of business from a single client? Life's good now; enjoy it. Beat the bushes and generate another client. If you're worried that you might lose your client—because of an acquisition or the arrival of a new general counsel—that's what a free market means. Buck it up and get tough.

I personally am a softer touch than my harsh hypothetical readers. I understand what these folks are saying—just as I understand what the recent graduates and junior associates are saying—and I wish I had a solution.

But I don't. I don't have jobs to offer, and I can't change the nature of your law firms. All I can do is share your stories. Maybe sharing the stories will either educate junior lawyers about the footsteps in which they're walking or prompt the leadership of some law firms to act slightly differently.

COMMENTS

J_HOW: Perhaps these partners whining about being trapped in jobs paying several hundred thousands of dollars per year should get out of their firms if they are actually so good at what they do.

> **GUEST:** It's a valid point. If that business is actually portable, and can be done without high overhead (some matters just require 10 lawyers), they can make a lot more profit doing that with one or two other lawyers in a small office rather than shelling over most of their billables to the firm.

FREQUENT_RUNNER: If your 3 partner friends really want out, they should start pitching themselves to the clients of their firm. The best thing for a law firm is to have one of their lawyers as an in-house attorney for one their clients – it provides an inside scoop. If they are doing a good job, there is a good chance that one of their clients would be willing to take them as in-house attorney.

I suspect that the real problem is that your friends are scared to drop down from the lives of their high salaries, leased Benz and kids' exclusive private schools to a Japanese sedan and public school.

> **GUEST:** That and many highly achieving individuals find it hard to, in some sense, admit defeat—that the people who run the place won out over them. At some point, you just need to realize that your interests and the firm's interests change. Go some place where you feel valued and your life will be dramatically better.

LOYOLA 5L: This article doesn't surprise me. It just sheds light on the way lawyers are. I'm a recent grad and was an undergrad business major. What this article highlights is that the kind of people that go to law school versus those that choose business school are two totally different breeds. From my experience dealing with and being a law and business student, the (future) businesspeople are proactive and the (future) lawyers are reactive. The business mind seeks to go out there to get and make work. The lawyer waits to be handed it, to be assigned it. And so, when after being handed work all one's life, one finds himself/herself as a senior partner who has to produce his/her own work, there is a shock to the system. Also from my experience, albeit limited, lawyers are a risk averse crowd and don't much like shocks to the system.

GUEST: Great article. Hadn't considered this stuff before.

LAW FIRMS, THROUGH THE EYES OF AN INSIDER TURNED OUTSIDER

ENTERING TIME

First, a story. Then, my point.

(If I promise a point at the end, maybe you'll persevere through the story.)

When I was a partner at a large law firm, sending out bills, I took the job seriously. I sat in a coffee shop one Sunday afternoon each month and went through every !*@!! time entry in every bill to be sure that (1) I could understand what task the lawyer had performed and (2) the time spent was not disproportionate to the work performed. Only then would I approve the bill.

Editing bills is like torture. In fact, strike the "like." This *is* torture. At the end of three or four hours of editing bills, you're ready to jam toothpicks into your eyes. So I took a lesson from Tom Sawyer and whitewashing fences: I conned my teenage son into thinking that editing bills was a very important job. He bit! (Other than falling for this, the kid is actually pretty smart.) During Jeremy's sophomore through senior years of high school, he and I did some father-son bonding on the third Sunday of every month at the local coffee shop. I bought the kid a caramel frappuccino ("venti" if we were doing north of 500 grand in bills; otherwise, grande; always with whipped cream). He took half the stack of bills; I took the other half; we edited. (Stay calm. I didn't charge clients even for my own time spent doing this, let alone the kid's. This was on the up and up.)

What did we do?

First, my firm's (and, I now know, most firms') computerized billing system spits out stupid phrases joined by a slash. So I told Jeremy that, for example, "review/analysis of" was wrong. We either reviewed or analyzed, but there was no reason to inflict on a client the "review/analysis of" abomination. Jeremy naturally asked whether we should delete "review" or "analysis." If there's a fair choice, I told the kid, delete "review." If I were a client, I'd rather pay for a lawyer "analyzing" something and not merely "reviewing" it.

One of my junior partners habitually submitted his time sheets late, so Jeremy and I would be plowing through DXR's April time while we were sitting in the coffee shop at Borders on a September afternoon. Jeremy asked what he should do about the late time. I told him to leave it in there, and we'd see if the client would pay.

But Jeremy exacted his youthful revenge: "DXR is an idiot. He always submits his time late. From now on, he's not going to 'analyze' anything. He's too stupid to do anything more than 'review.'"

I didn't object to this decision. After all, I was paying Jeremy only a frappuccino, so I figured he was entitled to some vindictive pleasure. And it wasn't entirely clear to me that his new rule was wrong. For three years, dozens of lawyers "analyzed" stuff, but DXR only "reviewed."

Other fathers play catch with their sons, or go fishing, or play golf. Not me; I breed 'em a little weird. So what else did Jeremy and I do at the coffee shop, for father-son bonding?

We deleted prepositional phrases. "Analysis of opening brief" is bad; "analyze opening brief" is good. We chose better verbs: "Prepare summary of deposition of Smith" is bad; "summarize Smith deposition" is good.

We made sure we could understand what we were reading. For example, Jeremy asked what he should do when he encountered a time entry showing "7.5 hours" for "MIL." Honest to God: 7.5 hours for "MIL." I studied the preceding and following time entries, looked at the work other lawyers were doing on the same days, thought about the tasks we'd undertaken the previous month, and had a flash of inspiration: Motion in limine! Motion in limine! We edited: "Researching and drafting motion in limine to exclude evidence of fraud on the FDA."

Some of my partners told me that I was nuts to personally review the bills I sent out, because that's what billing assistants are for. But I'm not sure that billing assistants know if time spent is appropriate for the task, and I'm not sure that billing assistants fix prepositional phrases and prefer meaningful verbs. So I personally edited bills. (Or so everyone thought at the time. Now Jeremy's secret is out.)

Was all this effort worthwhile? Who knows? Maybe it was gratuitous self-torture, and that's why I went in-house. Or maybe someone noticed. Maybe St. Peter will reward me at the Pearly Gates. ("Herrmann, you idiot! You wasted Sunday afternoons editing bills, when you could have been writing the great American novel or serving food at the soup kitchen?! No way you're getting in here!") I will say that, at one annual review of my law firm conducted by a client, we went through the checklist of items that the in-house lawyers were required to discuss with all outside counsel. We hit "bills," and the in-house lawyer started laughing: "My God, bills! That's not a problem with you guys. Your bills are great! You should see what we get from some of the other firms."

So that was my satisfaction from all those wasted Sunday afternoons. Plus one other, entirely accidental thing: Jeremy can write. I've looked at a few of his college essays, and the kid almost never uses unnecessary prepositional phrases. He chooses his verbs intelligently. And he gets to the point.

I haven't done a controlled study of this, but I'm pretty sure that three hours per month spent reviewing and editing sentence fragments that are connected by semi-colons is one way to teach writing.

That's the story; now the point. (You knew I'd get there eventually.)

I now review bills that exceed a certain dollar limit before my current employer pays them. And what do I see?

I guess this is not really a point, after all, but more another story. (So I lied. Sue me.)

I have, over the course of the last months, repeatedly been subjected to bills that seek good money for "attention/consideration/review of" assorted documents, because of those damned computerized billing systems. I have been asked to pay a half hour's fee based on the time entry (and I quote in its entirety): "11KBW." (You know this is true; I couldn't possibly be making it up.) After an exchange of e-mails, I learned that 11KBW is an abbreviation of the address of local counsel, and national counsel had called a lawyer at that address. I was convinced, and we paid.

Within the last couple of weeks, I've been asked to pay .2 hours for (and again I quote in full): "E to HJ." Gimme a break: "E to HJ." I'm not even asking this time around. We've got corporate crises up in the C-suites and opposing counsel busting our chops in courts around the world. "E to HJ" just ain't getting paid.

Put yourself in my shoes. I may know next to nothing about the case in which you're recording time. I don't know your personal shorthand, which may or may not make sense even to folks very close to the case. And I've got a whole lot of better things to do than to send e-mails to my colleagues halfway around the world asking them to call you to figure out if we can have the privilege of paying you a few more bucks.

Insist that your colleagues make comprehensible time entries. Review bills to be sure that the time spent fits the task. Edit the entries, if necessary, to make them intelligible (to a person of average intelligence who knows nothing about your case). And get rid of the unnecessary words, so I can review these godforsaken things quickly and easily.

If you think I've worked myself into a lather here, you may be right. But remember: Jeremy's off to college now. I don't have any help.

COMMENTS

BEAVERSHOT EMERITUS: You're an idiot, former partner. Your anal retentive concern with the grammar used in bills is a perfect example of the mindset that has created the massive inefficiencies in the practice of law. Pondering the difference between review and analyze or questioning the use of prepositional phrases in bills is the province of the window licker. I used to work for a partner who would spend hours (and bill the client for) checking for the proper use of "that" and "which" in registration statements. Of course, this caused all associates who worked for him to do the same. Total waste of time and money.

Idiot.

GUEST: Wait, so careful attention to detail and proper word choice aren't skills that good lawyers should possess? Great! Inclusive/exclusive–who cares right? It's all about the BIG PICTURE.

–Bingham 1st year associate "reviewing" contracts.

BEAVERSHOT EMERITUS: You're an idiot also, Bingham 1st year. CONTEXT. We're talking about bills, not pleadings.

GUEST: You really think that most lawyers can turn on and off their obsession with details and perfectionism and that it won't carry over to other aspects of their jobs (and lives)? That's a personality trait most lawyers have before they get to law school.

GUEST: I agree. Who has the time and energy to spend on such trivial issues? There are much bigger issues. I would rather have outside counsel who put their energy into getting me answers and results on time, even if that means their time entries are not perfect. My experience is that, if you stay within the budget and do a good job, your time entries are not going to get heavily scrutinized. The only time bills are going to get much attention is when you do a bad job or the bill is unexpectedly large. Otherwise, we don't have time to sit and ponder why you used "review" instead of "analyze."

BOB: "Trivial issue"? It's GETTING PAID, you idiot. That's not trivial.

VILLAGE IDIOT: What you need to realize is that in-house counsel don't trust firm lawyers to be truthful. Or at least not to exaggerate their time. So if you're trying to get bills paid you have to be accurate and descriptive. Obviously you'll never have the problem of getting bills paid, being so quick to call people "idiots" and all, but it bears pointing out.

GUEST: The purpose of describing what you did in your bills is so that clients will know what they are paying handsomely for. That's why it matters whether you spent 6 hours "analyzing" a 20-page motion (possibly reasonable) or "reviewing" it (unreasonable).

If partners are overly picky about this, you're right; it could be a waste of time. But it's not a waste of money since no one is paying for it.

GUEST: You are probably right that it is rational from an associate's perspective to spend time revising entries, since partners may be reviewing these entries and making judgments about the associate's use of time. From the in-house perspective, however, I am much more concerned about the number at the bottom of the bill than I am whether somebody "reviewed" or "analyzed" something. The only time I am going to make an issue of time entries is if that bottom number seems unreasonable – that's when I will start examining the entries to find an explanation. If you do a good job and are efficient, the wording of the narratives won't be that important in the end.

GUEST: I take it you don't object to firms requiring associates to do this, since you're not paying for it – just that you don't care whether they do. Is that right? Others (including the author of the article) want clearer information in their bills, though.

More details are also helpful when a job unexpectedly takes extra time, say, because the firm turned up some hidden issue or encountered a procedural hitch. You can see where the extra hours came from (and decide whether you agree they were reasonable). And it's also worth remembering that it doesn't really take more time to do it right; what eats up the time is doing it wrong and then trying to fix it later.

GUEST: That's right. I don't object to them doing this (of course, I would object to anybody charging for time spent doing it). It doesn't hurt – and in some cases it may be useful to review the narratives (if the cost seems high). The reason I wanted to point out that clients don't obsess over narratives (at least in my experience) is that I remember being an associate, spending a lot of time and energy on these narratives. Now that I am on the other side, I can see how a lot of that time/energy seems wasted. On the other hand, perhaps I would still have put the same time/energy into it for the partners' benefit...164not because the clients were scrutinizing them. To me, it seems like a lot of effort is put into time entries, and much of that effort is not valued by the clients. However, there are plenty of other areas where Big Law lawyers expend a lot of effort (because lawyers tend to be risk averse) that isn't always seen as a value add to clients, so it isn't really surprising that partners obsess over this.

TALKTOYOURKIDSABOUTELIE: With such a meticulous approach to good writing, Herrmann must be very pleased by the carefully drafted output of his colleagues at ATL.

GUEST: You mean: ". . . his ATL colleagues' carefully drafted output."

TALKTOYOURKIDSABOUTELIE: Outstanding revision, Jeremy! Good luck in college.

LAW DEPARTMENT CONSULTANT: I'm a former GC, and completely agree with Mark Herrmann's comments on billing. Back when I was a Big Law partner (after my first trip in-house), I used to present a "how to write effective, intelligible time entries" program to new associates in our section, and I made many of the same points.

A TANGENT ON MERIT-BASED COMPENSATION

I like what Steven Harper's doing these days. After 30 years at Kirkland & Ellis, he retired from the fray, and he now comments on big law firms from an outsider's perspective, at The Belly of the Beast. Although Harper's critiques are often cutting, I think they reflect his underlying concern, not animosity, about law firm life.

But, to my eye, Harper recently missed a trick. In a recent column at the AmLaw Daily, Harper speculated that big law firms may prefer lockstep compensation to merit-based systems because merit-based reviews require partners to invest nonbillable time thinking carefully about associate performance. There's no incentive for partners to invest that nonbillable time, says Harper, so firms settle for lockstep—and firms thus delay giving meaningful (and ultimately helpful) guidance to associates.

I think it's worse than that. I think there's actually an invidious incentive for partners at large firms to mislead associates about their performance. Why?

The skeptics among you are thinking: "Sure. Firms tell associates they're doing great, great, great, and then—whoops! no partnership!—because those early reviews encourage associates to stay at the firm, generate hours, and increase profitability. Firms have no reason to lower the boom early." Perhaps that's true; perhaps not. I never served on an associate review committee, so I really don't know.

But there's something else happening here, and I think Harper (and others) overlook it. Jack Nicholson understands it. He was onto something in "A Few Good Men." The problem is: "You can't handle the truth!"

Suppose a partner calls an associate into his or her office and says this: "I'm going to give you an honest and constructive critique of your performance. Let's start with your written work. I'd rate it middle of the pack. Here are some things you should think about.

"First, when you draft introductions to briefs, you typically recite all of the arguments that we'll later make in the body of the brief, and you give all the arguments equal dignity. Sometimes, that's the perfect introduction. But sometimes it's not. Occasionally there's one particular argument that represents the jugular, and everything else is an aside. In those cases, go for the jugular, and ignore the rest of the arguments (in the introduction). Remember: We're paid to win, not to follow some brief-writing formula.

"Second, you're fixated on the verb 'to be.' That's a boring verb, and you should use it less. Please don't tell me over and over that the rule 'is applicable' here. Instead, the rule 'applies' here; that's both shorter and more interesting. Please review all your drafts to find the verb 'to be' and substitute more interesting verbs where possible."

And so on.

What's your reaction to that? If you've spent your whole life in the top ten percent of your class, you're not going to be delighted that a partner sat you down and tried to help you. Instead, you'll be annoyed that the partner doesn't appreciate the magnificence of your work, and you'll start worrying about your future at the firm. You can't handle the truth!

Partners aren't stupid; they know this. I've heard from law firm partners (not necessarily colleagues at the places where I've worked) that honesty can be the worst policy. "What are you doing, Mark? You can't tell people that their work needs improvement. That makes them unhappy and unwilling to work for you. Even if they work for you, they won't give up nights and weekends for a guy who's always critical. Some day, you'll need those associates to run through brick walls for you. And you can make 'em do it. Just encourage them! Tell 'em they're great! That's how you build loyalty. That's how you build a team."

Unfortunately, that advice contains a certain amount of truth. And, true or not, many people believe it. So I'm adding this tangent to the Harper critique: Merit-based compensation does not simply require that nonbillable time be spent carefully evaluating each associate's work. Even beyond the difficulty of evaluating an individual's work, personal and institutional incentives may deter senior lawyers from giving truly honest critiques.

COMMENTS

RICHARD J. MACGUESTERSON, IX: "Some day, you'll need those associates to run through brick walls for you."

True.

"And you can make 'em do it."

Also true.

"Just encourage them! Tell 'em they're great! That's how you build loyalty. That's how you build a team."

Not really, no. Paying us respectable bonuses when we're working our tails off and the firm is doing really well is also, indeed more, vital.

AMD: "What's your reaction to that? If you've spent your whole life in the top ten percent of your class, you're not going to be delighted that a partner sat you down and tried to help you. Instead, you'll be annoyed that the partner doesn't appreciate the magnificence of your work, and you'll start worrying about your future at the firm. You can't handle the truth!"

I disagree. If you're hungry to make partner, and a partner is willing to give you honest, frank advice about how to improve in that direction, you'd listen, evaluate, and incorporate the feedback. Of course not all feedback will make sense, or there will be some counter-argument you might make. But on the whole, it'd be a positive thing that a partner has taken an active role in a critique of your work.

Also, making partner means making "partner"—you aren't in this alone. Your reaction to a partner's feedback might be indicative of whether you'd fit into the culture of the firm. Big ego? A rebel? Perhaps you're not a team player.

And regarding your ego, I have three words of advice: get over it. If you're in the top ten percent of your class, then likely so are a lot of the people you're working with or for. Feeling insulted because someone gives you feedback is just immature, and, if you find yourself feeling that way, better to deal with it now because it's not going to help you in your career.

Nonetheless, you raise an interesting point about why a partner might want to avoid a review, to avoid alienating a good employee. But I find it hard to believe that this wouldn't be better avoided by careful framing of the content of the review itself. In the best firms, you already know what you need to work on before you even sit down to chat about it.

GUEST: I don't disagree. So many junior associates have such entitlement syndrome that they can't take any criticism whatsoever.

GUESTARIFFIC: AMD's post is better than the entire article by Herrmann.

FROZT: I agree both that many of these associates are that fragile and that they need to get over it.

I remember working in a clinic for a practicing lawyer while I was in law school who would bluntly tell us that a brief or a motion we wrote (often the first or one of the first the student had ever actually written) was not very good and would patiently work with us to bring it up to standard. I personally loved him because he gave me truckloads of useful feedback and helped me to improve, but many of my more thin-skinned peers hated him for not giving them a hug and a pat on the back with each assignment.

THICK-SKINNED DUDE: The best partner I worked for was a guy who was always straight with me: If my work needed improvement, he'd tell me; if I did a great job, he'd tell me that, too. I enjoyed working with him because I always knew where I stood. According to other partners, I never do anything wrong, which is obviously not true. Of course, the first partner had a terrible reputation among associates, and had only a few people who wanted to work with him (and those associates would run through walls if he needed us to).

GUEST: The premise of this post is wrong. These days, most mid to senior associates' reviews are peppered with criticisms that lay the groundwork for a termination within a year or two. Firms are no longer concerned that senior associates will give up on the brass ring. Firms just want to be able to fire senior associates for "performance reasons" without having to admit to a layoff or risking a discrimination claim.

But why would I want honest feedback? Feedback is mostly relevant to improving my chances of making partner, and almost no one makes partner (my firm had over 100 associates eligible for partnership consideration this year, 12 will be considered, half will make partner, half of those will make equity partner). All I need to know is what I need to do to avoid being fired. Firms will never tell me this because they always want to keep that option open in case of a work slowdown or if I am too dumb not to leave on my own by year eight.

GUEST: No, feedback is also relevant to improving as a lawyer, which you should care about even if you don't want to make partner.

SIN NOMBRE: Partners who have time for post mortems on deals/briefs/other work have time for regular, honest evaluations. Also, if the reviewing partner cared about the layout of the brief's arguments or weak verbs, all he/she has to do is mark the document up for the associate to revise, or even tell the associate that he/she should run a redline of the partner's revisions against the associate's draft. Or are we saying that the partner let the work go out without improvement, but the partner didn't like the work that much? Lazy partner.

The people who will run through brick walls, after a certain level, are ones who are either happy with their firm lives or motivated to advance. Both groups are not so weakly constituted that they won't want to know that revisions were made – in fact, that's what conscientious associates do – whether or not the partner has time for a post-mortem. I certainly don't have time to handhold for every document and assignment I give to others, and I don't expect that from my supervising partners. But I do know that my success depends on me improving things that people want improved, and if people don't show any initiative to get better at what they do, then I don't work with them.

The more likely thing to do is not to improve junior associates who don't get it and can't take any critical guidance (unless you don't have any others to work with), but rather just find another associate you prefer working with, and calling dibs on them. This is what most people do. Then associates end up with no one willing to work with them, they are asked to find new jobs, and laterals are hired if needed. Isn't this the way things are supposed to work?

Many firms don't pay merit-based compensation because it's too much of a hassle to cajole people billing real hours to remember those pawns that worked with them and write something about work long finished. Further, people across different practice groups can't complain that they aren't being fairly treated even though their billing rates are a fraction of others', nor can people who think that they are superstars. Personally, I find lack of merit-based compensation grossly unfair, and it's why I don't work in that type of firm. Why would I work somewhere where I could bill 300 hours more than a colleague for no different compensation?

VERMANDO: I call bull. Feedback is a regular part of business practice nowadays, including in professions like management consulting that attract from elite talent pools. If McKinsey can give its associates regular feedback, why not most law firms?

GUEST: I think that while feedback does take time, it is necessary to develop an attorney's skill set. If people don't have thick enough skin to accept that some of their work product is not up to par, they better leave the profession. We all had to learn at some stage. It always irks me when junior associates think they know it all rather than asking a more senior person for guidance and feedback. In the end, with proper feedback, you can produce the highest quality work product for the least amount of effort.

HUMAN RESOURCES AND THE LAW

It's odd to be one of the legal world's shoulders to cry on.

This began when I went in-house a little more than a year ago. I started getting calls from lawyer-friends asking me how I'd managed to pull this off and how they could replicate the move. Then Lat and Mystal invited me to write this column, and complete strangers started to pose the same questions to me.

It's like being Ground Zero for the disaffected.

This gives you a skewed view of the world, because folks who are delighted with their jobs don't chime in (or, at least, don't chime in to express disaffection). But being on the receiving end of so many bad vibes does make you sensitive to how many unhappy lawyers exist.

This made me a keen observer last week at a presentation about how workforce happiness affects operational results....

Here's the story, in a nutshell: My client/employer, Aon, offers human resources consulting as a client service. At a recent corporate meeting, Aon basically turned its consultants on itself. And, although it wasn't meant this way, the presentation has implications for both law firms and in-house legal departments.

The starting point is this: Employee happiness correlates to share price; as a group, corporations with happy employees outperform corporations with unhappy employees. So HR consultants will survey your workforce to assess employee happiness, identify issues, and suggest solutions. The surveys are pretty sophisticated, but my layman's take on it was that the consultants assess three basic attitudes, which they characterize as "Say, Stay, Strive." (Forgive me when I oversimplify, or completely butcher, these measurements in the next several paragraphs. If you want professional HR advice, hire HR professionals; if you want a cretin's interpretation of what some HR folks said last week, keep reading.)

"Say" assesses what an employee would say when asked about his or her employer. The basic thrust is, "If asked by an outsider, would you say that our company is a great place to work?" Naturally, an employer wants to see a lot of yeses in response.

"Stay" asks how likely the respondent is to change jobs in the next year. The employer wants to see little anticipated movement.

And "strive" asks how likely the respondent is to give extra effort (work late, or the like) for no extra pay to help the employer. (I've made this post too easy for you so far. I'll let you guess what an employer wants to see in response here.)

Two things struck me. First, if law firms ever assess these sorts of things, I'm not aware of it. And if the calls and e-mails that I receive are any indication, it might be worth a look, for reasons of both compassion and economics. As a matter of compassion, it's good to make employees happier. As a matter of economics, if employee satisfaction correlates to corporate share price, it probably would also correlate to, say, profits per partner.

The second thing that struck me is that law firms may have a slight advantage over in-house legal departments on the "say/stay/strive" front. My sense is that a fair number of lawyers at firms "strive" not for their law firms per se (as to which many lawyers, at all levels, appear to be indifferent), but for their clients. ("I don't care if I'm at Firm X or Firm Y, but I can't let down the folks at Superior Products Co., who I've been working with for years and who depend on me.") The law firm benefits when the individual lawyer "strives" for clients.

In-house legal departments don't have that luxury. When the employer and the client are one, there's no chance that a lawyer's high performance on behalf of a client will spill over to the employer's benefit. An in-house lawyer who's disaffected from the employer is simultaneously disaffected from the client, so job performance will suffer. (I suppose that you could find "client" dedication on a more personal level at a corporation: "I really don't like Superior Products Co., where I work, but I could never disappoint Joe Smith in the widgets department, with whom I've worked for years and who depends on me." But given that Joe and the lawyer work for the same company, that strikes me as less likely.)

Ultimately, I drew two lessons from what the HR folks had to say. As to law firms, leaders might want to be more sensitive to the job satisfaction of their lawyers. And, as to in-house legal departments, we should be uniquely sensitive to job satisfaction, because we may be more at risk than firms.

COMMENTS

LEGAL VIKING: For someone who allegedly worked in Big Law you really don't seem to get it.

"Say" assesses what an employee would say when asked about his or her employer. The basic thrust is, "If asked by an outsider, would you say that our company is a great place to work?"

Most Big Law associates are gravely dissatisfied with their life/work, and wouldn't recommend their place of employment to their worst enemy. Law firms know that and therefore pay a premium for having us come to work each day. They don't give a crap about the "say" so long as we don't "say" what we think to clients or potential clients.

"Stay" asks how likely the respondent is to change jobs in the next year. The employer want to see little anticipated movement.

Given the rate of turnover at any Big Law firm, this is obviously the least important factor to Big Law partners. I've been told, and I'm sure I'm not the only one, that I'm free to leave at any time as there are hundreds of young attorneys ready and willing to take my place. Say no more.

And "strive" asks how likely the respondent is to give extra effort (work late, or the like) for no extra pay to help the employer. (I've made this post too easy for you so far.

I'll let you guess what an employer wants to see in response here.)

In your "strive" analysis you forgot about the billable hours metric of law firms. High billable hours = bonus (at least in most firms outside NYC), low billable hours = getting canned. To say that associates "strive" for clients is naive to the extreme.

That being said, I really like this column. Keep it up!

– Soon to be fellow in-house counsel

GUEST22342: Amen to everything except the second to the last line. This column sucks. Good luck being an in-house counsel. You should love it as you have wised up about BIGLAW. That's why I never am going back to it.

GUEST: Mark: Best column on this site. Should be required reading for law firm managers.

EVILEMPLOYEE: Should be required reading for insomniacs.

BIGGESTLAWSER: I'm with Guest. It's nice to have the perspective/thoughts of in-house counsel. Mark, one other, final point I was hoping you would make when you were summing up and that is supported by your article: Clients should be nice to their outside counsel and concerned about their happiness, since happy outside counsel is more likely to strive for the client that makes them happy. I can tell you that while my difficult clients still receive competent legal work, my great clients receive the extra attention and service they deserve.

NON: I've been in-house at a mid-size electronics company for 4 years now and so far every article Mark has written has been completely on-point, this one included.

As for those 3 questions, I think the biggest problem for retaining in-house talent is the lack of advancement possibilities. At a law firm there is always the chance to become partner, but there is only 1 chief counsel.

THE ILLUSION OF PERFECTION

When you write for as large an audience as reads "Above the Law," you get a huge variety of responses to your posts. But two recent posts illustrated that point in a remarkable way.

Last month, I published one post about the care with which I edited bills (that is, daily time entries) that I sent to clients when I was in private practice. And I later published a post about how lawyers could improve communications by taking a moment to reflect on the "subject" lines of e-mails before hitting the "send" icon.

The response to those posts was fierce and immediate. Folks who published "comments" to those posts overwhelmingly reacted negatively: "What kind of idiot spends several hours a month editing time entries to ease a client's life? This guy was a typical big firm drudge!" (I'm paraphrasing here, because some of our readers may be minors.) And, "He's writing about the 'subject' lines of e-mails? What comes next—a post about the quality of the office staplers or the tissue in the restrooms?"

Simultaneously, I was receiving a host of e-mails—not anonymous comments, but signed e-mails—from folks saying that they were sharing the posts with other lawyers in their offices or asking permission to reprint the posts in internal newsletters.

This caused me to wonder: Why the divide?

Perhaps personal biography matters. I practiced at a small firm in San Francisco in the 1980s, and the firm's mantra was "perfection." ("We're competing against Pillsbury and MoFo. Clients are taking a risk when they retain a small firm instead of a huge one, because, if we suffer a bad result, the in-house lawyer will be faulted for not having gone with a better-known quantity. We must be better than the other firms. Return phone calls immediately. No typos. Perfection. It's the only way to survive.")

From 1989 through 2009, I worked at one of the largest international law firms in the world. And the firm's mantra was again "perfection." ("We're competing against Paul Weiss, Sidley, and Skadden here. If their work is perfect and ours is not, they'll get more cases, and we'll get fewer. Return phone calls immediately. No typos. Perfection. It's the only way to survive.")

No one is perfect, of course. We're so far from perfect that it makes you want to break down and cry. But, in the fiercely competitive world of law, firms strive to deceive their clients into thinking that the firms are perfect. You don't send out drafts that aren't yet final, send e-mails that are filled with typos, or do anything else that might destroy the illusion of perfection.

It doesn't stop there; you do everything you can to reinforce that illusion. If the other firm sends out unintelligible bills, and you send out edited bills, the client is unlikely to thank you and may notice the difference only subconsciously. But that doesn't matter; you've reinforced the illusion of perfection.

If the other firm sends e-mails that all have the subject line, "See attached," and you send e-mails with subject lines that actually convey information or give a sense of comparative urgency, the client will never thank you and may notice the difference only subconsciously. But that doesn't matter; you've reinforced the illusion of perfection.

Eventually, at least for me, the mind-set of "perfection" became ingrained. It's hard to ignore even when you want to.

But I'll go beyond that—which will cause me to take a beating in the comments to this post and receive congratulatory e-mails from partners at major firms around the world: This mind-set is not simply ingrained in me; it is also right.

We live in a world of free markets. And free markets are tough things. If you plan to compete effectively at the highest level in a professional services environment, you must produce the highest quality work and pursue the illusion of perfection. That's the route to success.

Why will the preceding two paragraphs cause such a stir? Why will they simultaneously prompt cheers and jeers?

Is this a generational thing? On the one hand: "Those spoiled youngsters don't know anything about client service. Only the older generation does." On the other hand: "Those old codgers are padding bills, fixing mistakes that no one would ever notice or care about."

Or does this turn on practice area? "People doing high-volume, low-margin work for legally unsophisticated clients properly don't worry about the details of client service. Those clients won't notice the difference, and the charges for those legal services won't carry the freight of slowing down. People doing bet-the-company cases for sophisticated corporate clients live in a different world."

Or is this a technological divide? Above the Law focuses on a relatively young demographic, because it disproportionately covers job prospects for new lawyers and bonuses paid to associates. (Older folks visit ATL, too, in numbers that would surprise you—although some of them might deny it when asked, or claim that they're just monitoring what the associates are thinking.) Perhaps the vocal piece of the readership at Above the Law skews particularly young (or disaffected) because those folks are accustomed to participating in an on-line discussion, and the old timers don't live that way (or can't yet figure out how to post a comment).

I really don't know the answer to this, although the existence of the divide is unmistakable. I typically write these columns at ATL for the benefit of readers; this time, I'll be intensely curious in your reaction.

COMMENTS

POSTHASTE: Clients care about good advice, correct understanding of substantive law and procedure, ability to provide creative options and solutions, and outcomes. One of the very last things a good in-house attorney worries about is appearance of typos in bills, personal appearance of counsel (out-of-court anyway), or other minutiae.

Mark, you need more time in-house to sort out the priorities. You clearly don't get it. Start off easy, with the pen and stapler reviews, and work your way up the knowledge curve.

GUEST: Agree. I can't believe this guy is in-house. I'm in-house and came (or escaped) from that perfection mentality. The business people I deal with HATE this fetish many lawyers have for "perfection." They want good advice and good—but not necessarily perfect—work. The only part of his advice for outside lawyers that he got right is his advice to promptly return calls and respond to messages. If I have a business person wearing out the carpet in my office with an urgent issue and you don't answer my question promptly, I'm looking for another firm. If you have typos in your bills or sometimes don't have a perfect précis for a subject line, I probably won't even notice, much less care.

SANCHO: I disagree. Perception is important. I worked in one non-law consultancy. The boss pulled up one consultant on a report, correcting a typo by explaining that it had a "split infinitive." The employee asked what a split infinitive was to which he was told, "a split infinitive is the difference between a $10,000 report and a $100,000 report."

Maybe when you're low on the food chain you think these things don't matter, but try handing a report that has typos to a client and then asking for your fee of a few hundred grand. You'll be walking out of there with a lot less—and then only after a fight.

GUEST: I think the general problem, Mark, is that everything you say is entirely obvious to anyone with a brain. Law is a competitive industry; partners want perfection and they should. If you send me a document with obvious typos in it, I'm going to think you're an idiot or lazy and I may not hire you again. Did you need to take an entire article (or, what is it, like 8 articles now?) to get that and other similar messages across?

LOVING LATERALS

Why are lateral partners like pigs?

No, no! I didn't mean it that way!

I'm just remembering the line from George Orwell's *Animal Farm*—"Four legs good, two legs bad!"

Thirty years ago, law firms took pride in having only homegrown partners: "Homegrown good, laterals bad!" There was a certain logic to that. If you'd worked with a lawyer from his first day out of law school or a clerkship and seen the lawyer progress in the law, then after six (or eight, or ten) years, you had a pretty good sense of that human being, both as a person and as a lawyer. When you made a partnership decision, you could be fairly comfortable that you were working from a decent base of knowledge.

Law firms knew this, and they flaunted it.

Places bragged that all (or nearly all) partners were homegrown. Firms tried to convince their lawyers to stay put. (In 1979, one former Cravath lawyer told me that the firm had a mantra, "You leave Cravath only once." There was no going home again.) Firms didn't hire laterals, and firms bragged about it: "Homegrown good, laterals bad!"

That was then; now is now. Based on where I sit, on the receiving end of many law firm marketing communications, times have changed….

I understand that the world has changed, that firms now fret about profits per partner, and that some partners view themselves as free agents, available to the highest bidder. I'm not here to deplore that situation. But I'm scratching my head about why firms affirmatively brag about how they're bringing in large numbers of lateral partners.

Here's what I'm thinking:

After a decade of working with a homegrown lawyer, you know what you've got. If you invite that person into the partnership, you've made a fairly educated decision. You know what you're getting, and you're exercising real control over the quality of your partnership. When new people are considered for partnership in the future, you can generally trust the feedback that you're getting from existing partners. If one of your partners says that "associate X" is a fine lawyer and person, you know what that means.

Laterals are a different story. You haven't watched those people mature from taking their first legal steps to becoming fully competent lawyers. You generally haven't worked as long, or as closely, with partners from other firms as you have with your own colleagues. You're not as confident in the laterals' qualities—both personal and professional—as you are in your homegrown folks'. In those respects, at least, you're taking some risk when you bring in a lateral. You hope the person's good and trustworthy, but you may not yet truly know.

This doesn't mean that it's bad to hire lateral partners. If you need more biotech IP capacity in Los Angeles, you may have to hire a lateral to fill the gap. If a guy with an outsized reputation (or book of business) comes on the market, signing that free agent may improve the whole team. And, after you do this, I understand why you'd brag about having brought on the new recruit: You made a move, so capitalize on it. Publicize it. Issue a press release that you have a new biotech IP guy in LA, so clients know about your new capacity. Tell the world that you brought in a hotshot; maybe that'll attract more business.

What I don't understand is this: Why do law firms brag—both on websites and in brochures—about the sheer *number* (not the names, and not the expertise, but just the number) of lateral partners they've recently hired? "We snagged Joe Smith, biotech guru" serves a purpose; I might want to hire Smith. But, "We've hired 15 lateral partners in our midwest region in the last three years alone" mystifies me. What purpose does that serve?

Why would you brag about hiring scads of laterals in the aggregate? If that serves a marketing purpose, I'm missing it. I'm surely not more likely to retain your firm because you've recently brought in a bunch of unnamed and undifferentiated laterals. If anything, I'm somewhat less likely to retain you, because your firm may have started to lose quality control and a sense of collegiality or professionalism.

So why do firms engage in this type of boasting? Is it to prove to the world that your firm must be profitable, because otherwise you couldn't have poached partners from other firms? That might impress someone, but I can't believe it impresses clients or potential clients. Are firms doing this to offset bad publicity, because they recently lost a bunch of people to lateral moves? Maybe, although that logic seems pretty murky, and this type of boasting doesn't seem to be limited to those situations. Or does this just reflect the pride of the partner who's doing the lateral recruiting? ("I was asked to beef up the midwest region. I've done a great job, if I do say so myself. So by God we're going to flaunt my success!") Maybe that's what prompts this boasting, but you'd hope that calmer, more disinterested minds would intervene.

I just don't get it. This new type of marketing is like chanting, "Homegrown good, laterals better!" Which is why I started with pigs, and the revolution at Mr. Jones' farm: "Four legs good, two legs *better!*"

COMMENTS

CLASS OF 2010 GRAD: "I understand that the world has changed, that firms now fret about profits per partner."

Correct me if I'm wrong, but hasn't that always been something that firms fretted about?

GUEST: Yes and no.

Yes, to a certain extent people have always been concerned about money. However, before a certain date—say, 1975 +/- 5 years—law was not nearly as cutthroat of a profession as it is today. Court rules still prohibited a lot of advertising, and lawyers jumping ship because they could earn a couple thousand more a year would have been scandalous and considered mercenary.

FROZT: I think it's related to the lack of mentorship and development at big firms.

The firms can brag that their partnership ranks aren't made of the homegrown associates who spent the last eight years doing document review and typing memos for the partners without ever trying a case. No—those associates get passed over for partnership because they never had the chance to get real courtroom experience and no one wants to trust them with a big case. Instead the firm brags that they're lateralling in attorneys with the experience to try those big cases. In essence, it's an admission that their homegrown lawyers didn't learn anything, but don't worry—you don't have to rely on them.

MOVING LATERALLY

I spoke on a panel with two other in-house lawyers at the Indiana University Maurer School of Law a little while ago, and I learned two interesting things about lateral mobility. I'm not one to keep secrets (other than client confidences, of course), so I figure I'll share.

The first item came from a question a law student asked of Steve Beard, who's the general counsel of Heidrick & Struggles, a recruiting firm. The student asked when the best times are during your legal career to make a lateral move. I didn't have a clue, and Beard works for a headhunter, so I figured it was time to listen.

Beard said that headhunters will call you most aggressively at three times in your life. First, you'll get calls when you're roughly a third-year associate. At that point, the market perceives that you've been trained in the fundamentals of being a lawyer. If someone is looking for a competent person still early in a legal career, that's more or less the time.

You'll then apparently have to endure a few years of relative silence. The phone won't start to ring regularly again until you're six or seven years out of law school. The market will then perceive you as having become a fully formed lawyer, capable of performing most of the tasks in your niche. Corporations figure that they can hire a sixth-year associate, train the candidate about a particular business, and fit the person easily into a corporate structure….

If you don't move then, however, it's another couple of years of telephone silence. You're not likely to be recruited aggressively again until after you're a partner. At that point, you've distinguished yourself (by having successfully run the odd gauntlet that you chose), and you have a higher profile in your practice area. Potential employers assume that you have technical mastery of a field and possess useful specialized knowledge, so you become a hot item.

Beyond that, according to the pro (and the third panelist, who nodded in agreement, while I sat there mutely), things become more sporadic. You'll occasionally receive calls from headhunters looking for a particular person who possesses a particular attribute, but you'll no longer routinely receive generic cold calls. And, say my sources, job changes later in your career are more likely to be prompted by personal recommendations, where someone who knows you suggests to a colleague that you'd be good for a particular job.

The second interesting thing mentioned at the panel was that women tend to move laterally more successfully than men do. This apparently isn't just flagrant stereotyping, but flagrant stereotyping backed up by empirics. (At that point, do we call it "knowledge," rather than "prejudice"?) Some studies supposedly show that women generally perform more effectively than men do after they change jobs. And the studies suggest a reason for this: The data show that men invest more heavily than women in "internal capital"—men tend to build relationships and develop friendships with their co-workers. Women, in contrast, supposedly invest more heavily in "external capital"—women disproportionately form networks with people outside of their own organizations, staying in touch with people they meet through trade or bar associations, on non-profit boards, and the like. The theorists suggest that women thus move laterally more effectively than men do because men abandon their networks more completely when they move from one job to another, while women have a broader network that continues to support them in the new work environment.

I have no clue whether any of this is true. I haven't seen the data, and it's largely irrelevant whether they match up to my own personal experience. But I hadn't heard this stuff before, and it may be relevant to a career move or a hiring decision, so I figured I'd share. Enjoy!

COMMENTS

GUEST: "Women have a broader network that continues to support them in the new work environment." Good to hear. Can we stop complaining about the glass ceiling now?

BROSEF STALIN: Well I think that really explains the glass ceiling. Making partner or otherwise advancing within an organization requires you to have a "rabbi" within the organization who can rally support for you. The study shows that women struggle to develop these kinds of relationships, instead looking outside of the organization to network. In the unique context of a law firm, however, you need both internal contacts AND external contacts (to generate business). The results of this study, and the dismal statistics of female partners, seems to imply that while women can generate external contacts, they are far less adept at monetizing them.

PITCHING DIVERSITY

Diversity matters. It matters for reasons of social justice. It matters because folks are tracking it, and it can be important to look good on those scales. It matters for reasons of trial strategy, because our defense team should look at least slightly like our jurors. In particular types of cases, diversity may be a terribly important consideration. Employers may, for example, want an African-American to defend a race discrimination case. (Or, in my old product liability life, we may have wanted women to defend breast implant or hormone replacement therapy cases. Or we may have looked for female expert witnesses for those cases. Pandering, thy name is litigator!)

Law firms know this, and those that are able now stress their commitment to diversity. Which brings me to today's story.

A female colleague and I recently had lunch with folks from a firm that was looking for our business. (You'd be surprised how good I'm getting at those lunches. Whether or not I remember your name the next day is another matter, but I'm becoming a pro at eating.)

The outside lawyers pitched the diversity point fairly aggressively, telling us about their many highly compensated female partners and paying particular attention to my colleague when they did so.

When we left the lunch, my colleague said, "Well, that's exactly the wrong way to sell diversity."

"Ha!" I thought. "Here's a blog post waiting to happen!" So I cleverly asked, "What offended you?"

"Are you kidding me?

"First, we just had lunch with two old white guys. Don't just tell me about your women. Bring one along. If you have women that you're proud of, how about letting them participate in business development efforts? How about letting us decide whether the women impress us and whether we'd like to retain them?

"Second, don't tell me about your highly compensated female partners. That's easy to lie about, because matters of compensation are often kept confidential. And it's also meaningless. It's much easier for the old white guys to give up money than it is for them to give up power. If you want to impress me, tell me that a woman is on your executive committee, or is the managing partner of your firm. Don't tell me that you pay a few women a lot of money.

"Third, don't patronize me. Didn't you notice that, every time those guys talked about diversity, they stopped looking at you and started talking to me? And that wasn't limited to when they were talking about diversity generally. One of them turned to tell me that I'd like his wife. Why would I like his wife? Why wouldn't *you* like his wife? And they asked me about my kids, but they never asked you about yours. Who do they think they're fooling?

"And how about that parting shot? To you, they say, 'It was a pleasure meeting you. I hope we can do some business together.' But to me it was, 'Good luck taking care of those kids.' These guys just don't get it."

I must say that my colleague is generally a calm and level-headed woman, not easily disturbed by unintended slights. Which suggests that firms should be very careful when trying to convince folks of their commitment to diversity.

Forewarned is forearmed.

COMMENTS

NICEJEWISHBRO: "One of them turned to tell me that I'd like his wife. Why would I like his wife? Why wouldn't you like his wife?" This kind of conversation is the best reason AGAINST getting caught up in the diversity game. Do you really want your lawyers walking on eggshells trying to make sure every casual remark is equal opportunity? How about we all just do our jobs and leave social justice alone.

GUEST: In-House here: Diversity is nonsense. Unless you are a publicly traded company that has implemented some diversity metrics for outside vendors, no one really cares if their lawyers are black, white, female, or transgendered quadraracial. I want my litigators to win and my corporate lawyers to close. And, I want the bill to be proportionate to the task. If I need my trial team to look like the jury, I will give my local counsel a significant speaking role. If I need favorable rulings at hearings, I will hire the judge's drinking buddy or former classmate no matter what his or her skin color. I will hire whoever gets the results I need within the budget I am given. Pretending to care about diversity is as fake as the diversity your example law firm was pitching.

JUST ME: There are so many things that are problematic with this diversity nonsense that it is always difficult to know where to begin. Take the colleague's first point, for instance, that the two making the pitch were "old white guys." The assumptions made by the colleague are just as offensive as the assumptions made by racists and sexists.

How does she know women don't participate in business development efforts? Does she really expect to have female partners paraded around just because they're female and not, say, because they have more relevant experience or skills? Is the assumption that because "two old white guys" might have the most relevant experience for a particular potential client that the whole firm must sexistly be suppressing the advancement of women? And how does the colleague justify assuming that the "two old white guys" don't provide their own form of diversity to the firm—perhaps one is gay or even transsexual, follows an unorthodox religion, or something else.

"I had lunch today with a potential client. She met me for an hour, barely knows me, and still left with all kinds of assumptions about me because of my age, my skin color, and my sex." Isn't the whole objective of diversity efforts, as grossly misguided as they are, to encourage us all not to make exactly the sorts of unjustified assumptions the colleague made?

DISQUIETED COMMENTER: So nobody genuinely believes that diversity encourages breadth of thought, and is thus valuable in its own right, rather than simply as a selling point? I think that notion can be overstated, but there is something to it, no? And, I'm amazed that neither Herrmann nor any of the commenters have mentioned it, if only to mock it cynically.

ON OUTER-DIRECTEDNESS

Law firms, and in-house law departments, should be outer-directed.

I realize that I just invented the word "outer-directed," and sensible people might choose to call this concept being "client-focused." But "outer-directedness" is broader than mere client focus—and I invented the word, so it'll mean what I want it to mean.

At a firm, lawyers should naturally be client-focused, in the sense that client work comes first and most internal matters come second. "Outer-directedness" implies not just client focus, but a more general external focus—devoting efforts to impressing the world, rather than to impressing others within the firm.

We should naturally spend our professional time serving our clients. And, in a law firm setting, we should spend our semi-professional time gazing out through our office windows, not peering inwardly down our own corridors. If a case just settled and you have some free time, spend that time impressing the world, not your colleagues. Join a non-profit board, work for a bar or trade association, write an article, give a talk. Raise both your personal and your firm's profile. That benefits the world and serves institutional purposes. Don't spend your spare time impressing your colleagues.

We should of course be nice to each other, but that's civility, not having an undue inner focus. I'm opposed only to the stuff that goes beyond civility, which I'll delicately call "office politics"....

Every minute that we spend tooting our own horns internally is a minute that we're not spending pursuing our clients' interests or raising our collective profile in the world. So those minutes are wasted.

Everyone knows this. "Client focus" or, more broadly, "outer-directedness," is the name of the game. That's what adds institutional value, and that's the attitude we must instill in ourselves and in our colleagues.

So why is it so impossibly hard to instill that attitude? Why do so many people spend so much time trying to impress the colleagues with whom they work?

Because, in many contexts, playing office politics is an awfully good path to success.

Context does matter here. In a small law firm with, say, 20 lawyers, everyone knows everyone else. And everyone knows what everyone else is doing.

Publish an article? Everyone knows.

Win a case? Everyone knows.

Serve on a bar committee? Everyone knows.

In fact, everyone doesn't just know. At many small law firms (or at least the one where I worked, many years ago), everyone also swings by your office to say "attaboy, too" giving you lots of psychological satisfaction. Small firm life might not be for everyone, but it has certain advantages. One of those advantages is that it's easier to be outer-directed, because colleagues are more likely to know what you're doing and to appreciate your efforts.

Increase the size of the institution, and that probably is no longer true. In a large law firm, most folks will never hear of your accomplishments if you don't toot your own horn internally.

This isn't necessarily bad. You may actually enjoy practicing, and thinking about, the law. You may have no taste for administrative crap, and no interest in running a practice group some day. So do it your way: Impress the world, and let the firm come along for the ride. You can still build a practice and a career without playing internal politics.

But people realize, correctly, that maintaining a purely outer-directed bent at a big firm is fraught with peril.

As an associate, you write briefs and work on the young lawyers' committee, while some other associate is sucking up to the folks on the partnership committee. Maybe yours is the theoretically preferred route to achievement, but you're surely running a risk there.

Even as a partner, you can choose to spend your time taking depositions and writing law review articles, while some other clown is ingratiating himself to the managing partner.

After three years, you're respected in the community and being cited in the scholarly literature, but the sycophant controls the tickets to the loge.

After ten years, you've become a pretty famous fellow, but the toady is the partner in charge of the office.

When Flotsam and Jetsam, Inc., a potential new client, calls to request a meeting, the call may be routed to someone with a leadership position in the firm. The leader may choose to invite himself disproportionately to those meetings. Over time, the leadership position can yield real benefits. (As a former partner at an AmLaw 20 firm recently told me, "The guys on the client development committee were great at cross-selling services. To the other guys on the client development committee.")

Those benefits are not limited to business opportunities. The flatterer who holds an administrative position, for example, may now control a budget, and you do not. So when the adulator wants to fly off to Scotland with three potential clients for a weekend of golf, it's no problem finding 15 grand in the office budget to pay for the trip. But when you ask for 500 bucks for a day-trip to New York to speak to 300 in-house counsel, there's somehow no room in the budget for it.

This may not be an insurmountable problem; you can probably finesse the issue. You can pay your own way, ask the sponsor of the talk to pick up the tab, schedule a flexible business trip to take you to New York the day before your talk, and so on. But you're doing it the hard way.

Moreover, control of the budget has other implications. People outside the firm aren't stupid. Who would you rather have on your non-profit board—the diligent lawyer who's conscientiously built a name for himself over the years, or the guy who controls the office budget and can prompt the firm to kick in 25 grand to the non-profit's annual benefit?

Again, this problem isn't insurmountable. It's just that, by being outer-directed, you're forcing yourself to do things the hard way. Other lawyers at the firm see this, understand the implications, and act accordingly.

Because playing office politics often yields benefits, folks devote time to office politics; lawyers become inner-directed. Firms ought to discourage this, because inner-directedness helps the individual only at the institution's expense, thus hurting the common good. But it's awfully hard, and perhaps impossible, to design systems that are insulated from office politics.

I've heard the managing partner of a large law firm lament that "twenty years ago, Joe Smith spent a huge amount of time working for the good of the firm, and he never asked for a title other than 'partner.' Why is everyone now grasping for administrative positions?"

Perhaps the answer is that the firm was smaller twenty years ago, and everyone knew about their colleagues' accomplishments, and there were fewer issues about controlling budgets and who would invite whom to beauty contests.

Firms should think hard about how they can encourage their lawyers to become outer-directed. The answer plainly lies in rewarding people who are outer-directed, showering wealth and power in their direction. But it's awfully hard for a manager to reward the subordinate who's been most outer-directed instead of the sycophant who just moved into the house next door to yours and regularly joins you for golf.

In-house law departments must think about the same issue, although in slightly different terms. Who should lawyers report to—other lawyers, or business people? If lawyers report to business people, the lawyers are motivated to respond promptly to the needs of the business. But the business folks may be less able to assess the quality of the lawyers' work than other lawyers are, and there may be other reasons to have lawyers report to other lawyers.

We can't eliminate human nature, but sound management practices should permit us to improve institutional performance by encouraging optimum behavior.

COMMENTS

GUEST: I like your advice, and law firms and legal departments would be better off if everybody followed this advice, but you also answered the question why this will never happen. Bad behavior is often the behavior that gets most rewarded in law firms (i.e., while other people are trying to do good work and get good experience, the person who often gets rewarded with opportunities is not necessarily the hardest worker or best lawyer, but the "clown [who] is ingratiating himself to the managing partner").

I actually think this is less of a problem in-house. Maybe this is because there are fewer people on an in-house legal team than at a firm, so it works more like the small firm in your example—usually people know what others are working on and of their successes. Also, a person with a successful outward focus on an in-house team makes the group look better to the rest of the company, so it is more likely that he or she will be rewarded for the effort. In a law firm, being outward focused can sometimes be threatening to partners who may see you as competing for opportunities that they want.

HIRING LAW FIRMS OR LAWYERS?

Can we just put this one to rest?

At every conference, and in many articles, people pose the question: "As a client, do you hire law firms, or do you hire lawyers?" The clients dutifully respond that they hire lawyers, not firms. Hasn't this become sufficiently obvious that we can stop asking the question?

Why does any rational client hire lawyers and not law firms?

Because law firms are an aggregation of lawyers. Once a firm grows beyond a relatively small size, the quality of lawyers will vary. As a client, what matters is the quality of the lawyer working on your matter, not the quality of people not working on your matter, or the identity of the firm. (An exception may exist when a timid client is protecting itself against the possibility of a bad result: "We hired the biggest, baddest law firm available to handle this matter for us. Now that things have gone poorly, you can't blame me, because I hired the best and sunk a lot of money into the matter." But that reasoning is foolishness, and I hope this doesn't happen often.)

The truth is that law firms themselves are uncertain about the quality of their own lawyers. Why?

At many firms, partners rarely see or evaluate each other's work. A partner does work for a client, so the client sees the work. But other partners often don't. So long as the client is happy, associates are engaged, and the bills are being paid, there isn't a perceived need to review the partner's work.

The firm is thus relying heavily on what it knew historically about the quality of the partner's work. That may not be much.

It may not be much for many reasons. First, the partner may have been hired laterally. Perhaps the firm hired the lateral partner exclusively because of the quality of his work, but it's more likely that the incoming lateral partner's book of business had something to do with the decision to hire. And, even if the quality of the lawyer's work matters, the new firm may be only very gently aware of that quality. The new firm, after all, may have worked with the lateral on a transaction or a case or two, but the new firm hasn't seen the lawyer in action on a daily basis over the course of many years, as it has with homegrown associates.

Second, many partners may have joined the firm as a result of mergers. When Big Firm chooses to open a Denver office, Big Firm may acquire a smaller firm with, say, fifty lawyers in Denver. A few of those Denver lawyers may be truly extraordinary; others, not so much. But they all come on board, many as partners, and Big Firm's lawyers in New York are then touting the folks in Denver, pretty much oblivious to whether or not the Denver guys are any good.

Third, over time the quality of lawyers may vary dramatically in a firm's different offices. Think about the Denver branch in the situation I just discussed. Next year, the Denver partners (who, by hypothesis, are really not as good as partners in other offices) will be asked to evaluate new partners. The Denver partners will apply their own judgment and assessment of quality, and the number of partners in Denver will grow. But the new partners are being judged by lower quality people; over time, the quality of the Denver office may decrease significantly.

Fourth, even in a firm with generally high quality, few laterals, and little growth by merger, less competent lawyers will make their way into the partnership ranks. This can happen for reasons of finance ("He's only average quality, but he's a client magnet."), because of other perceived benefits of admitting the person into the partnership ("With a one handicap and membership at that elite club, we can put him to use."), or because of pure politics ("There are plenty of partners in this firm who can't think through tough issues or try significant cases. But if Fred Big can make a lawyer a partner in this firm, then so can I. And Joe Associate has worked hard for me the last few years; I'm going to make him a partner." Or: "If we don't make more partners in Atlanta this year, people will think that our Atlanta office doesn't have any clout, and our Atlanta associates will be demoralized. We have to push two people into the partnership."). In that environment, hiring by the name of the firm, rather than the quality of the individual lawyer, is nuts.

Frankly, this same institutional lack of knowledge of the quality of a firm's own partners also explains why clients must be wary when partners cross-sell services. The lawyer who's doing the cross-selling may or may not actually know the quality of the work of the person whose name she's pushing. In some situations, the lawyer who's doing the cross-selling may not care that much. When a client calls to ask for IP advice in Shanghai, the correct answer for the partner in Chicago to give is: "It's your lucky day! We have the leading IP lawyer in China in our Shanghai office. Let me get back to you with contact information." And then the Chicago partner starts frantically calling around the firm: "Hey! Do we have anyone who does IP in Shanghai?"

Some partners may be restrained from aggressive cross-selling for fear of ruining their client relationships. "The client loves me. If I foist off Joe Schlock in Denver on the client, the client may be unhappy, and I may lose business." But the institutional pressures to cross-sell are often great, and concern for a client's welfare may take a back seat.

So let's just stop asking whether clients hire lawyers or firms. If clients have any sense at all, they hire lawyers. Let's put that issue to rest and start asking instead how clients should react to cross-selling, which at least remains a live issue.

COMMENTS

GUEST: If this were really true, wouldn't Big Law be replaced by a series of boutiques?

GUEST: That is one trend we are seeing.

LATINTHUNDER: "Hasn't this become sufficiently obvious that we can stop asking the question?" Yes, but don't let that stop you.

GUEST: The way you write makes me hearken back to 9th grade English—"okay class, remember, every paragraph has to begin with a topic sentence...and make sure to include your thesis statements." What's even more sad is I bet you talk like this, too.

POO: And may the gods damn him for writing with clarity!

Those with such audacity must relegate themselves to a pitiful existence of excellent law school grades, convincing law review articles, and the general ability to convey a clear and unimpeded message!

ASSOCIATE: But when clients hire a lawyer, instead of a law firm, who is actually doing the work? Clients hire "Corner Office Partner," and typically interface with him, but he hands off literally everything to one or two "lieutenants" who are lower-level partners in his firm, who in turn farm the work out to associates...So, even if the corner office partner is the one who answers the phone, most of the time he actually has no clue what's going on in most of the work. He's too busy getting other clients to sign on, so he can hand off their work, too. Under that analysis, shouldn't the quality of the "firm" matter more?

HOW DE-EQUITIZING PARTNERS CAN UNDERMINE A BUSINESS MODEL

Last week's AmLaw 100 list revealed publicly a trend that partners at big law firms have been feeling acutely: The largest law firms have de-equitized partners in the last two years in an unprecedented way. In the words of one of the articles, "Equity partner head count alone slipped 0.9 percent last year, after dropping 0.7 percent in 2009." That trend may undermine the business models of some law firms.

Law firms have many and varied business plans and compensation systems. But one reasonable way to run a firm is to market your most marketable lawyers—concentrate business development in the folks best able to develop business. For that model to work, however, all partners must trust the institution. De-equitization reduces the necessary trust and may kick the stilts out from under this business model.

Here's how the model works. If a potential new client asks your firm to respond to an RFP for litigation matters, you turn to your half-dozen heaviest-hitting litigators and decide which one will be offered up as the lawyer to lead the new engagement. You know that, if you're invited to a beauty contest, the heavy-hitter will clinch the deal, because he's clinched so many deals in the past.

If you read in today's *Wall Street Journal* that the plaintiffs' mass tort bar has just put another industry under siege, you spring into action. Pull together the firm's marketing materials, identify lawyers with relationships in the relevant industry, draft up outlines of motions to dismiss and oppositions to class certification, assemble an outline of key issues and proposed responses, and then have your relationship lawyers call and e-mail their client contacts, offering to have one of the heavy-hitters meet with the client to explain the firm's capabilities. The heavy-hitter takes it from there.

If a corporate lawyer gets a serious litigation nibble, the corporate lawyer will naturally advise the head of litigation about the opportunity, so the firm can make an appropriate pitch. The head of litigation asks one of the heavy-hitters to lead the charge.

If a client asks a junior partner in the commercial trial department about the firm's ability to defend a multi-billion dollar case, the junior partner reports up through the ranks. The firm puts together a response that proposes a talented litigation team to handle the case—led, of course, by one of the heavy-hitters.

This approach to running a firm isn't crazy. To the contrary: Institutionally, this system makes a lot of sense. You offer up your most impressive lawyers to handle the most important opportunities, land the business, and distribute that business among the masses to keep everyone busy. Collectively, everyone at the firm benefits.

Enter de-equitization....

If, as the AmLaw 100 list suggests, large firms have, on average, de-equitized nearly one out of every fifty partners over the last two years, then all partners know this is happening. At those rates, de-equitization isn't an occasional event; it's happening to your long-time colleagues and friends down the hall, and, unless you're among the anointed, it could happen to you.

Every sentient partner sees that the heavy-hitters are not the ones being de-equitized. It's the loyal guy on the street who's been slaving away for decades, working for the good of the team, and converting what could be personal opportunities into institutional ones, because he thought it was important to serve the greater good. That poor schlub is powerless against the institution. He isn't fortified by the implicit threat that, if the firm mistreats him, he'll leave the firm and take a chunk of business with him. In the past, that guy was told that he was safe: "Bring in the business at the top. We'll spread it around. The pie will get bigger and we'll all prosper. Play by the institutional rules, and we'll protect you." Historically, the guy who played by those rules was not merely told that he was safe; he was in fact safe. (He may not have been exceptionally well compensated, but he wasn't at risk of being thrown off the team.)

De-equitization changes the game.

If you're at risk of being de-equitized, then it's time to hedge against the risk. That means looking out for yourself, even if your self-interest doesn't align perfectly with the institution's best interest. When you read in the *Journal* about a new case, or a client contacts you about a potential big piece of business, it's time to grab the opportunity and run. You may or may not land the business, but at least you've given yourself a chance. No more reporting up through the ranks, giving away the opportunity, and then being at risk that the firm will decide you're superfluous.

The prevalence of de-equitization will thus change the culture of some large firms.

To be sure, de-equitization won't change the culture of all firms. Some firms have been eat-what-you-kill for decades; those firms never asked partners to sacrifice for the common good. Some firms aren't de-equitizing partners, so the rules of the game haven't changed at all. Other firms are unique in their own ways.

But firms that asked partners to share individual opportunities with the institution to benefit the common good, and are now punishing partners who were foolish enough to play by those rules, may be facing a brave new world. It's hard to cultivate loyalty to an institution that can't be trusted to show loyalty in return.

COMMENTS

DUH: Anyone who needs to read this to learn that hustling for business is a good way to avoid being de-equitized should never have received an equity interest in the first place.

LT OBVIOUS: Equity partners are forced out all the time. Whether equity or non-equity, you have no job security. Many equity partners don't play by your "rules," and I don't see non-equity partners acting any differently than equity partners when it come to hoarding work and trying to handle large opportunities for which they are not the best-suited within the firm.

PRIVATE PLAIN: This is all encouraged by the way folks are treated from the associate level on up—if you start out by beating the snot out of people and leaving them insecure, giving arbitrary reviews, letting people go who killed themselves for years, making almost no one partner, etc., they don't evolve into people that trust the institution – they evolve into people that DIStrust it, even the ones who actually make it. Clients are not well served by this model.

GUEST: Exactly! How is this different than how people are treated at all levels?! I doubt many of us who were associates in Big Law during 2009 felt much stability then or now have much loyalty to our firms. A number of associates from my firm, including myself, have now gone in-house. Now, the partners try to get business from us, after all that. While I continue to work with one of the more reasonable partners from my firm, I have absolutely no institutional loyalty and am happy to consider advisors from other firms. Creating instability and treating people badly (to protect your own short-term piece of the pie) isn't wrong just because it is directed at partners—this goes beyond de-equitizing partners.

GUEST: I have been a partner at 2 AmLaw 100 firms. While I believe there is an issue here, I believe the big firms have long lost any sense of being professional organizations. Lawyers at these places are no longer one of the 3 historic professions of lawyers, doctors and clergy. Big Law firms are simply consulting firms that are after one and only one thing: money. Firm leaders at these places have their egos entirely tied to PPP, etc., numbers. Big firms have fired associates and are de-equitizing partners to keep up with the Joneses, nothing more.

ON INTELLIGENT DELEGATION

Some tasks are meant to be delegated; others are not.

Sometimes, whether the task is meant to be delegated depends on what the supervisor has in mind.

Let's think about three examples....

Example number one: I *can* write a letter. I can*not* write a letter in your words. Whether the task of drafting a letter is meant to be delegated depends on what the supervisor has in mind. If the supervisor needs a letter that generally conveys an idea, then any competent person can handle that project. On the other hand, if the letter must be worded exceptionally delicately, or if the supervisor is unable to restrain himself from editing everything intensely, then the supervisor shouldn't delegate the task. Graduating from law school and passing the bar exam makes one a lawyer, but it does not make one a psychic. If writing the letter will require mind-reading, then the drafting duty can't be delegated to a mere lawyer. (If the letter will contain some parts that simply convey ideas generally and other parts that require a special touch, then the supervisor should pause for a moment and think about how to handle this.)

Sometimes, the supervisor simply doesn't know what he or she wants. I remember distinctly, from some 25 years ago, a partner telling me that I should make "these five points in a short, snappy introductory sentence to the brief." That task can't be delegated. It's likely impossible to make five points in one short sentence; if it's not impossible, then the partner had something in mind that I couldn't divine. If you need something written in your words, then you must write it yourself.

Example number two: I *can* conduct settlement talks. I can*not* conduct settlement talks precisely as you would conduct them. If the supervisor honestly believes that something significant will turn on the precise words that are spoken during settlement talks, then the supervisor should conduct those talks herself. If the instructions to the subordinate (whether the associate at a firm, the junior lawyer in-house, or outside counsel taking instructions from a client) will basically include a script for the conversation, then the task probably shouldn't be delegated. "You should start by saying that the client is outraged and doesn't think it should be paying a nickel in this case. The senior executives at the client were already having the lawyers' heads when the lawyers proposed paying anything. We should then say blah, blah, blah. When opposing counsel says X, it's crucial that you then act angry and say Y. Opposing counsel will then say A, and you must furrow your brow, squint your eyes, and say B." And on and on.

This is either necessary or unnecessary. If it's truly essential that the negotiator speak precisely the words being dictated at precisely the times specified, then you probably shouldn't delegate the task. You're not asking the subordinate to conduct settlement talks; you're instructing the subordinate to conduct settlement talks in your very words. It can't be done. Either don't delegate or carve out a task that is in fact delegable.

Last example: I *can* handle a case (or argue a motion, or take a deposition). I cannot handle a case (or argue a motion, or take a deposition) exactly as you would, reacting instinctively and deciding every close judgment call precisely as you would have. If you want the case managed, or the motion argued, or the deposition taken in a responsible way, then a responsible lawyer can do that for you. But if you need the case handled or the other actions conducted exactly as you would have, then do it yourself. Either the task is not meant to be delegated or you, the supervisor, are not able to delegate it. Either way, don't try; the attempt at delegation will quickly cause both you and your subordinate to become unhappy.

What does this mean for relationships among lawyers? If you're a supervisor, think hard about what you're delegating. If the task is meant to be delegated, then do so—but give only guidance that's necessary and able to be heeded. If you find yourself scripting the letter, or the discussion, or the trial tactics, then perhaps either you don't want to delegate this or you're unable to let go. Either way, don't try to delegate. Handle the task yourself.

The amount of guidance that's necessary depends on the nature of the task you're delegating and your level of confidence in your subordinate. If you're supervising someone fresh out of law school who you've never before seen in action, it might be appropriate to say: "Please draft a letter to convey this thought. Then, let me review the draft before you finalize the letter and send it." On the other hand, if you're supervising a senior associate on the verge of partnership, you might say: "The amount in controversy in this case just barely justifies our firm handling the matter. We're really taking the case to accommodate a client for which we do a lot of other work. So this case is all yours, with one caveat: See me before you commit malpractice. If you have a question about anything, I'm always here and always ready to help. If you're making a tough call, talk to me rather than make a mistake. But otherwise I trust your judgment. This case is really all yours."

If you're a subordinate being asked not simply to do a task, but to do it according to a script, this issue is trickier. You'll have to decide whether the supervisor really means what he or she is saying. If the supervisor doesn't really mean what he's saying, then do what he wants, not what he says. (My long-ago partner did not really want five thoughts in one short, snappy sentence. I suspected that he didn't really want that. So I drafted something sensible—five thoughts contained in two or three introductory paragraphs that spanned a page or two. When the partner read those paragraphs, he realized that was what he actually wanted, edited the paragraphs gently, and we were both satisfied.) It is, of course, high-stakes poker to ignore what the supervisor asks and do instead what he wants, but it's often possible.

If the supervisor scripts settlement talks, the supervisor typically doesn't really care precisely what words you speak or with what intonation. (The supervisor is probably just a compulsive nutcase who can't resist scripting everything.) If you settle the case on the specified terms, the supervisor will probably be satisfied.

But if there's a real chance that the supervisor honestly believes that everything must be done according to the script, raise that issue with the supervisor before you proceed. Tell the supervisor that you're happy to take the deposition and you appreciate the guidance, but it's likely that unexpected things will happen and your instincts won't be the same as the supervisor's would be in the same situation. Commit to do everything intelligently, but, depending on how events develop, perhaps not exactly as the supervisor is proposing.

If the supervisor chooses not to delegate, you've lost an opportunity, but you've avoided creating two unhappy people. If the supervisor agrees to delegate despite your warning, you've at least raised in advance that the task will be accomplished, but perhaps not precisely as it had been scripted.

Supervisors, be sensible. Subordinates, be sensitive. We can all get along; I promise.

COMMENTS

VALERIE: Let me be contrarian: Sometimes the end result can't be delegated, but the first draft can. It's more difficult to write something from scratch than it is to re-write something in the words you like.

> **PHRAXOS:** Not true at all. It is far more difficult to fix crap from a second-year associate—paragraphs full of lumpy, leaden sentences fixed on the page, studded with poor word choices, and all in the wrong sequence—than to write it well in the first place. This is also true if what you get is not crap but is still organized or phrased differently from how the argument had come to you in the shower that morning.
>
> If it's important that an introduction, or a particularly key section of the brief, be written right, then I invariably write it myself. Those couple of paragraphs can be dropped into someone else's discussion of the black letter law, and with a little massaging of the rest it won't look so obviously like the diamond in the coal heap. But no great author ever produced his memorable work by rewriting an assistant's first draft.

NANCY: Mark, I recommend you delegate your column to someone more interesting.

NON: Thank you Mark. This is the precise cause of all the conflict in my law firm—a partner who can't let go.

360-DEGREE REVIEWS

360-degree reviews: We solicit anonymous input from your boss, your peers, and your subordinates. A reviewer goes through all of that information, discusses it with you, and, perhaps, shares with you documents containing parts or all of the anonymous responses.

These are remarkably helpful tools. They're helpful, first, because you know that they're coming. If you're going to be evaluated by everyone in the neighborhood, then you're more likely to be civilized and fair to everyone in the neighborhood. ("Civilized and fair" doesn't mean "easy" or "letting others break the rules." It means "civilized and fair." If someone's performance needs improving, you talk reasonably with that person about his or her weaknesses and how to improve. You don't belittle people or scream at them, because incivility will surely come back to haunt you at 360-degree review time, and you know that 360-degree review time is lurking in your future.)

360-degree reviews are helpful because you critique others. It's relatively easy—or, at least, routine—to be asked to critique folks situated beneath you in a hierarchy. But it's a little different to be asked to critique folks who are situated horizontally or above you. When you're asked to critique those people formally, it makes you think a little harder: What are those people doing right? What are they doing wrong? What information should they hear about their performance?

Because you're forced to think about those topics, you become more sensitive to them. And, because everyone knows those topics will later be identified during reviews, you may be more willing to raise sensitive issues with your peers or your supervisors. ("I agree with you that Sally didn't distinguish herself on that project. But, if I were you, I would have been a little gentler on her during the group meeting. She deserved the criticism, but don't you think she also deserved the dignity of hearing the criticism privately?") Intelligent peers and supervisors, aware that 360-degree review time is right around the corner, may be pleased to receive this type of feedback.

360-degree reviews do not simply sensitize you to, and perhaps make you more willing to speak about, these subjects. Those reviews also make you feel more engaged in your workplace. "The firm is asking me how my boss performs? That's pretty cool. Who knew the institution cared?" The institution shows concern for employees by soliciting their input on important matters, and your relationship with your supervisors surely falls into that category.

I've heard (from a person who participated in these things) that some consulting firms use 360-degree reviews to inform partnership decisions. And, I'm told, those reviews are done the intelligent way: You select a reviewer who is truly disinterested. The reviewer is not located in the same office as the candidate for partnership and doesn't work in the same practice area. The process thus reduces the parochialism that might otherwise infect partnership decisions: "We really need another corporate finance partner in Dallas this year. We haven't had one in forever, and the associates are getting disheartened. Fred may not be the best candidate for partnership we've ever seen, but we should push hard for him so it doesn't look like corporate finance is powerless here."

The reviewer gathers the information, distills it, and presents it to the partnership committee. That provides a fairly comprehensive view of the candidate, may weed out some of the ogres, and alerts candidates in advance that the partnership decision will turn in part on the perceptions of folks horizontal to, or beneath, the candidate in the hierarchy. That can work wonders to create a more civilized workplace.

Many corporations use 360-degree reviews. At least some consulting (and other professional services) firms use them. But I've never heard of law firms using them, either annually or as part of the process for selecting partners. Perhaps some law firms do use them, and I simply haven't heard. Perhaps law firms are uniquely protective of their partners' egos, or uniquely concerned about infuriating a rainmaker and causing him to leave the firm because he's been insulted by the review process. Or perhaps law firms in fact would not benefit from these reviews, for reasons not obvious to me.

In the corporate setting, however, we manage to conduct 360-degree reviews right up to the C-suites, and most folks seem pleased to receive feedback and delighted to participate in the process. Unless law firms are a truly unusual breed, they, too might consider using this management tool.

(Yeah, yeah: I know that you're concerned about reviewers not respecting the pledge of anonymity. But you're wrong. First, information can be solicited anonymously through a web-based tool administered by a third-party vendor. No one at your outfit would know who wrote what. Second, you must of course be smart when you evaluate others. If you say, "Partner Jones was a jerk when he screamed at me about my draft motion to dismiss in the IBM case," then partner Jones will probably figure out who you are. But I suspect that you're clever enough to avoid this problem. Finally, so long as the 360-degree review process is used to convey constructive criticism, rather than to vent hysterically about perceived wrongs, then most people will accept criticism in the spirit in which it was offered. You'd be surprised: I, and others, have been pleased to learn how those surrounding us in the corporate structure perceive our performance.)

COMMENTS

GUEST: Here's why 360-degree reviews don't seem to work in a law firm environment: 1. Partners generally work with only a few associates. No amount of effort at anonymity can be effective as there is only one possible source for many comments (as someone who was confronted by a secretary over a poor review, I can say that anonymous downward reviews have the same problem). 2. The compensation committee does not base decisions on reviews. So partners won't change behaviors based on the results.

I'm sure there are more reasons, but these seem like enough.

NOWHERE: Agreed. Anonymity only works if it is a really huge firm and the partners don't know the associates well. Even in big firms, some departments are smaller than others and the partners will know who wrote the reviews (unless they are multiple choice).

GUEST: Yes – since there are no consequences for bad behavior, nothing will change. Partners seem to be completely incapable of policing each other's behavior. In a company, most everybody is accountable to somebody, and there is an understanding that people aren't going to go out of their way to help somebody who is unreasonable...so karma really has a way of biting back at bad behavior (not always but much more than in a firm). I think there is a belief among partners that they are overpaying associates, so they should just take what they get, and that once you get to the top (partnership), one of the prerogatives is to be able to behave as badly as you want without being questioned by others.

DON'T BE A MENTOR!

I am not a mentor!

Never have been. Never will be. Don't care to be.

I'm a lawyer. I'm a co-worker. In some cases, I may be a friend. But I'm not a mentor; I have no time for that crap.

When I was clerking (for the Honorable Dorothy W. Nelson of the United States Court of Appeals for the Ninth Circuit), my judge was (and remains) a delight. She was a warm, engaging person who treated everyone as an equal. She was living proof that you don't have to give up on human kindness just because you've become powerful. She taught, by example, many lessons about work-life balance and the meaning of humanity.

But a mentor? I'm not sure they had invented the word "mentor" (at least with its current connotation) back in 1983. I don't think Judge Nelson gave the idea a moment's thought....

When I started work at Steinhart & Falconer in San Francisco in 1984, Neil Falconer wasn't a mentor. He was a pain in the neck. He'd ask you to report on the results of your legal research, and you'd break into a sweat after 15 minutes of his questioning. You honestly believed that you'd read those cases and thought carefully about their implications; it quickly became clear that you hadn't understood a thing. Many associates dreaded the thought of working for him; he was too smart and too demanding.

There was no way that guy was a mentor. All he did was teach me everything that mattered about being a lawyer. A "mentor"? He'd have had no use for that stuff.

From the time I arrived at Jones Day in Cleveland in 1989, until the time I moved on in 2009, I wasn't a mentor. Summer associates occasionally asked about possible topics for their law review notes; if I had any stray thoughts kicking around that I'd never have time to write about, I might offer them up. Why not? I wasn't going to use those ideas for anything. I sure wasn't mentoring anyone.

When junior people wrote bad drafts of briefs, I'd sit down and explain what they'd done wrong and how they could improve things in the future. I wasn't mentoring; I was mainly trying to make my life easier the next time around.

If I needed help with an article, I'd ask (competent) junior people to co-author things with me. That was just to get the work done; there was nothing charitable about it. (I confess that I'd always give my co-authors full co-authorship credit on the authors' by-line. But that choice was driven by my sense of fundamental fairness; if you'd contributed significantly to the finished product, we shouldn't relegate your name to a footnote thanking you for "research assistance.")

If opportunities came up to let junior folks write articles, or give talks, or teach classes, or play a serious role in a piece of litigation, I'd naturally pass on those chances to people who seemed, to my eye, to deserve them. That's minimal payback for the many chores those folks helped me with over the course of the decades.

If someone needed a recommendation, I'd provide an honest one. That's neither mentoring nor helping people out; it's just speaking the truth.

Being a "mentor"? Not for me.

"Mentoring" strikes me as analogous to "networking." "Networking" means sucking up to people to curry undeserved favors. I don't believe in it at all. I don't object to joining a few organizations and then working with others to help those organizations achieve their goals. That's okay. It's just "networking" that I don't like.

So, too, with "mentoring." Mentoring means that you go out of your way to help people. Bah, humbug! Who's got time for that? Surely "mentoring" isn't just working with colleagues in a way that makes sense. That's just doing your job; it's not mentoring.

So I was more than a little surprised several years ago when Richard Cordray—the guy who President Obama just nominated to head the new Consumer Financial Protection Bureau, after Elizabeth Warren was sent packing—wrote in a book review (page 5 of the pdf) about the "accumulated advice that [I'd] shared over the years" and said that I'd never spoken to him in a "high-handed way." If anything like that ever happened, it was purely by accident. If that [then]-young pup wrote run-on sentences, I told him so. And I never minced words about it. Trust me.

And why is Sean Costello now saying in public that I was his "mentor"? I deny it; I was not his mentor. We just worked together on a few cases. If he made mistakes, I told him what they were. If he did something right, I told him so. And, because he was competent, I asked him to co-author an article or two with me. I sure didn't mentor the guy.

I know the people who are mentors. I don't like them. They walk around telling you about all the young lawyers they trained, and they regale you with stories about the many people who would be nothing if not for the mentor's sage guidance. Then you ask the young lawyers about the mentor, and the young lawyers say: "He's a disaster! You walk into his office, and he hands you a note to return a phone call. It turns out he just let our client's default be taken, and he wants you to make the embarrassing phone call asking for relief."

Don't be a mentor!

Just be a decent human being who respects the feelings of others, and work collegially with people to achieve your common goals. That's plenty. That's really all there was before they invented the concept of "mentoring," and it's really all there'll ever be.

COMMENTS

GUEST: Herrmann, you are the icon for parasitic baby boomers who took and never gave. You have left the country in ruins, and you are proud of your selfishness. Do us all a favor and take that amalgam of wrinkles, lack of hair, fat and old man smell of corpse of yours and throw it off of the highest floor of your building, so that us gen x/yers can at least do without paying you $60,000 per year for social security and medicare.

NON: Gist of the article:

Who has time for the next generation of partners? Screw 'em.

Throw work at 'em, see which ones do a good job, ream 'em if they do bad work, give 'em more work if they do good work, promise 'em partnership, and then screw 'em!

GUEST: Ignore the comments, Mark. Those guys have no clue what they're talking about, nor do they understand what you're saying. I hated the "mentoring" program at my big firm. It was useless and the partners involved all resented the loss of billable time—both mine and theirs. But I loved the head of my practice group who didn't even know there was a mentoring program and never volunteered for anything to do with associates ever. What he did instead was talk to us. We knew things the senior lawyers didn't. Like what was in the documents. When he needed to know about that, he'd come to us and ask what we saw and, gasp!, what we THOUGHT about it. He knew the firm prided itself on hiring the best and the brightest coming out of law school so he thought "we're paying these kids a ton of money because they're supposedly so smart. Let's get some use out of these brains we paid for." And we adored him for it because once someone needed us to think, we started learning to really think. We learned what was important about the case and what wasn't. It made us better at our jobs, which was what we really wanted anyway.

GUEST: I suspect he's trying to distinguish between those who "mentor" by providing broad, unhelpful, and unusable, career advice, versus those who just teach younger attorneys how to be a great attorney through day to day interactions while simply trying to provide the client with the best service possible. The problem is that he's apparently incapable of doing that without sounding like a complete jerk.

THE MUTUAL MENACE OF ONE BAD PARTNER

Suppose your firm has one incompetent partner, and our joint has the misfortune to be working with that person.

This guy consistently misses important issues. He sends us briefs that read (as did one draft I recently received): "In response to ALR's motion to dismiss the OC, [plaintiff] added an allegation in the FAC that . . . ." We comment, over and over again (as we did recently), that briefs on our behalf must be written in English, not gibberish. Even if you've set up short forms, no reader sees "OC" and "FAC" and thinks "Original Complaint" and "First Amended Complaint." Use words, not alphabet soup.

To no avail.

We suggest that the partner include on the litigation team a gifted writer (because we're too nice to suggest that the partner include on the litigation team "a lawyer who's worth a damn"). But nothing ever changes; the partner never hears us. Confronted with an avalanche of criticism and suggestions, no law firm partner has ever said to us, "Why, thank you. Now that you mention it, I realize that I am in fact inept. To better serve your legal needs, I'll replace myself with a real lawyer."

No, no, no. Instead, the partner continues to send us bad briefs, making the same mistakes over and over, but seemingly thinking that we may not care the next time around. It's Einstein's definition of insanity: "Doing the same thing over and over again and expecting different results."

Up to that point, the fault is the partner's. But then I personally make two mistakes....

First, I continue to talk directly to the relationship lawyer to try to improve the situation. That's Einstein back at you again: If the relationship lawyer doesn't understand what you're saying the first time you talk to him, why should he understand it the fourth or fifth time? But I'm too "nice" to do what's really necessary, which is to call the managing partner of the firm and explain that the firm is about to lose a big client unless the firm staffs our cases differently. Why do I do the crazy thing repeatedly, and never do the thing that might actually fix the situation? Because it feels somehow impolite or unfair to tell the managing partner that one of her colleagues is inept. So I let the situation fester.

Then I make my second mistake: I do not draw the correct mental conclusion that my relationship lawyer, John Doe, is inept. Rather, I draw the incorrect conclusion that the law firm of Bigg & Mediocre is an inept institution. I let the one case that the firm is handling for us stagger to its conclusion, and then I put out the word that we should never again retain B&M.

(The joint where I work is actually slightly more fair than this to outside counsel. We insist on conducting annual reviews of the firms that represent us, which ensures that the firms receive feedback. But the relationship lawyer often attends those meetings, so we're frequently giving constructive criticism to the very person least able (or willing) to hear it.)

What should corporate counsel do?

Don't be as stupid as I am. (I admit that that's setting the bar mighty low.) Don't blame an entire law firm for the ineptitude of a single lawyer, and don't avoid confrontation by limiting your criticism to speaking only to the relationship lawyer. Realize that the firm might actually be okay; speak to someone with the capacity to fix the situation; and thus give the firm a decent chance to prove itself.

And then there's the other side of the coin: What should law firms do?

First, have disinterested lawyers—partners not involved in representing the client—solicit candid feedback from clients. Solicit that feedback mid-year, so the conversation doesn't conflict with an annual year-end review. During that session, listen carefully to what the client says. (Hint: "I rate the quality of your firm's work as just below middle of the pack" is not praise.) Ask the client what your firm can do to improve (or expand) the relationship, and heed the advice you receive.

Second, impose real quality control on partnership decisions. A client that has a bad experience with just one of your partners may mistakenly choose to condemn your entire institution. This makes the quality of your partnership awfully important. Try to apply uniform criteria, applied equally across all offices, when you make partnership decisions. Hire lateral partners sparingly (because you probably know little about the true quality of those folks' work).

Finally, think about how you can encourage clients to switch lawyers, rather than firms, when clients are unhappy with the service they're receiving. If it were easier (and less embarrassing) to replace the lawyers working on a team, then firms would not lose clients unnecessarily.

But don't keep doing over and over what you've been doing unsuccessfully in the past. That's just insane.

COMMENTS:

BILLY JO : Mark, you're the client. You have enormous leverage over the lawyers you hire. If they're not performing to your standards, simply say, "If the briefs do not improve, per our specifications, we will hire another firm to handle this matter." Problem solved. If it is not solved, replace these idiots with lawyers at a competent firm.

Your incessant frustrations are self-imposed, my friend.

ONLYMODERATELY: This is a serious problem for clients. When we have a problem with an associate, we can call the partner and get it fixed. But when it's the PARTNER that's the problem, we have no recourse but to move the work to another firm. The firms give us no other option. It's frequently difficult to find out who the managing partner is for an office, and I can't recall ever hearing ANY client say that they called a managing partner and got the partner handling their work replaced.

I am reminded how I once had a matter with some tricky issues transferred to a partner at another firm. I was dreading an afternoon marketing call from the partner who had been handling our matters. Instead, I got an e-mail an hour later asking us if he should transfer ALL of our matters.

So I said "Yes."

SILLY E-MAIL OF THE YEAR AWARD

The "commenters" at Above the Law are—as you know if you've ever looked—a tough crowd. If you're a partner at a big firm, then you're a loser, because you're a workaholic stiff with no life. If you're a partner at a small firm, then you're a loser, because you couldn't succeed at a big firm. If you're an associate at a big firm, you're a loser, because you're a lifeless drone who doesn't have the courage to pursue your dreams. If you're a scholar, then you're a loser: Those who can't do, teach. If you're a judge, then you couldn't cut it in private practice, so you had to bail out.

You get my drift.

The correspondents who choose to write to me personally (by clicking on this link) are an entirely different breed. (Perhaps it's because they're not anonymous.) My correspondents have been consistently civilized and reasonable, and often quite thoughtful. But I recently received a well-crafted, nicely written e-mail from a law student who utterly missed the boat. I devote this column to that correspondent, and to others who might be suffering from a similar misconception.

Here's the backstory: I wrote a column about how improving the quality of law firm interviews might improve the quality of associates that a law firm hires. A law-student-correspondent suggested that law firms might in fact not care about the quality of associates. To paraphrase: "Law firms count on having high attrition in the associate ranks. So you need a fair number of associates who will either leave on their own or have to be shown the door. And law firms make very few partners, so, after an entering class has been winnowed down over the course of a decade, the firm is likely to have one or two remaining candidates who can be offered partnership. That's true regardless of the quality of the entering class."

That e-mail is proof that insanity can be made to sound plausible ....

Law firm partners don't care about the quality of their associates? Are you nuts?

If a partner is supported by decent associates, then the partner is like Superman. The partner receives glittering draft briefs that can be sent to clients for review and then filed without editing a word. The partner gets to work from perfect deposition transcripts, filled with clean questions and answers that will support motions for summary judgment or devastating cross-examination at trial. Legal research is comprehensive and conclusions thoughtful, so the partner can rely on spadework done by others. This is bliss!

What's the alternative? A partner cannot permit poor quality work to go out the door. If the partner receives crappy draft briefs, the partner will be forced to devote nights and weekends to burning the associates' drafts and then re-writing the damned things. If associates can't be trusted to take depositions, then partners fly around the country like lunatics covering for their colleagues' failings. If research can't be trusted, then the partner must duplicate it himself or risk drawing wrong conclusions. If a partner had an infinite number of perfect associates, then the partner would be able to handle an infinite amount of work. Partners care very, very deeply about the quality of the associates with whom they work.

What about the supposed need for associate attrition to make the big firm model work? That's a straw man. First, if a startlingly good number of associates were top-notch, I suspect that most firms could handle that "problem." Those firms would, after all, be able to handle more business more efficiently, which would presumably support the load of retaining more associates. But, on the off-chance that didn't work, then it's easy enough for a law firm to induce attrition: Tell the unnecessary associates that it's time to leave. Law firms are not going to be threatened by a lack of associate attrition.

So, too, for the straw man about needing only a very few qualified candidates for partnership at the end of the associate gauntlet. (On a Sunday morning talk show in December, George Will accused another panelist of being a "pyromaniac in a field of straw men." I swore that I'd find a place to steal that line and use it in this column. Done!) If a firm has too many truly outstanding candidates for partnership, then the firm certainly should find a way to accommodate a few extra brilliant partners, thus improving the quality of the partnership overall. But, on the off-chance that wasn't possible, then it would be easy enough for a law firm to avoid being swamped by having too many new partners: Simply don't offer partnership to most of the outstanding candidates. Law firms are not going to be threatened by having too many extraordinary candidates for partnership.

In an odd way, I enjoy the commenters at Above the Law. After a couple of decades as a law firm partner, I became unaccustomed to being savaged in public; the commenters fixed that problem. And I enjoy my correspondents in a more traditional way: They have educated me, challenged me, and provided some of the pleasure that comes from writing these twice-weekly ditties. But thinking that law firms don't care about the quality of their associates would be a grave mistake. Please don't fall into that trap.

COMMENTS

ALISON: While I agree with you that law firms want "quality" associates (and could probably do a better job interviewing to get them), I think it's silly of you to so casually gloss over the promotion-to-partnership issue. It's pretty simple. If the metric by which you measure success is profits per partner (as, let's face it, most firms do these days), you're not just going to casually make room for all the qualified candidates to become partner. Each one admitted drops your PPP numbers, so there's very little incentive to take on more partners, from the short-term perspective of the existing partners. Obviously, it looks different if you think of the long-term survival of the firm, but how many partners these days really care about that, when it comes right down to it? Not many.

BEEN THERE DONE THAT TROLL: Counterpoint—Wachtell Lipton. They hire the best of the best, pay them extremely well, and yet many burn out and/or move on to other things, thus only a small number of new partners are made each year. Whether by design or otherwise is somewhat irrelevant.

A SEAL-EATING SHARK: Yeah, the Navy SEALS are the same. Problem is there is only a small population of candidates at the level you need, so this model won't be extensible to most Big Law firms for the same reason you won't get a Navy with 300,000 SEAL-quality sailors.

ODD

HIRE THIS UNEMPLOYED CHICAGO-KENT EDITOR-IN-CHIEF!

First, a story; then, an attempt to find a job for an unemployed former editor-in-chief of the Chicago-Kent Law Review.

Here's the story: After I wrote *The Curmudgeon's Guide to Practicing Law*, I thought about how to maximize sales of the book. I had the clever (if I do say so myself) idea of sending free copies to the editors-in-chief of a bunch of law reviews. I figured that those folks were likely to (1) read a book and (2) be "opinion leaders" on their respective campuses, so word of the book would spread.

But there was a fly in my ointment. If you send a law student a book, the student is likely to read the book and pass it on to a friend, who will do the same in turn. That generates readers (which is nice), but it doesn't generate sales (which is nicer).

How do you prevent this?

My wife had a great idea. (I wish the idea were mine, but I really can't take credit. Actually, I'd take credit in a heartbeat, but she might read this column and call me on it.) My wife suggested that I personally inscribe each book to the targeted editor-in-chief: "For Jane Doe. Enjoy the practice of law! Mark Herrmann."

This is great! The recipient is delighted; he or she feels as though you've gone out of your way to send a personalized copy of the book. But the inscription also serves the author's purpose. No one gives away a copy of a book that has been personally inscribed and signed by the author; inscribing the thing is as good as tearing the cover off of it.

So I sat down a year ago September (as I now do every year), inscribed a bunch of books, and mailed them off to some editors-in-chief. That typically results in a couple of "thank you" notes, a small uptick in the book's sales ranking at Amazon.com, and an echoing silence.

Earlier this month, however, last year's mailing prompted a different result. I got a letter in the mail from the editor-in-chief of the Chicago-Kent Law Review for 2009-2010. This kid (sorry—but, at my age, recent graduates are all kids to me) wrote that he graduated last year and has been unemployed for seven months. He's done everything possible to find a job—volunteering, interviewing, applying to all the clerkships, checking all the online job sites—and remains unemployed.

Remarkably, he somehow blames me for this. (His logic was a little convoluted here, I must say, but it had something to do with my book exciting him about the prospect of working only for him to discover that he had no place to work.) The letter asks that I make this up to him by calling or meeting him and offering a job, or at least providing some advice. (The letter does include a postscript, which I quote in full: "Oh. And thanks for the book." Nice touch, kid.)

Anyway, I admired the kid's spunk, so I met him for coffee last week. And David Freedman, the 2009-2010 editor-in-chief of the Chicago-Kent Law Review, seems like an articulate, decent guy. He has the EIC credential. And he's available. (I must say that I'm dumbstruck to learn that the editor-in-chief of the Chicago-Kent Law Review is having trouble finding a job, even in a terribly tough job market. David's letter acknowledged that his situation might be different if he had "finished at the top of [his] class," so perhaps that's an issue. I really don't know; I didn't chat with David about his grades.)

That was the wind-up; here's the closing pitch:

On the one hand, if there's a chance that you have a job (or a lead for a job) that can help this guy, please send an e-mail to David Freedman at dfreedman@hotmail.com. Let's make this column at Above the Law serve a purpose. Let's find a job for at least one unemployed recent law school graduate.

If, on the other hand, you just want to savage this guy, that's what the "comment" bar is for at the bottom of this column. Have at it. (David will probably forgive the abuse if we manage to find him a job.)

Finally, if you're another unemployed recent law school graduate, please do not contact me for help. David came up with his idea; he contacted me first; he wins (to the extent you can call spreading news of one's plight a victory). I don't even know if I can help David; I certainly can't help everyone else. Sorry about that.

P.S. to David Freedman: If you get a job, you really must let me know. And, oh, yes—as to the free copy of the book: You're quite welcome.

COMMENTS

GUEST: So instead of reaching out to your long list of professional contacts that includes partners with hiring authority, you're spamming a blog mainly read by associates? Way to really stick your neck out for this "kid" (your explanation for referring him to this way makes it no less insulting).

> **FROZT:** To be fair, it's not necessarily an either/or situation. He may have been doing both.

> **GUEST:** True, but I doubt it. The whole tone of the post is "Don't say I never did anything for ya, kid. By the way, buy my book."

GUEST: As an employed Chicago-Kent alum, I am aware of the current economic conditions and how lucky I am to have a job. I am also embarrassed for Mr. Freedman–the sense of entitlement that accompanies many law review staff members is appalling. Instead of blaming others for a lack of employment options, do something to make yourself indispensable. No one is guaranteed a job and last time I checked, ability to wallow in self-pity isn't considered a specialized skill by prospective employers.

> **CALLINGOUTTHEDBAG:** When did Freedman say he was entitled? From the anecdote above it seems like he is making unusual efforts to find a job.
> You say you feel "lucky" to have a job. This kid wasn't so lucky.
> In sum, you are a douche.

WE'RE HIRING ...: Interesting. This column shows a real disconnect with the modern law job search, and it shows one other thing too: (1) even if you admire his pluck, plenty of readers will spot a high maintenance employee in the rough (he comes across as all about what others should do for him); (2) if you really wanted to help him, you should have considered whether to saddle his whole career future with the association of his name and e-mail address with this column; it will show in any search for his name/current e-mail with this post for quite some time (perhaps created a new e-mail for this purpose); (3) the one other thing: even good columnists have to scrape the bottom of the idea barrel once in a while. Looking forward to future columns... with better content.

DAVID LAT: Just FYI, David Freedman consented to this shout-out. In fact, he reviewed and signed off on this column before it was published.

PLUM DUMB: Bravo to the kid. It's a hard market, you have to be creative. And thanks to you for giving him a hand.

> **GUEST:** Mark? Is that you?

NON: It's comments like this...
> "I must say that I'm dumbstruck to learn that the editor-in-chief of the Chicago-

Kent Law Review is having trouble finding a job, even in a terribly tough job market."

...that prove that people currently practicing law—particularly, older people—have absolutely no clue how bad it is out there. If this was the EIC of a T10 law review, maybe, mayyybe, I'd agree with Herrmann's comment. But to be "dumbstruck" by the fact that someone who is clearly not in the top 10% at Chicago-Kent (who?) doesn't have a job just goes to show how completely unaware people like Herrmann are as to how bad it is out there. I have friends at my T10 law school, some graduating with honors, who still have nothing, or are eking out a living as a contract attorney doing doc review.

The "lost generation" is truly lost if Herrmann's is the predominant view. When the market picks back up again, and jobs become available, people like Herrmann will look down their noses at people who couldn't get a job—or worse (?), worked as contact attorneys doing doc review—and assume that they just didn't have enough "pluck" or "didn't try hard enough" or that there was some reason that they didn't get an offer from their summer gigs (as opposed to the harsh randomness of the no-offers).

GUEST: It's impossible to tell how "screwed" he is without knowing his grades; his LinkedIn page doesn't show any honors, which given the rest of his elaborate profile, I'd expect to see on the page. Also, while putting himself out on ATL is questionable, I don't see anything wrong with him hustling his butt off and contacting this "Inside Straight" columnist for help.

NWDC: I don't even understand this post—the EIC of the law review of a complete joke of a law school sends an offensive letter with ridiculously poor logic (and paranoia/blame issues) and someone should hire him because you had coffee with him and he seemed halfway decent? Who is an employer going to blame when Freedman's work product sucks?

  PLUM DUMB: Let me guess, you graduated from Kent? The guy's just looking for work, you dbag.

JENNIFER, LOVE & HEWITT: I think a number of the commenters take themselves a little too seriously. The kid needed to get someone's attention so he reached out with some tongue-in-cheek self-aggrandizing. His ploy worked. Good for him!

JONMAN438: They're just annoyed they didn't think of it first or didn't have the guts to do it.

FAIL WHALERSON: Mark, way to demonstrate that lawyers are heartless jerks. You just confessed to countless individuals that the only reason you signed the gift you sent them was to try to earn a $.10 royalty from an extra book sale or two? Was it really worth outing what a cheapo you are? Not to mention that your strategy, while weak, wasn't even one you were able to come up with on your own (way to go, Mrs. Herrmann!).

As an aside, I pity the poor guy you called out here. When he fails to land a job after this, he will take on additional taint ("not even national recognition got this guy a job–he must be damaged goods!" is what the hiring partner will say).

MIKE BORELLA: I worked with David on the CK Law Review. He was an excellent EIC, who solved quite a few real-world problems to dramatically improve the state of the journal. The guy is a natural leader and oversaw a very successful year.

> **GUEST:** Please tell me the types of "real-world problems" that editors of law reviews face? Books not going out on time? Typos in the masthead? Publishing offers snatched up by expedites to other, higher-ranked schools? The world of law review is so far removed from "the real world" that I have a hard time believing this.
>
> Also, nice try David, posing as Mike Borella.

MARGO: What on earth is shameful about what David did? He secured an in-person meeting for the purpose of potential employment, and the writer of this blog got a kick out of it and wrote this about it. The job market sucks, people go to different tiers of law school, it is or it isn't hard to get onto Law Review depending on the tier in question.... blah blah blah.

Bottom line: David MOST LIKELY worked pretty hard and was pretty successful if he served as EIC anywhere, and he wants and MOST LIKELY even deserves a job, like many of us. Why all the hate?

Most of you sound extremely bitter about something or other, and my guess is it isn't David. Your profession has made the lot of you jealous and judgmental. It's sad.

CK1: Know for a fact that EIC status actually hurt him in his employment search during the summer between 2L and 3L years. The firm I worked for didn't want to hire him because he would not have been able to stay on and put in 20 to 30 hours a week during the 3L school year. Pretty much a microcosm of law school in general these days: think you're doing something ambitious that will advance your career, only to find out that there's nothing waiting for you on the other side and your ambition may have just screwed you out of a few years of employment while racking up a studio apartment's worth of debt.

RACHELLE: I've tried a number of stunts in order to get an interview in this crappy job-market. Unfortunately, you almost have to do so in this economy. Contacting Mark makes him gutsy... not "entitled." Kudos to David for thinking outside the box. This shows creativity and drive, which are both traits that make for a good lawyer. If he did agree to this being published, it clearly shows he's willing to do just about anything to get a job. I'd hire a lawyer with that much nerve.

Author's note: Within three months of when this post was published, David landed a job at one of the world's leading law firms.

SUCCEEDING IN THE LAW

WILL YOU BE THERE ON MONDAY?

Put yourself in the other guy's shoes.

I don't want a chorus of, "But that's common sense! Tell me something new! Complain about bonuses!"

Of course it's common sense that you should put yourself in the other guy's shoes. But few people do it.

You call an IT guy for help because your !!%@! computer isn't working. And the IT guy starts blathering on about IT gobbledygook. Interface this and reboot that and a bunch of gigabytes.

Gimme a break: I don't want information technology; I want magic.

Just make the damned thing work. I'm not interested in your job.

You call the internal training folks and tell them that you have to revise the training module about discrimination or overtime pay or insider trading or whatever. And the training person starts blathering on about approvals and launch dates and other training modules and personnel schedules.

Gimme a break: I don't want logistics; I want magic.

A business person calls a lawyer and asks how to accomplish something. And the lawyer starts blathering on about statutory this and precedent that and whether *Smith* is distinguishable.

Give the business person a break: He doesn't want law; he wants magic.

So give him magic….

You do have to discuss the issue with the business person. You do have to learn the relevant facts and business issues. And then you have to drive the issue to a responsible conclusion with a minimum of fuss. The business person doesn't care about your precedents any more than you care about the gigabytes. It's a matter of whose shoes you stand in, and you should think about the other person's perspective.

That's true for just about everything you do.

An outside lawyer recently sent me an e-mail that read in its entirety (and I quote): "Will you be there on Monday?"

That means as much to you now as it did to me when I received it.

What the heck's happening on Monday? Is someone throwing a surprise party for me? (If so, outside counsel just blew the secret.) Do we have a mediation? A trial? A big argument? If so, in what case? I've got hundreds of cases to think about, and I'm not tracking every event in every case on my desk calendar.

Most corporations have a very few cases (typically, those disclosed on quarterly securities filings) that are material and whose names easily drop from everyone's lips. We have other cases that we supervise with varying degrees of rigor depending on the nature and status of the case. We also have many meetings or calls every day to coordinate with business units, other lawyers, overseas colleagues, external auditors, outside counsel, and the like. We have endless crises because some business deal must close this week, or some colleague needs urgent business advice, or some regulatory inquiry is exploding halfway around the world.

I just got off a half-hour conference call about piracy in Sudan, and my administrative assistant is waving at me that the CFO and GC are holding urgently on the other line.

And you want to know, "Will you be there on Monday?"

I don't think you're putting yourself in my shoes.

How about: "You may recall that we have the Second Circuit argument in *Doe* in New York City on Monday. Are you planning to attend? If so, where can I meet you and when?"

Put yourself in the other guy's shoes.

This applies equally to your colleagues at law firms. Your secretary really doesn't need to be asked to run photocopies at 4:57 p.m. and miss the bus, if the copies could have been run earlier in the day. Your partner really doesn't want printouts of three cases accompanied by the excuse, "I didn't have a chance to do comprehensive research, so I can't answer your question, but I found three cases that you should read for yourself."

There is of course the other side of the coin: Your associates don't need to be summoned on Friday at 5 p.m. to do emergency research that could have been started on Tuesday morning. And they don't need to be told that the draft brief must be on your desk on Monday when you'll be on the road (and not reading the draft) until a week from Friday.

Just slow down.

Think.

And put yourself in the other guy's shoes.

That may be common sense, but following that advice will set you apart from most of humanity.

COMMENTS

QUINNTWEET: "Your associates don't need to be summoned on Friday at 5 p.m. to do emergency research that could have been started on Tuesday morning. And they don't need to be told that the draft brief must be on your desk on Monday when you'll be on the road (and not reading the draft) until a week from Friday."

But that's a large part of the fun of being a partner! Take that away and most partners under 55 will only have a modest after-tax income benefit over senior associates and Counsel when you subtract capital buy-in, and that will be the only reason to be a partner rather than Counsel.

When you're miserable, the power to make other people's lives hell for no reason is one of the best forms of compensation.

INHOUSEDUDE: I do not like the author's tone. This guy is arrogant and condescending, and I bet his underlings dislike working for him. Above the Law should look into dropping this author in favor of someone else.

> **BENEDICK:** I worked (as an associate) for Mark when he was at Jones Day. And liked it. He tended to be direct with criticism. So lousy associates tended to like him less. So yes, InHouseDude, you probably would dislike working for him.

> **LOGIC:** Nice logic–if you don't like working for someone, you're probably lousy. I take it you like working with everyone.

GUEST2433: Gee whiz–I'm so glad this guy has told me how to interact with my internal business clients. I am glad he has shown me the light after six years of being an in-house counsel and six more of being in private practice. This guy must have a Ph.D. in the Study of the Obvious. I think I knew the first day I went in-house that a good in-house lawyer mostly asks questions about what the business client wants to accomplish, thinks about it in that light, and tries to come up with a solution that gets them there as quickly as possible without giving away the store or taking ridiculous risks. Nobody on the business side gives a crap about precedents or legal technicalities on deals and only marginally more so on litigation (which you let outside counsel waste their time dithering about–to a point anyway). In litigation, an in-house counsel should act as a filter for his internal clients. As for his point about wasting people's time with 11th hour assignments, I agree. But this mostly goes on in law firms and rarely in-house because most people at in-house gigs are in them because they wanted to escape that crap. Usually with the law firms it is because some power-obsessed partner likes to give some pointless or marginally important research or memo project to an associate at 5:30 PM on a Friday just to test the associate's commitment and/or satiate his sick desire to exercise the power to screw up the associate's personal plans for fun. I had to deal with that all the time.

KETTLE BLACK: Okay, let me get this straight, you're saying that the author 'must have a Ph.D. in the Study of the Obvious' and in order to bring that point home–you've decided to detail everything he just said in your own 2433 words? Any chance you're available to type out some deposition digests for me?

DAVID: Mark, I've been enjoying your posts, and just bought a copy of your book because of them. Thanks!

GUEST: When you're finished with his book, can you pass it along to me? I have a table with one leg shorter than the other three.

THINKING ABOUT E-MAIL 'SUBJECT' LINES

Please think for a second before you hit "send" and launch your next e-mail.

There are actually a bunch of things you should think about before sending your next e-mail, but today I'll rant about just one: the "subject" line.

My rant comes in three parts.

First, the "subject" line has the potential to be helpful. At a minimum, an intelligent subject line can get my mind in gear for the information that I'm about to read, and perhaps can give me some sense of the urgency of your communication. At a maximum, an intelligent subject line can convey an entire message.

So use the thing! Please don't send me e-mails with subject lines that are entirely blank. You've missed an opportunity to make communication easier, and you've forced me to pop open your e-mail to learn what you're writing about. Put a few words in the subject line, to tell me what's coming.

Second, please remember who I am and who you are. If you work at Kirkland & Ellis, it wouldn't be too helpful to receive many e-mails with subject lines that read "Kirkland & Ellis." That subject line wouldn't distinguish one e-mail message from the other. You are Kirkland & Ellis; you don't need to be told that every e-mail is about Kirkland & Ellis....

That's you; I'm me. I work at Aon. So it really doesn't help me to receive e-mails with subject lines that read "Aon." Those subject lines don't distinguish one e-mail message from another. I am Aon; I don't need to be told that every e-mail is about Aon.

I understand that you think of the case you're handling for us as the "Aon case." And that's fine; that's intelligent; we are, after all, the client. But I don't think of any of my cases as the "Aon case," because that's meaningless from where I sit. Depending on who's suing us, or who we're suing, I might have a "Smith" case or a "Jones" case, but I guarantee you that no one in our legal department is educated by hearing that we're involved in the Aon case. So please don't send us e-mails with the subject line "Aon." That's terribly unhelpful, and (because what I've just written is so self-evident) it doesn't reflect well on you.

Third, if it's possible (and it almost surely is), please provide more than just the case name in the subject line. It's okay to receive one e-mail labeled "Smith" to indicate that the e-mail is about the Smith case. But the Smith case may have been filed in 2008 and may remain pending, two trials and three appeals from now, in 2016. It's not very helpful for me to have an e-folder about the Smith case that contains 1500 e-mails all with the subject line "Smith."

Consider writing subject lines that give just a whisper more than that, such as "Smith: draft mo dsms." Or "Smith: 1/20/11 conf call with Doe." Or, if the situation permits it, the enthusiastic and helpful: "Smith: Summ jdgmt granted!" When I see those messages waiting on my computer, I have a preview of your communication (which aids comprehension), and when I file those e-mails in an e-folder, they're easy to find when I'm searching for one years from now for some future use.

I'm not nuts about this. When I was in private practice, I had one client that tried to dictate the contents of e-mail "subject" lines. Every subject line was supposed to start with the case name, then include a code for whether the e-mail was high, medium, or low priority, and then include other, specified information in a particular order. That system struck me (and continues to strike me) as unfair. Lawyers work for a lot of clients; they shouldn't be forced to memorize a unique structure for the "subject" lines of e-mails being sent to each client.

But it doesn't strike me as unreasonable to ask my correspondents (whether they were other lawyers at my firm, when I was in private practice; or my colleagues with whom I work now; or outside counsel communicating with me about our cases) to pause for just a moment before sending an e-mail to craft a subject line that's logical and helpful. That's a matter of both courtesy and efficiency, and no one should object to giving the world just a little more of both.

COMMENTS

GUEST: Is it me or does this guy sound like Andy Rooney with all his whining and complaining about stupid crap like this?

FEVER PITCH: Tantalizing subject. Next installment: which stapler brand is best? Mark reviews 7 different models and expounds on the test results on copy paper, letterhead, and coated papers.

Stay tuned!

CONFUSEDIOUS: I have a strong urge to send an e-mail to inhouse@abovethelaw.com with "jerkoff" in the subject line. However my fear is that he receives so many e-mails with that subject line that it will detract from the efficiency of his online folder system.

> **BONOBO_BRO:** I'd be interested to see how exactly Mark "gets his mind in gear" upon seeing that subject line on an e-mail.

DUH: Preachy and what anyone with half a brain cell already knows. Next, tell us how to work that mysterious zipper contraption.

GUESTY: I love these columns. I have worked in-house at a giant SF-based bank, and also at several law firms. It was very interesting to see things from the in-house angle, and many of the columns touch on items that I noticed peripherally while there, but could not completely articulate—I was still in "Big Law mode."

Also, many management communication books advise the same as this column. A B-school classic is "Management Communication" by Mary Munter. Small, brief, pricy, excellent.

And no, I'm not Mary. Just a former student of hers :)

PHUCNAIL: Exactly! How about doing some useful columns for in-house counsel—like how to deal with the 3:30PM commute rush hour, how to deal with CEOs and boards that continually ask for in-house counsel to provide quantitative estimates for the probabilities of various legal outcomes so they can plug them into their B-school quant formulae so they can make decisions solely based on imaginary guesstimate numbers, or how to explain legal issues, disclosure requirements, and information requests to non-legal technical and business people who have no clue what is important from a legal standpoint.

Nah, stick to the stapler reviews and e-mail header advice, Mark. You obviously know what is really priority information for in-house counsel to read after 11 months in-house.

SOMEONE: "Nah, stick to the stapler reviews and e-mail header advice, Mark. You obviously know what is really priority information for in-house counsel to read after 11 months in-house."

The reading comprehension of the average commenter here is pretty low. If you pay attention to the column, it is being written for outside counsel in their dealings with in-house counsel. It is giving advice, from the in-house perspective, for outside counsel.

This advice is actually quite reasonable, as almost every attorney I deal with sends e-mails with no useful information in the subject line, making it difficult to search for those e-mails later.

GUEST: I think the readers here are making fun of him because he is a tool and rants about total nonsense that has little practical use and makes him sound like a pompous jerk. His pet peeves about e-mail subject lines do not strike me as being that important except to the extent it makes this particular high maintenance client happy. So outside counsel, if you represent Aon make sure you follow his rules. I am sure there are more than this—all just as ridiculous. He'd be better served advising us on how to keep costs under control. That might be worth listening to, but don't hold your breath.

THE SINS OF OUTSIDE COUNSEL— CREATING SURPRISES

"No surprises."

When you interview for an in-house job as head of litigation, that's what everyone—CEO, CFO, General Counsel—is likely to say: "All we want is to know in advance what's happening. Don't hit us with last minute litigation surprises."

That characterization is only half true. Half the job is what you would actually expect, and why someone would actually pay money for a person to do this gig: Half the job is to minimize liability. That task, at least, requires a law degree and a little bit of skill.

But, remarkably, the other half of the job—avoiding surprises—is the aspect that seemingly draws the ire of the folks who run the joint. And that task is one that the kid down the block ought to be able to do with about fifteen minutes of training: How hard can it be to avoid surprises?

Piece of cake, right? Just track developments in all of the pending cases, estimate settlement values or likely verdicts, and flood the C-suites with information. Put together a calendar of every major event in every major case over the coming six months. Winning cases can occasionally be hard, but just tracking them? Nothing to it.

Remarkably, that isn't true. There are five main reasons why it's hard merely to track cases (and their values) and thus to avoid surprises, and outside counsel are responsible for three of the five....

Let's start with the two reasons that are beyond outside counsel's control. The first reason why it's tough to track all major litigation events over the coming, say, six months or a year is because some court systems simply won't cooperate. If we get a call from counsel in Mexico telling us that a case was just set for a trial starting three weeks from today, that may be the fault (if "fault" is the right word) of the judicial system, rather than counsel. In some countries, cases are set for trial on remarkably short notice, so it's not possible to keep an accurate timeline projecting when all cases are moving to judgment. Judgments, of course, can contain surprises.

The second reason why it can be tough to track all major litigation events has to do with a corporation's own internal failings. (Needless to say, we have no failings at the joint where I work. I'm just speculating about things that might occur at other, imperfect institutions.) You might get an e-mail that says, for example, "We lost $750,000 in a trial in Sweden yesterday. No one in the business unit ever told anyone in the legal department that we'd been sued." That's a surprise, of course, but the solution lies in improving internal controls and processes. You probably can't blame outside counsel for that one.

But what can we blame outside counsel for? How do outside counsel subvert my ability to do half my job? Let me count the ways:

First, outside counsel ask for settlement authority on extremely short notice. If we're set for a mediation (or will otherwise need settlement authority by a specific date), please plan ahead. You can't send us an e-mail on Monday saying that you could use a couple of million bucks for a mediation on Wednesday. It's a whole lot better if you tell us in August that we're set for a mediation in the fourth quarter, and you'll likely need $2 million in authority a few months out. In September, send a memo analyzing the value of the case and recommending a settlement value. Give us ample time to think about your case (and the many other cases that we're handling simultaneously) at a decent pace, and to track down everyone (up to and including the CEO, in certain instances) whose approval will be needed to authorize an offer or a payment. Let us alert our financial folks (who are planning cash flow) to anticipate the expense. Avoid surprises.

Second, outside counsel change their estimated values of cases for no reason. Outside counsel report on Monday that a case should settle for $1 million. Then they tell us on Wednesday that the case will in fact cost $4 million. And there's no reason for the change.

We can understand that the value of a case will change if we unearth the e-mail from Hell, or if the state supreme court hands down an opinion that turns our world upside down. But the value of a case can't multiply simply because outside counsel decided to think a little harder about it or got more nervous because we're now actually approaching trial.

All of our in-house lawyers are responsible for many cases. Our in-house folks simply can't know the facts of any one case as well as the outside lawyer who's living the case from day to day. If we ask for your estimate of the value of the case, we're relying on you. (We're not relying on you unthinkingly; we do what we can to confirm your ideas. But you have the luxury of time, which we often do not.) Tell us the value of the case, and we'll plan for it. But you can't change the value of the case on short notice for no reason at all. That's a surprise, and it's our job to avoid surprises.

Third, outside counsel blow through their litigation budgets. If we ask for an estimate of defense costs, then give a reasonably accurate estimate of defense costs. (We know that litigation is unpredictable, blah, blah, blah. Some of us spent decades in private practice defending lawsuits and preparing litigation budgets. We feel your pain. Really, we do.) It's possible to provide an estimate of defense costs in a case, and we should be able to rely on what you say. If the estimate proves wrong—and that sometimes happens—then tell us immediately. Immediate notice alerts us that we'll have to adjust, but it probably doesn't force us to change our budget by a huge amount tomorrow. We can handle evolution; we just don't like surprises.

Avoid surprises.

That's much, much harder than it seems. Help us out, and you'll have our gratitude—and, over time, an increasing share of our business.

COMMENTS

GUEST: I think the third point is a good one, and I always make sure that counsel alerts me if costs are going to materially exceed initial estimates up front and not at bill time. Any in-house counsel who has been burned once that way knows to convey that requirement to counsel.

LALA: Settlement authority is also usually provided with a range in mind, i.e., you have authority to settle this case for up to $100,000. Anything over that threshold, you go back to your client for authorization. It is quite impossible to go "off reservation" under those terms.

GUEST: I guess I could say this entry is a step in the right direction, but that would be more a function of how bad the other columns generally have been, rather than an indication that what we have here is...well....any good. In this case, I can see the kernels for a good column, but the excess verbiage and "well duh" factors once again pervade.

HG: Sigh. We try. We give honest appraisals, from budgeting to end game, and then get the request that we reduce the numbers for estimating purposes. We can reduce any estimate they want, but we can't reduce the actual cost of defense or outcome. They know. They don't care. Just reduce the estimates. Push it off to some future quarter, where it will be someone else's problem to explain.

And then, when the bills come due, they're surprised? Honesty (not to mention competent, on target estimates) is an undervalued commodity.

ASSOCIATE: More like this please. Associates need to know this stuff.

ISOLDE: Very interesting. I nominate myself to author a series on what I hate about in-house counsel. 1) When I tell you, six months in advance, that the court has scheduled a mediation and that CLIENT ATTENDANCE IS REQUIRED, put it on your calendar and arrange for someone to attend. 2) When I tell you that there is no point submitting a summary judgment motion now, because discovery isn't over yet and the court will punt it off the docket, don't instruct me to file it anyway and then write off my time when the court punts it off the docket. 3) When I fly cross county to meet with you to discuss the upcoming key deposition, don't call in sick that day and leave me sitting around in a conference room with some guy with a girl lawyer fetish. AND 4) Keep in mind that it takes time to assess a case and prepare a proposed litigation budget. I can't get it over to you on the day you're served.

Thanks much. [points finger like trigger; winks once]

INSIDER: There's always a flip side to every story. Sometimes, I told the business person months ago about the date, and he ignored me or scheduled something "more important" on top of it. And while it's obviously wrong to demand work and then refuse to pay for it, I really would like outside counsel to be more amenable to the idea of trying to limit discovery expense—what's the point of compromising to avoid trial if I still have to pay you to prep for and take 18 depositions and review a truckload of documents? It's always disappointing to travel a long way to meet someone who cancels at the last minute, but people do get sick sometimes, and as long as you're still getting paid for the work, is it really that big of a deal? And finally, yes it's unrealistic to expect a case budget, on day one, but don't act offended every time I ask for one. My boss wants to know about the case as soon as possible, and one of the first things she'll ask is how much it may cost in attorney's fees. If you make me beg you for a budget, you make me look bad.

ON ALPHABET SOUP (HEREINAFTER 'OAS')

Quick! What short form will you use in your brief to identify your client, Porsche Cars of North America, Inc.?

If your guts are screaming "PCNA," then your guts need reworking.

But I chose this example for my column today because I've seen this very thing happen. I've seen a lawyer (at a perfectly good firm) assign the short form "PCNA" to this entity.

What was he thinking?

If I'm at the steering wheel of the case, then we're not representing PCNA.

Who do we represent?

We represent Porsche, for heaven's sake. Porsche.

It's a word. I understand it. It creates an image in my mind. It communicates with me quickly and compellingly. That's (generally) good....

(I tucked in the "generally" because if Porsche were somehow being blamed for the death of a pedestrian in an accident caused by driving at excessive speed, I might prefer not to represent an entity called "Porsche." PCNA might be fine. Or maybe SMCI, for "Slow-Moving Cars, Inc." But that's a different situation. The case in which I was involved was a dispute among various car manufacturers and their dealers. I had "GM"—a perfectly good short form, because "GM" is used as widely as "General Motors." The guy who represented Volkswagen should have paused to think—"Volkswagen" or "VW"? That's a close call. If you're bumping up against a page limit, go with VW, to save space. If your brief is constrained by a word limit, this issue is a judgment call. The guy who had Ford in my case had a no brainer—it's "Ford," not "Ford Motor Company (hereinafter 'FMC').")

So who am I?

(That was a rhetorical question. I don't want to hear a chorus of, "You're a compulsive nutcase; that's who you are.")

I'm Aon. I'm not "Aon Corporation (hereinafter 'AC')." If one of our affiliated companies is named in a case, and only that one entity is involved (so there's no chance for confusion), that other entity can also be Aon. Thus, we should refer to "Aon Services Corporation" as "Aon," because "ASC" is gibberish, whereas "Aon" is a word. (Well, okay, Aon isn't actually a word in English; you've got me there. But it was a word in Gaelic, and it meant "oneness." And today, Aon is a reasonably well recognized trade name. In any event, "Aon" is a whole lot easier to understand than "ASC," which doesn't mean anything in either English or Gaelic.)

I'm not stopping there.

I'm going to take my thesis a step further, because I'm a radical. (A radical compulsive nutcase, maybe. But a radical.) When I was in private practice, I'd drop the parenthetical with the "hereinafter" crap. When I'm writing a brief, I'll put some limited trust in my audience. I'm ready to assume that I can safely write the following sentences without losing my reader: "On May 1, 2010, Joseph R. Smith crossed the street. Smith did not look at the traffic light . . . . "

I understand that, in the eyes of the folks still wearing fedoras, this is heresy: "If you're going to use anything other than the exact name of a party, you must define it! Otherwise, there's ambiguity! Your reader won't understand that Joe Smith is 'Smith'!"

Calm down. Maybe there's some risk of ambiguity in a contract, where complete precision is necessary (I'll defer to others on that), but I'm pretty comfortable that no one will be confused when we refer in a brief to Aon Corporation as Aon or Joe Smith as Smith without pausing to explain our convention.

In any event, I'm happy to run that risk, for the sake of persuasion and not interrupting the flow of a brief by creating unnecessary short forms.

One final point: The rule that I've just stated is not limited to the names of parties. Words are (generally) better than letters, period.

Most law firms seem to understand that the "Complaint" in a lawsuit can safely be called the "Complaint." But throw in an amendment, and lawyers lose their minds. Must we really call the First Amended Complaint the "FAC"? What the heck is an FAC? Those letters don't mean anything to a reader. Let's just define the First Amended Complaint to be the "Complaint" (I'll grant you a parenthetical to do that, because there is in fact the possibility of confusion if we don't define the term) and then move on in English.

If the iteration of the complaint matters, be smart. We can distinguish a First Amended Complaint from a Second Amended Complaint without descending into madness. The judge really won't be moved by sentences that tell us, "In the SAC, unlike the FAC, plaintiff alleged.... " How about: "But plaintiff abandoned the allegations in the First Complaint when she moved on to the Second...."?

Words! Words are great! Use 'em.

IMHO.

TTFN.

(LOL.)

CLASSIC BAD INTRODUCTIONS

I know, I know: This column is not supposed to be about written advocacy.

And I know, I know: No one needs my smug suggestions, because no one who reads Above the Law ever makes any mistakes.

But the legal writing community keeps urging me on. The people who fret about this stuff seem to think that these lessons are worth repeating, so I'm adding one more column on legal writing to the collection.

Here are three possible introductions to one brief. I saw all three types repeatedly while I was in private practice, and I've seen all three since I've been in-house. (I've seen the worst type—the first—only once during my in-house days, and we chatted with outside counsel about what we expect to see in the future.)

So, without further ado, two bad (but typical) introductions, followed by one good one, all for use in the same case….

(Note: I'm drawing the example from an actual lawsuit, although I've changed the parties' names out of an abundance of caution.)

Bad introduction 1:

"Defendant DrugCo (hereinafter "DC"), by and through its counsel, Lat Mystal & Gang, hereby moves for summary judgment pursuant to State Rule of Civil Procedure 56, on the claims brought by plaintiff Susan Jefferson (hereinafter "Plaintiff" or "Jefferson")."

Why is this bad? Because, if a judge reads nothing else, he or she is likely to read the first paragraph of a brief. And you've just wasted the first paragraph by saying essentially nothing. You've identified the parties and defense counsel and told the judge that this is a summary judgment brief, but that's it. The sentence is utterly generic (other than naming the parties, it could be used in any summary judgment brief) and so wastes your best opportunity to start winning the case.

Blech!

Bad introduction 2:

"Plaintiff Susan Jefferson has filed this product liability action against Defendant DrugCo based on Jefferson's use of the prescription drug Calmnerves. DrugCo hereby moves for summary judgment on Jefferson's claims."

This is slightly better than bad introduction 1, although still plenty bad. At least we didn't take a detour to provide the irrelevant name of counsel filing the motion, and the judge learns that this is not an untethered summary judgment motion, but a motion in a product liability case. This introduction thus moves the ball slightly, but it does nothing to persuade.

So it's better, but still not acceptable.

Decent introduction:

"On September 20, 1999, Dr. Susan Jefferson brought home a scalpel and slit the throat of her six-year-old son. She then slit her own throat. Both she and her son survived. In April 2001, Dr. Jefferson pled guilty to the charge of assault and battery with intent to kill.

"Eighteen months after her guilty plea, Dr. Jefferson sued DrugCo, the manufacturer of Calmnerves, a medication that had been prescribed to treat Dr. Jefferson's depression. Despite her guilty plea and her admission of intent to kill, Dr. Jefferson claimed in her civil suit, for the first time, that her bloody act was not willful, but impelled by her medication. DrugCo is entitled to summary judgment on Dr. Jefferson's claim, for two independent reasons.

"First, collateral estoppel prevents Dr. Jefferson from re-litigating issues that were determined in the criminal action, including the cause of the harm she inflicted. Second, judicial estoppel prevents Dr. Jefferson from disclaiming admissions that helped her avoid jail in the criminal action."

Aha! We're there!

Why?

We didn't waste time with generic stuff. Instead we focused on the (dare I say it?) argumentative jugular of this particular case. Within a very few short paragraphs, the judge knows the facts, knows the identities of the parties, and knows the legal reason why my client should win. Perfect!

Different readers may have different reactions to this introduction. Some readers will come away from this loathing Dr. Jefferson—which is fine, because that means that my client should win. Others readers may come away from this feeling sorry for Dr. Jefferson, but nonetheless thinking that she's unfairly trying to recover money in a terribly sad situation. But that's fine, too, because that still means that my client should win.

The authors of this brief thought pretty carefully about word choice. Reasonable people disagree over the appropriate short form for the names of individuals in briefs. Some say that "Joseph R. Smith" should be "Smith," because "Smith" uses the minimum number of words and impersonalizes the party. Others prefer the short form "Mr. Smith," because that shows respect for the individual, which the court may appreciate. But in my hypothetical introduction, the choice is easy: We're calling this person "Dr. Jefferson," because that emphasizes her medical training and advanced degree, making the bloody act particularly offensive.

The authors then chose to have the good doctor "slit" both her son's throat and her own. She could have "incised" the throats, or "cut" them, or "sliced" them, among other things, but "slit" seems delightfully vicious. (In fact, after we won the motion and submitted a proposed order in this case, plaintiff's counsel objected to our use of the word "slit" in the proposed order granting summary judgment. So we had the pleasure of briefing to the court whether the word "slit" was unduly prejudicial. We told the court that we preferred "slit," because we thought it seemed most accurate, but wouldn't object strongly if the court revised the order to say that the doctor had "cut" or "sliced" her six-year-old son's throat. I'm not certain that opposing counsel was wise to pick that fight and thus force the presiding judge to linger on this particular detail, reading briefs that debated this issue at length.)

What's the rule for introductions?

They are short. They are sexy. And they aim for the heart of your particular case. Good introductions show the court (by presenting facts) that your client should win; good introductions do not simply tell the court (by making an assertion, such as "DrugCo is entitled to summary judgment") who should win.

What does this have to do with inside counsel?

Heck if I know.

I suppose that (1) sophisticated clients insist on decent introductions, (2) outside counsel should surely know how to write them, and (3) corporations minimize legal expense by filing good motions and winning cases, so good writing helps to control costs.

But, more than anything else, people screw up introductions over and over. I'm keenly aware of this, and the legal writing community says that we should work together to educate people about these things. So think of this as a public service message.

Perhaps, in my next post, we'll go back to our regularly scheduled program.

COMMENTS

TROLLFACE: In most cases, the judge doesn't offer a critique of the brief. So you never really know if the judge decided in your client's favor because of your wonderful brief, or in spite of your crappy brief. Therefore, I take advice on what makes a good brief with a grain of salt. How does anyone know if their brief is good? The smartest thing to do is just to make things easy for the judge and show that your mindful of how busy he or she is (even if they're not busy). Bad introduction no. 1 does that– tells the judge what he is about to read. The decent introduction will prompt the following response from most judges—who is Dr. Susan Jefferson and what does a scalpel have to do with this case and whose motion is this anyway?

> **PLAIN ENGLISH GUEST:** The judge can read the caption and the title of the motion for that. Unless you're in some backwater hell-hole, the judge or law clerk can tell at a glance 1) which party submitted the document, 2) what kind of document it is (in this case, a motion), 3) what kind of motion it is (summary judgment).
>
> Just get to the motion and stop wasting people's time with crap they skip over.

GUEST: I find introduction #3 least likely to lead to a winning motion for the defendant, as it immediately invokes an emotional response in the reader (i.e., the law clerk or judge), who is likely to view the rest of the legal arguments through that prism and conclude that (whatever the merits of the legal arguments) the plaintiff has a case that should see a jury.

> **GUEST:** If the motion shows the defendant has a winning defense or the plaintiff

lacks sufficient evidence, I can't imagine any decent judge allowing a trial to go forward just out of sympathy. Even if the judge is very emotion-driven, a pointless trial helps no one. The defendant will either lose at trial, or in a post-trial motion, or on appeal. The only situation I can think of when a judge might rule as you describe would be a motion for summary judgment where the evidence doesn't exist now but might materialize at trial.

GUEST: I disagree. All three introductions are problematic. A good introduction should tell the judge what you want him or her to do (first!) and then a short precis of why you want him or her to do it. Save the gory details for later....

GUEST: Often the caption of the motion makes it clear what you're asking the judge to do. If that is so, no reason to open with that information.

OH GROW UP, ALL OF YOU: You are all so full of crap. Take it from an old broad who has written, and now reads hundreds of briefs, 3 is the preferable option. No, it will not "annoy the judge," or law secretary. You know why? Because it has all the salient info you need in an interesting readable format. What IS infuriating is when the appeal/motion is on liability grounds and the first paragraph is about "devastating injuries," or the appeal is on a No Fault dismissal that leads with the defendant's drunk driving conviction. Get the distinction?

As for the law clerk being the only one reading it, if that's the case then the law clerk/secretary/magistrate is writing the opinion too; so it's a distinction without a difference.

And my goodness, if your boss tells you to write a certain way, obviously you do it, no matter how awful the format is. But not all of us are constrained the way you junior associates are. Good luck!

STANDARD OF REVIEW DECIDES CASES

Here are two stories, from nearly thirty years apart. They're bookends on the subject of why standard of review counts.

Travel back with me, if you will, to the summer of 1983. I'm ten minutes out of law school, and I've just arrived in the chambers of Judge Dorothy W. Nelson of the Ninth Circuit, for whom I'll clerk. Our wise and sagacious predecessor-clerks—out of law school for an entire year!—are introducing us to the job. (We overlapped for one week.)

One of my predecessor-clerks, John Danforth, asked the new group: "Do you think standard of review matters in appeals?"

I knew the answer, and I was about to pop off: "Of course not! Once you convince the court that your side is right, the judges will do whatever it takes to rule in favor of your client. Standard of review is just a silly lawyers' game."

Fortunately, Danforth talks quickly. Before I was able to make a fool of myself, he said: "Standard of review decides cases. It decides cases. That's the most important thing I've learned in a year of clerking. Standard of review makes all the difference in the world."

Why?

After a relatively short time on an appellate bench, a judge's brain becomes hardwired to examine standards of review. For federal appellate judges, that means that, if the standard of review is *de novo*, the court should think hard about the trial court opinion and reverse if the result seems wrong. If the standard of review is for clear error, then the judge knows that the appellate court should probably affirm. If the standard of review is for abuse of discretion, then you don't really have to bother reading the briefs. Just get out the "affirmed in an unpublished memorandum disposition" stamp, and move on to the next case.

(There was a joke among the clerks, way back when, that standard of review actually varied by the identity of the trial court judge, not the nature of the legal issue presented. If the opinion came up from Judge X, reverse. From Judge Y, think about it. And from Judge Z, affirm. We of course were talking about particular trial court judges, and not the anonymous Judges X, Y, and Z. But we were just kidding. I promise.)

Flash forward to 2010. I'm talking to my outside counsel who'll be arguing an appeal the following week. (He (or she, but I'll use the masculine for the sake of convenience) is a partner at a large and well-known firm. You'd recognize the firm name in a heartbeat.) I ask the lawyer what he'll say if a certain issue comes up. He says that he'll give three answers to that question, and he recites the three substantive arguments that we'll make.

"What about standard of review?" I ask, still in debt to John Danforth after these many years.

"It's in the brief. The court knows that this issue is reviewable for abuse of discretion."

So we chat. And we recast the appellate argument. We ultimately decide to open the argument by saying, more or less: "We're on appeal on three issues. All of the issues are reviewable only for abuse of discretion, and they arise after a four-week jury trial."

If Danforth was right, this should do it. "Abuse of discretion" means "summarily affirm." And "four-week jury trial" means "reverse over the trial judge's dead body." The other arguments are nice, but let's start by telling the court (implicitly) that we're right, the other guy is wrong, and the court has to affirm. That sets the table pretty nicely.

It worked like a charm. We opened the argument as we had decided. The most senior judge on the panel smiled and nodded at the end of the opening two sentences. My guy realized that this was working, and he improvised: "You might almost ask why we're here." The senior judge raised his or her eyebrows, leaned forward, and asked: "Why *are* you here?"

We started to feel pretty comfortable.

What are the lessons to learn?

First, appreciate your predecessor-clerks. They teach you important stuff (and show you where you can get a good, cheap lunch in downtown L.A.). (I don't want to hear from some Google-happy reader that Judge Nelson sits in Pasadena, not downtown L.A. She sat in L.A. in '83. And you can Google Danforth, too, if you want to double-check this entire post. Everything I write at Above the Law is the God's honest truth, except for the stuff I make up and write about to entertain myself.)

Where was I?

Oh, yeah.

Second, you—outside counsel—should know this stuff, and I shouldn't be teaching it to you. If you're my appellate advocate, you have to know how appellate courts work. You can't expect much repeat business if I'm teaching you how to do your job.

Third, think hard about standard of review when you're working on an appeal. If you're the appellant, find an issue that's reviewable *de novo* and press that issue on appeal. If you're the appellee, analyze the appellant's issue and explain why it doesn't actually turn on a question of law and is properly reviewed only for clear error or abuse of discretion. If we come up with a decent argument why the appellant's issue isn't really reviewable *de novo*, that's probably worth a page or two of the brief. Standard of review, after all, decides cases.

Fourth, no matter which side you're on, use standard of review to maximum effect. If you're the appellee, depending on the circumstances, you might open your brief with a short paragraph about standard of review. For example: "After a three-week trial in this product liability case, the jury deliberated for just four hours before returning a unanimous defense verdict. Appellant asks this court to reverse that verdict and the resulting judgment on two grounds, both of which are reviewable on appeal only for abuse of discretion."

Think about all the buttons we just pressed: "three-week trial"; "jury"; only "four hours" of deliberation; and the verdict was "unanimous," which isn't required in all civil trials (many state courts don't require unanimity), so the jury wasn't struggling with this. And the appellee is raising issues that were committed to the trial court's discretion? This goose is probably cooked, and we're not yet into the second paragraph.

Similarly, if the standard of review cuts in your favor, plug it into your statement of the issues presented. That could be, for the appellant: "Did the trial court err as a matter of law when it held . . . ? " Or it could be, for the appellee: "Did the trial court abuse its discretion when it held . . . ?"

Appellate courts will notice these things. Don't take my word for it. Take John Danforth's.

COMMENTS

THE RESISTANCE: A post focused on actual practice on ATL? The end is nigh....

A nice change though, keep it up.

ESQUIRE: Translation of this post: "27 years ago, I got this piece of advice about appeals. I saw it work once in an appeal, so I'm now convinced that it's the number one tenet of appellate advocacy."

In some cases, it's clear what the standard of review is, and an advocate who leans too heavily on the standard gives off the impression that he has no confidence in the substance of the argument. "We've read the briefs and we're familiar with the standard of review. Why don't you tell me what evidence supports the jury verdict, because your opponent over there makes a good argument that there isn't any, and your brief's pretty thin on that point." Standards of review are important, but don't forget the actual "review" part.

Here's another tip for inside counsel: if the lawyer doing the appeal doesn't understand that courts of appeals aren't the same as trial courts and hesitate to overturn jury verdicts, then either you've hired the wrong firm or they need to staff someone with a clue on the appeal. That sort of thing is basic on the same level as "don't misspell the name of the court if you can avoid it."

GUEST: There's nothing more obnoxious than an in-house guy who's thought about a case for an hour chiming in at the last minute with obvious advice and thinking he's a genius.

> **GUEST 2:** Yes there is.
>
> When in-house guy is a contracts or securities guy who's never litigated a case or seen the inside of the courtroom but believes (because he's running outside counsel) that he's now the king of litigation strategy.

GUEST: It is not surprising at all that a partner at a well-known firm would overlook the standard of review. I was a federal appellate clerk and spent two years at a large firm before returning to the Government. The partners for whom I worked knew nothing about how appellate courts worked even after I dropped hints. I was tempted to get out sock puppets to explain.

GUEST: Isn't this obvious? I would find it appalling if my outside counsel didn't know to focus on standard of review when the standard favored my case. Maybe it's because I clerked for an appeals court judge myself, but my reaction to this post was "OF COURSE standard of review is key."

SCOTT H.: Great post. I had similar experiences when I was in-house. Standard of review decides how the rest of the brief is written and how oral argument is delivered.

TROLLFACE: The important thing to take from this article is that inside counsel hired outside counsel from a large prestigious law firm despite having to teach him how to do his job. Prestige 1, competence 0.

EVILEMPLOYEE: Wow...getting better. I'm actually reading beyond the second paragraph now.

So what do you do when the SOR goes against you? Put it in a footnote in the middle of a paragraph citing cases where the dissenting opinion's judge argues that the majority are a bunch of whining racists?

> **GUEST:** When the standard of review is against you, focus on your substantive arguments. Certainly don't open with the standard of review or stick it in a big paragraph by itself. Also, you should attempt to find a way to cast your substantive arguments as pure legal arguments.

WHO, ME?: I still think the name for this column needs to be changed from "Inside Straight" to "Barely Literate Captain Obvious." But I jest....

So the real question is, what is the standard of review for quality writing on ATL? Nonexistent? *ding ding ding.*

SO MUCH FOR TEAMWORK: Must it always be such a problem to have to communicate even good ideas (that can sometimes get lost in the shuffle of a complicated case) to outside counsel though? Believe it or not, we welcome and appreciate them, and they help. Sorry if it means you have to do some work too. And I know, you are paying for it, blah blah blah, but whatever happened to the client and attorney working hard and well together as a team? Or perhaps we are just the outside help to be ordered around, instead.

GUEST: Seriously, the best column on ATL. This is the stuff I was supposed to get sitting at the feet of the senior partners at my firm, but never did because teaching the young ones is not billable. Thank you, Mr. Herrmann. Keep it coming!

KEITH: I'm sure there are a lot of 1Ls in Research and Writing classes who found this very interesting and timely. Otherwise, if you're a practicing attorney who does ANY appellate work and you don't know how to handle the standard of review, you're incompetent.

DELIVERING BAD NEWS

Several readers have sent e-mails asking for advice on how to deliver bad news to clients.

Here's proof that, if ye shall ask, ye may receive.

Think first about the "bad news" that you're delivering. You're not a physician, so you're not looking a person in the eye and explaining that he or she has just six months to live. That's really bad news, and that's hard to deliver. Your job is easy.

Even in the universe of bad news delivered by lawyers, if you're working with a corporate client, you're probably getting off easy. You're not reporting to the client that "the Supreme Court just rejected the application for a stay of your execution" or "the appellate court just affirmed the conviction, so you'll be doing the time." The bad news that civil litigators are delivering to corporate clients just isn't that significant. So calm down.

I'm also ruling out other bad news that folks deliver to, or receive from, in-house counsel. I'm not thinking about telling employees that they've been laid off or fired or delivering unhappy performance reviews. I'm not thinking about how you deliver bad news to your own law firm or to a court. And I'm ruling out situations where the bad news results from your own error, rather than an adverse decision by a court. (It's much harder to tell a client, for example, "I blew the statute of limitations, and your claim is now time-barred," than it is to tell a client, say, "The court denied our motion for summary judgment.") So maybe I'm cheating here, by limiting the discussion, but the optimal way to deliver bad news will vary with the situation.

So what's the best way to deliver news of an adverse judicial decision to a corporate client?

I propose six rules:

1. **The client must hear the news from you first.** If the client hears the news from a Google alert or an e-mail from an old friend, you're starting off on the wrong foot.
2. **The news must arrive promptly.** If you'd promptly call to tell the client that you'd just won the summary judgment motion (and you probably would, to share the moment of glory), then you should promptly call the client to say that you've lost the summary judgment motion (because the news is equally important and equally time-sensitive).
3. **If at all possible, you should deliver bad news by telephone or in person.** I understand that it's easier to send an e-mail reporting the bad news, but that's why e-mail (or a voicemail message, or a letter) isn't acceptable. The worse the news, the more important to deliver it personally. (I stuck the caveat—"if at all possible"—at the beginning of the preceding paragraph because sometimes it's important to deliver time-sensitive news as quickly as possible, and that may preclude a personal communication.

If you've called the client's office phone, and asked the client's secretary to track down the client, and called the client's cell phone, and still can't deliver time-sensitive bad news personally, an impersonal communication may suffice. Even then, though, I'd be inclined to explain in an e-mail why I was taking the coward's way out: "I've just tried to call you on both your office and cell phones, and your secretary wasn't able to track you down. We learned moments ago that we lost the motion for summary judgment in the *Smith* case, and I wanted to deliver that news to you promptly. Please call me at your early convenience to discuss this, and I'd like to schedule a call tomorrow, if possible, to discuss our strategy going forward." Or some such thing.)

4. **Be clear and direct when you deliver the bad news.** Beating around the bush doesn't make life easier for either you or the client.

5. **Do not sugarcoat the bad news:** "We lost the motion for a temporary restraining order, and this is great! Now we can beat up on the other side in discovery, and they'll still have the threat of a future defeat hanging over them." You won't fool anyone when you sugarcoat bad news, and you may well infuriate someone.

6. **Propose a plan for dealing with the problem.** If a client (or anyone) hears bad news, the client will naturally start wondering how best to live in the new, gloomy environment. If we resisted a motion to compel massive e-discovery and lost, then suggest how best to respond to the discovery quickly and at the lowest possible cost. If we lost a motion for summary judgment, then think about any possible appellate review by writ or interlocutory appeal and propose a road forward for handling any remaining discovery, devising motions *in limine* to limit evidence at trial, and planning for other upcoming events. If appropriate, you might suggest moving to reconsider, although sophisticated clients will often view that approach as throwing good money after bad.

There's obviously a tension between delivering bad news quickly, on the one hand, and coupling the bad news with a plan for the future, on the other. But that tension is not insurmountable. You could think in advance about what you'd do if the court ruled against you on the pending motion, so you would already have a plan for the future in mind. Or you could deliver the bad news promptly along with a request for a longer call on the next day, which would give you a chance to collect your thoughts.

I don't doubt that there will occasionally be exceptions to those six rules, but the rules strike me as a pretty good starting point. And any communication will naturally be tailored to the situation: It may be easier to deliver bad news on the heels of the good ("You knew our luck would eventually run out. We won the last six summary judgment motions, but I'm sorry to report that we just lost the seventh."), or to a client with whom you have a long relationship or exceptional rapport.

But taking the coward's way out—procrastinating before sending an e-mail that delivers the news obliquely—will never be the right answer.

COMMENTS

LT_WEINBERG: Good stuff. Though not mentioned sufficiently in this article was the notion that you or the client shouldn't be caught flat-footed by bad news. It isn't just that you think of Plan B in advance, but that the client knows about Plan B in advance. If there's an important motion for summary judgment out there on a large commercial matter, and you're doing your job right, you've discussed the strengths and weaknesses of the document with the client, as well as what winning or losing means, before it is filed. Also, no harm in over-stating the difficulty of winning a proposed motion so you look like a genius when you bring home a victory.

Granted, you don't always know HOW you're going to lose a motion, so there's going to be contingencies you can't plan for. And some bad news can't be anticipated at all. I'm sure sometime, somewhere, a lawyer has called his client to say "your CFO just went into his deposition and admitted to smuggling human organs."

SENPAI71: I know everyone complains about MH's column, but this is actually pretty decent advice. Pretty decent advice that should be obvious to every lawyer (and human being), but yet often isn't followed.

Bravo sir–that's one for the win column.

GUEST: It's not followed probably because it takes a little bit of courage to do so, particularly if you didn't manage expectations well.

Calling your client to let them know you just lost is difficult and it's very easy to put off, or rationalize into "well it's 9 p.m. there now, so I'll just write him an e-mail."

A DISQUISITION ON PILE-O'-CRAP SYNDROME

Pile-o'-crap syndrome: We've all been victimized by it.

In private practice, it arrives in the form of four boxes of documents (containing about 2,000 pages each) delivered to your door with a single handwritten note of explanation: "Here are the documents you'll need to prepare Smith for his deposition on Wednesday."

What does that note really say? "Here's a pile of crap. I can't be bothered. You deal with it."

For an in-house lawyer, the pile o' crap arrives in the form of a one-sentence e-mail responding to your request for a brief description of a particular lawsuit that's headed to trial: "As you requested, I've attached my 100-page, single-spaced summary of the discovery record in this case."

What does that e-mail really say? "Here's a pile of crap. I can't be bothered. You deal with it."

In business environments everywhere, pile-o'-crap syndrome arrives in the form of e-mails that say only either (1) "see attached letter" or (2) "see attached chain of e-mails."

What do those communications really say? "Here's a pile of crap. I can't be bothered. You figure it out."

Why do people do this?

Some surely do this because they're thoughtless. These are the folks who don't give a second's thought to what the recipients of their communications really need and so deliver messages that aid the sender, but burden the recipient.

Other people suffer from pile-o'-crap syndrome because they're lazy. These folks understand that the recipient of a communication needs a short, cogent explanation of the relevant topic, but also realize that it would take time and effort to provide something useful. Those folks are too lazy to create something helpful.

What's the alternative to pile-o'-crap syndrome?

As always, it's the Golden Rule: "Do unto others as you would have them do unto you."

Think for a minute about what the recipient of your communication needs. Create that, and then send it.

The partner who's preparing a witness for deposition doesn't need an undifferentiated mass of 8,000 pages of documents. The partner needs a short outline that sorts information by topic, identifies key issues and documents, and provides tabbed and highlighted copies of the stuff that matters, along with background information that may be necessary to understand the whole situation. Provide the 8,000 documents if they may be needed for background information, but explain what they are and why they matter; don't unload a pile o' crap.

The in-house head of litigation needs a summary that explains, in a few cogent paragraphs, who's suing whom for what, the strengths and weaknesses of the case, key documents on both sides, and a little intelligent commentary. It's okay to attach the 100-page outline, which may in fact edify the truly curious, but explain the essence of the issue first; don't unload a pile o' crap.

Don't send an e-mail attaching an unexplained letter or chain of earlier e-mails, forcing your reader to sort through a mass of material to figure out what the reader is being asked. Explain that the attached letter is from someone to someone and requires attention because, on page two, the letter asks the following question as to which only you, the recipient, knows the answer. Explain that the attached e-mail chain relates to issue X, and the question that the recipient is being asked to answer is Y, and you've attached the whole e-mail chain in case the recipient requires more information. Don't just unload a pile o' crap.

How do you avoid becoming a sorry carrier of pile-o'-crap syndrome? Think before you write: Am I about to unload a pile o' crap on someone? Is there any way that I could make the recipient's life easier by providing an executive summary or otherwise explaining the materials that I'm sending? If you can make the other person's life easier, do.

To whom does this rule apply? To everyone. In law firms, legal assistants should not inflict piles o' crap on associates; associates should not inflict them on partners; partners should not inflict them on clients. (It works the other way, too: Partners should not unnecessarily inflict piles o' crap on associates or associates inflict them on legal assistants. The exceptions include, of course, when the project for which we've been retained is to sort through a pile o' crap: "A potential new client came in yesterday and handed us ten boxes of unsorted financial records. Please make sense of that pile o' crap." Or: "A client came in and left us three full-sized suitcases stuffed with handwritten notes, crumpled photocopies, flash drives, and cassette tapes that supposedly prove the conspiracy. Please make sense of that pile o' crap. (And keep your eye on the relevant wiretap laws.)")

The "no piles-o'-crap rule" also applies to everyone who works in-house. Don't inflict a pile o' crap on your boss. Your boss shouldn't inflict a pile o' crap on his or her boss. The boss's boss shouldn't inflict a pile o' crap on the CEO. The CEO shouldn't inflict a pile o' crap on a customer. And down the ladder, too: Your boss shouldn't inflict a pile o' crap on you.

Let's make each other's lives easier: Think before you hit "send." Let's eradicate the plague of pile-o'-crap syndrome.

COMMENTS

SUSPICIOUS GUEST: Dear Lat, Attached please find a Pile-O'-Crap I disguised as an ATL column about in-house counsel. I can't be bothered. You deal with it.—M. Herrmann

GRIZZLED VETERAN: Mark has chosen to illustrate his point with an example.

TIMOTHY: I'm always happy to provide careful, thoughtful summaries of information. I'll even have glitzy PowerPoint presentations prepared for you that you can use to wow your board if that's what you want. But you have to pay for it. If you're only willing to pay for crap, sorry but that's what you get.

The problem with Mark's advice is not (generally) the advice itself. It's the apparent obliviousness to the relationship between cost and work product.

GUESTA: Article summary: "Be helpful to the recipients of your communications."
Thanks, Inside Straight!!

GUEST: People on this website seem to think that quibbling about minutiae demonstrates intellectual prowess. I don't think there's any good counter to Herrmann's main point, which is that attorneys should consider the recipient when providing information to him/her. All the naysayers rushing to criticize the article are probably those among us who assume they have nothing to learn and, as a result, limp through their careers with a reputation for being average.

GUEST: As in-house counsel, the problem is usually that some business person with a problem dumps the pile on me with little explanation. Unfortunately, that business person may just outrank me, so responding to the pile dumping can sometimes be touchy.

> **SHILL:** This times 1,000. Except it's not so much an issue of rank for me, it's that some of the 'boots on the ground' people dealing with problems in the execution of our contracts generally have no ability to summarize anything in writing. So I'll get 25 e-mails, many of which are forwards and replies and forwards of forwards and include 100 pages of attachments and a note: "can we talk tomorrow?" Why sure we can. But unless I have some idea of exactly what it is you need me to do I'm not going to wade through the pile first. And when we DO talk, it's cool if you want to give me "a little background," but not when that ends up being you rambling on for 15 minutes about every conversation you've ever had with your angry customer.

THE GHOSTS OF INCOMPETENTS PAST

There's a reason why people get crotchety when they get old. People forget about things that went right in their professional lives; that's like water off a duck. But people remember things that got screwed up; that's what sticks in their craws.

You personally are not necessarily incompetent. But you're tarred by the ghosts of incompetents past. When your elder—a partner, a boss, a client, whoever—asks you to do something, the boss assumes that you won't do it. The boss doesn't assume this because she knows that you're irresponsible; she assumes it because the clown she asked to do something six months ago was irresponsible, and she has to hedge against you being an irresponsible clown, too.

How do you prove that you're not irresponsible?

At the outset, remember that the working presumption is against you. The elder will remember (whether correctly or not) that she has for decades been disappointed by everybody she has ever asked to do anything. Everybody has blown off assignments or completed them poorly. The elder is asking you to do something, so you'll naturally blow it off, too. That's the assumption; you bear the burden of disproving it.

You don't carry that burden by promising to do things. The clown from six months ago promised to do things, too—and then he didn't follow through. The clown from six months ago received the e-mail asking him to draft and mail a letter, and the clown immediately e-mailed back, "Will do." Then, despite the promise, the clown didn't follow through; he dropped the ball. Your similar e-mail—"will do"—doesn't mean anything either.

You carry the burden of proving that you're responsible by proving that you're responsible. When you're asked to draft and mail a letter, you send a blind copy of the mailed form of the letter to the elder. The elder sees the copy and thinks, "What a pleasant surprise! This person actually did what was asked of him!"

If you do not send a blind copy to the elder, then, a week later, the elder wakes up with a start in the middle of the night and thinks, "Shoot! I asked that young whippersnapper to send a letter, and I haven't yet seen it go out. So he probably blew off the project (just like the clown from six months ago did). I have to remember to remind the young whippersnapper to send out the letter." The elder turns on the light on his nightstand, waking his spouse, and writes a note to himself to confirm in the morning that you did what you were asked.

In the morning, the elder calls to ask if you did the job. You say that you did. The elder is comforted, but the process was wrong. Your failure to prove that you were doing things caused the old coot to wake up in the middle of the night and bother his spouse. You could (and should) have done better.

If you're asked to do something, (1) do it (on time and right) and (2) simultaneously prove that you've done it. Send out the promised e-mail, and blind copy the elder with the e-mail. The elder will see that you've done your task, and he won't fret that you were irresponsible.

If you prepare a report for a third party, copy the elder with the transmittal letter or e-mail. The elder will see that the report actually went out, and he'll calm down.

If a client sends an e-mail to three lawyers—you, elder, and eldest—asking for something, then you respond. You transmit the requested information, and you copy elder and eldest, so they see that the information went out. If elder and eldest don't see that you sent the information, the next day elder will silently curse you, root around through his office to find the requested information, and send it himself (copying you and eldest, so that everyone sees that the client got the requested information). When you e-mail back that you already sent the information to the client, elder will not think: "What a fine, competent person. He promptly provided the requested information." Rather, elder will think: "What a damned fool! Why didn't he send me a copy of the transmittal message? Then I wouldn't have wasted time looking for the information, and we wouldn't have embarrassed ourselves by transmitting the same information to the client twice."

When asked to do something, do it (on time and right) and simultaneously prove that you've done it. That is the only way to comfort your bosses. Over time, the crazy old coots may actually calm down and tell you not to copy them with every transmittal message. But that time may never come. In any event, the choice is the old coots', not yours.

This rule sounds as though it's aimed at young people, but it's not. How does a partner at a law firm convince another partner that she's responsible? By doing things (on time and right) and simultaneously proving that she's done them. How does the new general counsel prove to the CEO that the new GC is responsible? By doing things (on time and right) and simultaneously proving that he's done them.

You—like everyone else—must overcome the starting presumption that you're inept, which is the lingering gift bestowed on you by incompetents past. If you understand the starting presumption, you're far more likely to cause your elders—partners, bosses, clients, whoever—to trust you, which is ultimately the name of the game.

COMMENTS

NOWHERE: The real answer is to know your audience. Half of the partners don't WANT to see the transmittal letter or be bcc'd on every little stinking thing. Jesus.

GUEST: And you think you can divine this without them telling you?

GUESTY: Actually, I think this is good advice. Particularly for more junior people. And, let's face it, for junior people direct responses to clients are rare, but direct responses to the next person up the totem pole should include, usually, the person above them too. I.e., Junior associate send midlevel the insert for the section of the brief midlevel is putting together for the brief senior associate is preparing for partner. Junior should send his e-mail to midlevel and senior, midlevel should send to junior and senior, and senior should send to everyone.

LATINTHUNDER: If you do not send a blind copy to the elder, then, a week later, the elder wakes up with a start in the middle of the night and thinks, "Shoot! I asked that young whippersnapper to send a letter, and I haven't yet seen it go out."

Yes, particularly in Big Law, partners often wake up in the middle of the night in a cold sweat, preoccupied with a minor assignment given to a junior associate. Realistically, even when you copy partners, they will ignore your e-mails, or read them and forget about them, and just end up calling you if they're ever wondering if the document went out.

> **GUEST:** Depends on the partner. I've literally had a partner say he's lost sleep over something I thought was pretty routine.

> **GUEST:** And one should, apparently, revolve one's professional life around the possibility that a crazy partner might lose sleep.

TEXAN99: This seems like basic and sound advice for practicing in a team. The rest of the team needs a quick, efficient way to monitor what's been done, so they can cross it off of their to-do lists. Why should we worry about "clogging the e-mail files" of a supervisor? Any supervisor can glance at a confirmation e-mail and either file it or delete it in about 3 seconds. It consumes less time than wondering if something got done and having to check on it actively.

SGD: I agree with texan99 and others—this takes no extra time and lets the person who assigned the work know it has been done; in addition, should the client call them instead of the sender, they are up to speed and look good to the client (making others look good makes you look good, too). If they find it unnecessary or burdensome, they will tell you but it is generally better to err on the side of too much info (in this context) rather than too little.

ANALYZING THE GENERATIONAL DIVIDE

I'm thinking again, as I did on Monday, about why lawyers go insane over time.

Years ago (long before MapQuest was even a gleam in its inventor's eye), an older lawyer sent me directions for driving to his home. It was pretty easy to get from my apartment to his house; I had to make only three or four turns. But the directions were several typed pages long. Why?

Because this guy had been driven insane by mistakes in the past. He had told someone to turn east on a road, and the person had turned west. So now the directions eliminated that possible mistake: "Turn east (that is, turn right as you are proceeding northbound on route 1) at the light." Someone else had missed the turn. So now the directions eliminated that possible mistake: "If you see a shopping mall followed by a McDonald's on the right side of the road, then you have gone too far. Turn around, go back to the light, and turn east (that is, left as you are now proceeding southbound on route 1) at the light." Having experienced all of these mistakes, the older lawyer felt compelled to help me avoid them, which made his driving directions nearly incomprehensible.

What does this have to do with being a lawyer?

As you age, you are driven insane by mistakes that you've made (or seen others make) in the past. You've seen someone wait until 5 p.m. to call for vital information, and the one knowledgeable person had left for the day and was now unreachable. For the rest of your life, you make your phone calls for vital information before noon, just in case.

You've sent an e-mail urgently requesting information and not received a response for a week, because the intended recipient was out on vacation. For the rest of your life, when you send an urgent e-mail, you then call the person to whom you've sent the e-mail to confirm that the person is not on vacation. If you don't reach the intended recipient, you speak to the recipient's secretary to confirm that the recipient is in the office and will see the e-mail. You remember that once a secretary deceived you, saying that the person was not on vacation, but neglecting to mention the person was tied up in court and wouldn't see the e-mail for hours. For the rest of your life, you cross-examine secretaries about when the lawyers for whom they work will next be checking e-mails.

You've put the final touches—just fixing a last typo or two—on a brief and asked a secretary to make the changes, proof the changes, and file the brief. The secretary accidentally deleted a sentence as he corrected the typos, so the final version of the brief contained a nasty error. For the rest of your life, you read, from start to finish, the final form of every brief that's going out the door, even though the last set of changes that you made involved only fixing two typos.

Sure you're crazy; you've been driven insane by events. You're hedging against things that victimized you in the past.

I frequently hear that today's young lawyers are different from the last generation: "I don't get it. The kids coming out of law school today just don't sweat the small stuff. They don't make sure that things are perfect, and they don't worry about finishing tasks on time. When I graduated from law school, we had a name for people who sweated the small stuff; we called them 'lawyers.'"

I understand the criticism, but I'm not sure we've pinned down the cause.

One possibility is that the older lawyer is right: Today's kids are just bums, unwilling to do what's needed to succeed in our cold, cruel profession.

But another possibility is that the older lawyer has simply lived longer and so had the chance to be driven insane by more events. The older lawyer knows—deeply and fervently, down to his very core—that you simply must proofread the last draft of the brief before you file it, even though the final revisions did no more than fix a couple of typos. The younger lawyer thinks the older lawyer is nuts.

Although this is a generational divide, perhaps it's the inescapable one. Young lawyers are not a new breed of human beings who simply refuse to sweat the small stuff; rather, every generation is driven insane as it ages, and the young lawyers have not yet had that pleasure.

COMMENTS

NOYAM: I feel like this is also why basic documents that should be a few pages bloat up over time. "Hmm, we didn't account for this remote possibility, and it actually happened. Let's tweak the form, make sure we cover it." And so on.

OLDUDE: Client: We don't want more than a three page contract.

Me: OK.

Client (two years later): Why didn't we make him represent and warrant to that? He's killing us.

AB: I disagree that this is a generational divide. I am a younger lawyer, 34 years old, but with a perfectionist streak. I sweat the small stuff. It drives me nuts. Careless mistakes made by anyone—young lawyer or old lawyer—bother me. I proof almost everything. Rarely do the firm's Word Processing Service or secretaries run any edits perfectly. At Big Law, this makes my life rather awful. It is why Big Law is killing me. It is why I have to get out of here. There is not enough time in the day for me to behave this way and stay sane, but if I don't behave this way, my job is imperiled.

LATINTHUNDER: Who gives directions like "turn east" instead of simply saying "turn right"? This was inadvertently a great example of the way some lawyers' compulsion to needlessly complicate things invites the kind of mistakes they obsess over.

> **GUEST:** Unless the person giving directions knows which way you're coming from, the first direction can't be relative to your position.

MANAGING PARTNER: Mark–As a lawyer in his second decade of practice, I certainly have noted the behavior that you mention. However, it still feels like there is a difference. New lawyers today often don't seem to be as alarmed by errors and worried about the consequences. It's like they think that clients won't leave because of errors and will just accept them and move on. Don't know—maybe in 20 years when the clients in charge are the contemporaries of the current new lawyers, then the clients will accept errors and it will be "no big deal." That would actually be a lot more relaxed way to practice—but it is quite different.

SPEED4NICATOR: We're not lazy, we're smart enough to realize that being a lawyer is a job, not a career. I'm not defined by my job and I'll do it well enough to get paid what the going rate is for that job. At the end of the day, I'm going to go home and enjoy my LIFE. If you can't live with the occasional comma splice, that's your problem not mine. I'm ethical, conscientious and hard-working, but I'm not a machine and I have no desire to be one. Having a career so I could die at 47 is not the plan.

GUEST: If I found out that an attorney I had hired spent $1,500 of my money to perform that kind of a proofread, I'd fire him. What a waste of money. Typos are inevitable. Supreme Court opinions have 'em, for god's sake. And has a case or even a motion ever been decided one way or another over a typo or two? Of course not. So the real question is why do clients put up with "perfectionist" attorneys who spend too much of the client's money proofreading (and perhaps not enough time planning an end-to-end efficient litigation strategy)?

> **GUEST:** If I received legal work from an attorney that had typos in it, I would have doubts about the attorney.

> **GUEST:** (1) There are no typo-free attorneys. So stop deluding yourself. The dictionary has typos. The bluebook has typos. Supreme Court opinions have typos. And they're more frequent than you think. Write enough, and you'll produce typos, regardless of how much you proofread. (2) The cost of finding and fixing additional mistakes (form and substance) should be weighed against the benefits of doing so. It's probably worth three hours of time to cite-check a short brief to see if cases have been overruled. It's probably not worth three hours of time to reduce a .1% misspelling rate to a .05% misspelling rate. I would happily hire an attorney who thinks about this kind of calculus. I would have doubts about any attorney (and there are too many out there) who thinks that any marginal increase in the quality of work product—no matter how small—is always worth the cost.

> **GUEST:** You think they're doing some grand calculation about the cost effectiveness of your typos? Please tell me, where do they get the information to do this? Do they know your typing speed or error rate? Do they know you were exhausted when writing work product for them so your error rate was unusually high and your speed unusually slow?

All they know is one attorney gives them work product that's full of obvious errors and another doesn't. All else equal the lawyer with the error-free work product is better than the lawyer turning over a memo or brief full of typos.

OLD FOGEY: I agree with the gist of this article. When I came out of law school 20 years ago, with all the brio and confidence of a young lawyer, I wasn't lazy, and obviously had the chops to make it through the competitive rigors of law school, but I admit now I wasn't really prepared for the demands of the tedium of everyday practice. It's difficult to transition from the "big picture" approach of law school to the "small ball" of day-to-day practice. And I did think my partner/supervisors were "nuts" with some of their obsessiveness to detail, because I hadn't yet seen the consequences that result from the failure to be so obsessive. It only takes a few red-faced moments of explaining to a client, judge or your boss why you failed to notice a glaring mistake to realize that those mistakes are worth avoiding, but that's a lesson that can only be learned over time. Now, when I lecture and sigh to young associates, saying many of the same things my mentors did to me 20 years ago (almost verbatim), I think, "OMG, I've become [insert name of oppressive supervising partner here]!"

IF I'VE GOT IT, THEN BY GOD I'M GONNA INFLICT IT ON YOU

A few months ago, I attended a hearing on a motion for a temporary restraining order.

The judge came out on the bench and berated one side's lawyers: "You filed these papers at midnight last night. Your brief is more than 70 pages long and has a foot of exhibits attached to it. I arrived at court at 9 this morning, and you're now arguing this at 9:30. Do you really think I had a chance to read this stuff?"

How does this happen? How can lawyers be so silly?

This could well be another sad case of if-I've-got-it,-then-by-God-I'm-gonna-inflict-it-on-you syndrome. (I do believe that's the first time I've ever stuck a comma in the middle of a long, hyphenated adjectival phrase. You wonder why I write this column? It's for the education that it provides me.)

If-I've-got-it,-then-by-God-I'm-gonna-inflict-it-on-you syndrome is particularly common at large law firms. That's probably because they've got a lot of stuff, so they have lots of opportunities to inflict things on you.

Think about the 70-page TRO papers. You know those lawyers didn't sit down yesterday afternoon, start doing research from scratch, and crank out a 70-page brief before midnight. (In the right circumstances, that's possible, but it wasn't likely in the case I saw.)

Instead, I bet the lawyers (intelligently) thought they'd save time by looking to see who'd written a brief on a similar issue in the past. The best old brief they found hadn't been filed at the TRO stage, but instead was the more comprehensive brief that's appropriate for a preliminary (or permanent) injunction hearing. The lawyers (foolishly) ignored their actual situation and thought: "This is great! We have a 50-page brief that beats the living daylights out of this issue. We'll merge it with a 15-page brief about the standards governing TROs, update the research a little bit, and blow away the other side with one of the finest briefs ever created in eight hours!"

Presto! Another sad victim of if-I've-got-it,-then-by-God-I'm-gonna-inflict-it-on-you syndrome.

What's the problem here?

First, the brief doesn't fit the situation. Even if it legitimately takes 70 pages to present the best possible argument for your side, you're running a risk if you file an over-long brief as part of an emergency application. In an emergency, things happen quickly. A typical judge is unlikely to have the time (or inclination) to read a 70-page brief seeking a TRO. Unless you know that your judge is the child of Evelyn Wood and Benjamin Cardozo, don't file the long-form brief. File the 10-page brief that the judge will read (which gives you a chance to persuade), not the 70-page thing that's headed straight to the trash.

Second, even if the situation permits the filing of a long brief—perhaps a post-trial motion after a jury trial or an opening brief on appeal—consider whether length works in your favor.

Typically, the best brief is the shortest possible brief. If you really have the goods on me—because, say, the Supreme Court ruled yesterday that a litigant in my position loses—you could probably convince a court of your position in a relatively few pages of argument. The introduction's pretty easy: "Sad Sack's position is X. Just yesterday, the Supreme Court ruled that position X loses. [Cite.] Therefore, Sad Sack loses." The statement of facts need only show that this case is identical to the recent Supreme Court case. The legal argument describes the Supreme Court case, and you're finished. No muss, no fuss, and you win.

If you really, really, really win, there's no need to waste 70 pages chatting about circuit and trial court cases, similar cases decided on analogous facts, and assorted policy arguments. Prolixity ain't persuasion.

(Don't get me wrong here. You may well have to do exhaustive research to find the few cases from which you will craft your short brief. But don't lard up a brief with every case you read, thinking that, so long as you read the stuff, you'll inflict them on the reader. That just doesn't work.)

How does this apply to in-house lawyers?

First, don't let your outside counsel suffer from if-I've-got-it,-then-by-God-I'm-gonna-inflict-it-on-you syndrome. If counsel suggests filing a brief that's wonderfully long and impressive, but simply wrong for the occasion, put your foot down. The idea is not to impress people; the idea is to win.

Second, in-house lawyers occasionally possess long and impressive work product. An in-house lawyer may possess a 20-page chronology, a 30-page analysis of all of the legal issues, or a 100-page summary of all of the testimony presented to date at trial. When the head of a business unit asks what's happening in the case, you must control your if-I've-got-it,-then-by-God-I'm-gonna-inflict-it-on-you tendencies. The head of the business unit may need only three paragraphs, or three pages, to serve her purpose. Don't think you're helping or impressing people by giving them more information than they need.

Written work must fit the occasion. Think about what your reader needs before bludgeoning the reader with everything you happen to possess.

Let's stamp out . . . well, you know.

COMMENTS

LEARNED PAW: Mark Herrmann: We lost the case! Why didn't you make x, y and z arguments?????

Outside Counsel: We made the best arguments. The best brief is the shortest possible brief, remember?

Mark Herrmann: You're fired!

ARTPEN100: Same thing in providing advice to clients. Some want the writing or discussion as brief as possible. But I will still add in the important points that could result in a different course of action, even when I sense their annoyance. Why? Because those are often the same clients who will claim malpractice if I omit some point that turns out to have been relevant due to some fact they didn't tell me. Better to have a client complain that you are being too technical than a malpractice suit.

KEEPING PEOPLE IN THE LOOP

How much do other people have to know?

This question comes up in many different contexts, and answering it always requires a little judgment.

At law firms, the questions often involve what the partner or the client needs to know. These people are supposed to be kept in the loop, but that task may be trickier than it seems. You want people to be fully informed, but you don't want to become a pest, constantly alerting people to irrelevant trifles. What's a person to do?

The answer varies by many things, including the nature of the matter you're working on, the compulsiveness of the person you're working with, the degree of trust established between you and the person you're working with, time pressure, and the like. To the extent it's possible, though, let's establish some general rules....

First: There shall be no surprises at public meetings. In a law firm setting, if three firm lawyers are meeting three client representatives, then the three firm lawyers must know all of the important information that the law firm possesses before the meeting starts. You can't be sitting in front of the client and startle your colleagues with some new, critical piece of information that changes the landscape. Any important information that the law firm knows gets shared in advance.

So, too, in-house. If you have quarterly meetings with the auditors to discuss some set of issues, then all of the client representatives at the meeting should know all important information that the client possesses before the meeting starts. Let's not be sitting with the auditors when we first alert our colleagues that the billion-dollar acquisition has gone south or the appellate court just reversed the favorable hundred-million-dollar verdict. If you have news, share it with your colleagues privately first; we don't spring surprises on our colleagues in public.

Second: Your boss shall not be surprised by his boss. For example, if an outraged client will be calling the CEO tomorrow to complain about something, and the CEO will predictably then walk down the hall to ask the general counsel about this issue, speak up now. We should advise the CEO that she'll likely be receiving the angry call, so the CEO is prepared to field the call appropriately. We should advise the general counsel today, so that when the CEO walks down the hall to investigate, the general counsel is prepared to answer. To the extent that it's humanly possible, don't let people above you in the hierarchy be taken by surprise.

Third: Tell people the things they must know to perform their jobs intelligently. I know that's a mushy standard, but it's the relevant one. Put yourself in the other person's shoes; think about what the other person logically must know to do his job effectively; pass along that information promptly. If a law firm knows that a case is going to trial in two months, the client must be told. Within the client's hierarchy, the head of litigation must know about the trial date. If it's possible that an adverse judgment will be significant, the general counsel must know about the trial date. If the adverse judgment might be not just significant, but material, then the CFO and CEO must know about the trial date. If an adverse judgment might draw media attention, then you owe a call to someone in public relations. Give people the information they need to do their jobs.

Fourth: If in doubt, share the information. It's indeed annoying to receive endless e-mails relaying insignificant stuff—so I'm not saying you should pass along insignificant stuff. But if there's a chance the other person will need the information to do her job, then share the information. It's a whole lot easier to delete an e-mail that provides unnecessary information than it is to read minds to discern information that you've never been told. If your boss thinks you're providing too much information, your boss will surely speak up. But if your boss flubs his job because you chose not to share some critical piece of information, your boss will likely speak up more quickly and less happily. If in doubt, share the information, until you're told otherwise.

Those are suggestions for reporting up within a hierarchy. There are also ways to report down (or sideways) intelligently, but mistakes in those directions may not be as career-limiting. In any event, the general rule is always this: Think about what the other guy needs to know; then, provide it.

COMMENTS

VALERIE: All of this advice assumes that clients and partners are rational. Why didn't I cc the partner on that recent e-mail to a client? More than likely because it would have invited undue scrutiny from the partner, who would have asked, "Why did you do this? Why did you say that? Didn't you mean [something slightly and imperceptibly different]? Why didn't you say [something else, probably irrelevant]?" Sure, I could later back up every one of the decisions I made in writing that e-mail, but why subject myself to such an unnecessary annoyance?

GUEST: The problem is, if you don't cc them, they yell at you for that. Ahhh …life as an associate.

THE RULE OF EQUAL DIGNITY

Years ago, I saw a memo written by a law firm partner who was renowned for mistreating junior partners, associates, staff, and lost children who wandered in the front door looking for their parents. But this memo showed a whole different personality. The memo was directed to a practice leader who had solicited comments about how best to expand the practice. (In case you're wondering, the memo was distributed widely by mistake. The practice leader told his assistant to gather in one document all of the comments about how to improve the practice, so the comments could be shared and everyone could discuss the ideas at an upcoming meeting. The assistant then took all of the unedited inbound memos and assembled them in a single packet that she distributed to the entire group. *Voilà!* There was the ogre's memo, for all to read.)

The ogre's memo was breathtakingly—what's the right word here?—"solicitous" to the practice leader: "I'll satisfy your request for suggestions about how to expand this practice area further, but we should first acknowledge what you've achieved to date. When you were appointed to lead this practice ten years ago, everyone thought you'd been sent on a fool's errand. No one thought it was possible for our firm to compete in this space. We had no cases in the area and none of our lawyers had any expertise. But you've defied all the odds. You've made this practice one of the great success stories in the firm. You deserve endless praise for what you've done, and I want you to know how much we respect—indeed, admire—you." And so on.

Don't get me wrong: I understand the fine art of sucking up. (I'm not much good at it, but I understand it.) And I appreciate the wisdom of people like the ogre who try to do their sucking up in private. But I don't understand folks who do these things publicly. Can't we control at least the public manifestations of unequal treatment being accorded to people who matter to you and people who don't?

What am I thinking of?

Among other things, I'm thinking of opportunities. If it makes sense for you personally to spend money to try to seize some opportunity, then it should often make sense for others presented with similar opportunities to have the same access to money. In the law firm setting, if it makes sense for the practice leader to fly first class to Istanbul to give a talk to fifty people in some industry, then it probably also makes sense for someone else in the practice to fly to New York to talk to fifty people. If you find yourself authorizing expenditures for yourself and your favorites, but not for others, then you're not treating people with equal dignity.

The equal dignity rule also applies to personal interactions. If you're talking to the CEO or the global managing partner, you probably don't pull out your BlackBerry and start typing away into the high-ranking person's face. If you don't do this to people above you in your institution's hierarchy, then don't do it to people below you. If it's rude to ignore the CEO when she's talking to you, then it's equally rude to ignore the person three rungs beneath you in the bureaucracy. Treat people with equal dignity.

How about picking up the phone when someone's sitting in your office talking to you? I have an easy rule for you to consider: Don't. If someone's in your office (discussing a business matter), then ignore the phone. This rule worked just fine for me in the decades before caller ID existed: If you were in my office, you received my undivided attention. I didn't answer the phone, check the computer, or, in the old days, flip through the inbound Fed Ex packages, faxes, or mail. The person sitting in my office came first; everything else came next.

Suppose a client was calling about a crisis? That's why God created secretaries. If a client called with a crisis, the secretary could field the call, realize that the matter was a crisis requiring immediate attention, and interrupt the meeting. That's polite, and that's fair.

Suppose a family member was calling about something urgent? That's another reason why God created secretaries. If your spouse or kids call to talk to you, the secretary fields the call, decides (along with your caller) whether this is urgent, and makes an intelligent decision whether to interrupt you or have you call back at a convenient time. My kids are now 22 and 24, and neither one of them has ever called me about something so urgent that they chose to interrupt me in a business meeting. (Maybe I've been lucky, and we've had mercifully few family crises.)

What about my wife? She caught me at my desk on the day the babysitter died in the living room while watching our kids (then aged 1 and 3), so she didn't have to interrupt on that occasion. (Don't ever tell me that you have the "world's greatest babysitter story." I'm going to call you and raise you, and then I'll sit back with the calm confidence of a Christian holding four aces.) My secretary did track me down and interrupt on the day my wife went into labor with our "little" one; that strikes me as the right call. And I'm sure I'd hear if the house were ever on fire. But those are not the general rule. Absent an emergency, the rule is this: Finish your existing conversation; then tend to other stuff.

I'll admit that I make two broad exceptions when I apply the rule of equal dignity: First, it does not apply to my secretary. If my secretary is in my office talking to me, then I'm likely to turn away when the phone rings. That's a tad rude, but I think my secretaries over the years and I have understood the implicit logic: A good secretary is like an appendage; he or she is there constantly to help you keep the ball moving. If someone's calling about the ball, then the ball has to come first, and you can talk to the secretary after you hang up.

Second, caller ID changes things slightly. Because you can now see who's calling before you pick up the phone, you can effectively screen your own calls. In this brave new world, it seems to me permissible to look away from the person in your office to glance at your phone when it rings. If the caller is someone who's notoriously strapped for time and hard to catch (such as, for example, the CEO or CFO of a Fortune 500 company), then you might reasonably apologize to your visitor and field the call to avoid missing something urgent or finding yourself unable to reconnect with the caller in a reasonable amount of time.

For the most part, however, follow the rule of equal dignity: Treat people beneath you in the hierarchy the same way you treat people above you. Give others the same opportunities that you'd give yourself. Walk down the hall to talk to the folks who report to you, instead of always summoning them to your office. Make your outfit feel just a little more egalitarian, and your workplace environment may become a whole lot happier.

COMMENTS

GUEST: This is an excellent column and should be required reading for all attorneys at law firms. Broad implementation of the advice would substantially improve morale and working conditions at firms. In my experience most attorneys do treat their colleagues with equal dignity, but every office seems to have an "ogre" or two as described in the column. What I don't understand is why senior partners and other firm leaders allow these ogres to treat people this way. Sometimes even one abusive partner to ruin associate morale across a practice group.

> **BONOBO_BRO:** Book of business > firm leaders' personal opinions of your personality >>>>>associate morale.

GUEST: It's very sad that you had to write this, only because it's the equivalent of writing "Water====wet."

GUEST: I thought this was the reason before I started practicing, but from my experience I've found this isn't actually the case. The partners that have big books of business often treat associates pretty well—they realize it's important to develop associates to serve their clients and help them leverage their time. The ones that are the worst are the partners that have small and/or declining books of business and vent their frustrations by abusing associates. Other partners often recognize this but rarely do anything about it. I think there are two reasons: confrontation avoidance and/or partner solidarity. Either way it's counter-productive to the success of the firm.

IF YOU TOUCH IT, IT'S YOURS!

Here's the sad rule: If it comes across your desk, then you're responsible for it.

Period.

That's the rule at law firms. It was my rule when I worked at a firm, and it's the rule that I now impose on outside lawyers. Thus, when I was a partner, I did not tolerate this excuse after an associate sent me a crappy draft brief, supposedly ready to be sent to a client for review: "I know the draft is not very good. But I didn't write it. Local counsel did."

Yeah? So what am I supposed to do with the crappy draft? Send it to the client with a cover note explaining that we propose to file the attached terrible brief, and we should be excused from blame because local counsel wrote it? I don't think so. If a brief crosses my desk, then it's my brief. I'm responsible for it. It has to be good.

So, too, with you: When the brief hits your desk, you became responsible for it. The draft brief that you send to me is your best possible work product; there are no excuses.

The same thing is true in-house....

Remarkably, law firm partners have told me, after I explained that a brief was unacceptably bad, that the brief had been written by either local counsel or an associate. (Actually, on one occasion, a partner told me that the brief had been written by one of his partners "who doesn't write that well." That statement leaves me speechless, so I'm unable to comment.)

Those excuses simply cannot work.

If you send it to me, then it meets with your approval. You vouch for it. Period.

If that's not the rule, then I have no guarantee that I can trust the things that you send to me.

This rule applies not just to things that you write, but also to things that you say: If you, one of my fellow in-house lawyers, say that a lawsuit has a settlement value of $100,000, then you're responsible for that judgment. If we discuss the case for a little while, realize that the law is on our side, the plaintiff is a convicted felon, and we have a lock-cinch motion for summary judgment that's already been written, then you can't tell me: "Well, outside counsel said that the case was worth $100,000. Maybe outside counsel was wrong." Once the judgment comes across your desk, the judgment is yours.

In a fast-paced in-house environment, that rule can cause trouble. Someone sends you a draft e-mail, destined for your supervisor's supervisor's desk, that's essentially incomprehensible. The draft badly needs to be translated from English into English. You're trapped. You can't disclaim the thing, because it landed on your desk. And you really don't want to be saddled with responsibility for this lump of coal. You'd love to write back: "You are free to send this e-mail to my boss's boss, but please explain in a cover note that the e-mail represents exclusively your work, and that I played no role in preparing this travesty."

Nice, but it doesn't work: No matter what you ask, the author of the e-mail will say, "I have bounced this e-mail off of [you], and the e-mail has [your] approval." Tag! Now you're a moron, too!

It's very hard to take personal responsibility for everything that you touch. But it's the only way to build credibility and a reputation. If it comes across your desk, then it's yours. You have to make it right: "that is all Ye know on earth, and all ye need to know."

COMMENTS

GUEST: In fairness, if a client had asked that local counsel write a brief, I would first show them the brief and tell them it wasn't very good and offer to re-write it before spending dozens of hours duplicating work that had already been done with no client authorization.

GUEST: Client's are half of what is wrong with this profession. Many are jerks who expect perfection in everything but are rarely willing to pay for it.

GUEST: This is just one of so many reasons lawyers are inefficient. Should you accept the responsibility for your employee's or local counsel's work? Yes. But the way to ensure quality in that work is through selecting a good employee or local counsel, giving them reasonable, clear instructions, providing corrective feedback, and performing quality control. This should result in work product that doesn't need extensive fixing. Instead, however, lawyers at every level redo the work that comes from below. It completely defeats the purpose of delegation and is incredibly wasteful.

GUEST: I agree with the general principle, but I also allow for some exceptions. For example, people who deliver shoddy work are also more likely to be running up against deadlines. If you are brought into a matter urgently because things have gone to hell and receive a crappy document hours before it needs to be submitted/filed/signed, etc., then you fix any radioactive problems and do your best with the rest in the time you have. It won't be your best work but rather your best work under the circumstances. It's kind of like Winston Wolfe's advice in "Pulp Fiction" on cleaning up the car: "You don't need to eat off it. Just give it a good once-over. What you gotta focus on are the really messy parts."

WHEN YOU DO NOT ASK FOR A BETTER DRAFT

I occasionally take advantage of my little megaphone here at Above the Law to vent about poor quality drafts. When I do, "commenters" or correspondents routinely suggest that I'm tilting at windmills: "If you receive a poor quality draft, send it back to the person who wrote it, and tell that person to make it better. There's no reason why you, Mark, should be saddled with improving the thing."

Wrong, wrong, and wrong again!

I'm absolutely saddled with improving the thing. It often makes no sense at all to return a bad draft to the author and ask for a better draft. In fact, I submit that there are only two situations in which it does make sense to ask the original author to improve a draft ....

I'll ask the original author to improve a draft only if (1) the author is a young lawyer, still being trained, and creating a new draft will be a worthwhile training opportunity, or (2) there's a reasonable chance that the next draft (or some later iteration) will be respectable. Otherwise, either I'm saddled with finalizing the thing or I must find someone (other than me, but not the original author) to help.

Why?

The first situation is obvious: If we're training people, we're training people. The new lawyer writes a bad draft; we give general suggestions about how to improve it. The new lawyer writes a slightly better, but still bad, draft; we give more detailed suggestions. Then, either: (1) the new lawyer writes something that's close to final, and we finalize it, or (2) the new lawyer writes a third bad draft, and we give up, burn the thing, and start writing from scratch. (Training is one thing; pursuing lost causes is another.)

The second situation—returning a draft because there's some chance that the original author can make it respectable—is trickier: How do you know whether there's a chance that the person who wrote the first, bad draft is capable of producing a later, acceptable product?

The answer to that is not always obvious. When you receive, for example, a mediocre draft from a mid-level associate, you can't be sure whether that person has the capacity to make things right. I'm inclined to err on the side of giving people a second chance and, if time permitted, I'd ask that original author to improve the draft.

But there are other situations that you simply know are hopeless. You'll develop a nose for this over time, but certain situations recur. If, for example, local counsel is an experienced practitioner, 20 or 25 years into practice, and sends a bad draft, then that situation is hopeless. This person is fully trained; he thinks he's competent; you could return the brief to him 100 times, and he still wouldn't produce a finished product. That person doesn't know the meaning of "good," so he'll never reach that goal, and you won't be able to help by making gentle suggestions for the author to consider.

Similarly, if you receive a bad draft from one of your senior colleagues (at a firm or in-house), it's probably the same deal. (I say "probably" because there's always a chance that time pressure, or some other unusual situation, hurt the quality of your colleague's work.) A senior person is likely to be beyond the training stage, and that person simply never learned. If you return the draft to that person for revisions, you'll insult your colleague and receive back only another unusable draft.

The name of the game is not to have raw sewage bounce back and forth from your desk to the other guy's, never creating a finished product. The idea is to create a finished product and deploy it. There is simply no reason (other than training) to return a crappy draft to a person who will not be able to make the thing substantially better in the next iteration. That wastes time and money, and it doesn't advance the ball.

What's the solution? There is none. If you work in a place with ample resources, perhaps you'll identify a colleague who can spin straw into gold. Give your junior partner, or assistant general counsel, the bad draft, and ask that person to work her magic. Presto! You've unloaded the chore of editing onto some other sad sack.

But in a place with fewer resources, or if you can't find the necessary talented colleague, or if a matter won't bear the freight of involving an extra person, then you're stuck. When you receive a bad draft, there's no place to turn for help, and it's up to you to make things right.

And that's why it's fair for me occasionally to vent about that subject in this space.

COMMENTS

RAF: Kudos! Too many bad writers out there, though :(

PHIL: But you are assuming the drafts you receive are the person's best work. It is highly probable that those who send you low quality drafts are very busy and are doing just enough to get by. If you persist in correcting their work (and grumble about it), they do not know it is not up to par nor that you are disappointed.

You could give it back with a stern and fatherly look and ask, "Is this REALLY your best effort?" Nine times out of ten you'll get a sheepish, "No" and they will do it again.

You will never escape the final edit, but you can close the gap.

'RECREATIONAL' WRITING, IN-HOUSE AND OUT

Complete honesty is such a dangerous thing.

I'm going to give it a shot.

I'm posing three questions to myself today. First, why might a lawyer at a law firm choose to write articles? Second, what topics should lawyers write about, and where should they publish the articles? Finally, why might an in-house lawyer choose to write?

The honest truth is that outside lawyers choose to write for many, varied reasons. In-house lawyers might also choose to write for many reasons, but those reasons are different and fewer. Across the board, authors' motivations for writing will be mixed.

Do I have a right to speak on the subject of publications? My credentials, in a nutshell, are these: Three books; twelve law review articles; two book chapters; more than 70 other, shorter articles (in places ranging from *The Wall Street Journal* and the *Chicago Tribune* to *Pharmaceutical Executive* and *Litigation*); and maybe 600 blog posts (roughly 500 at Drug and Device Law and north of 100 here). Call me nuts (and I may well be), but I've spent a professional lifetime doing a ton of "recreational" legal writing.

Why did I do it? Should you?

As a lawyer at a firm, why write? I'll start with three answers that you weren't expecting and only slowly work my way around to "business development." Here's the first reason to write: Write because you're not 100 percent sure that you'll want to spend your entire professional life practicing law, and you may someday want to "re-tire" into academia. (Long, long ago, that was part of my motivation. Then the 1980s ended.) If that's your motivation, then write a law review article or two while you're relatively young, and jump ship while you still have a sufficiently long professional life ahead of you to build a reputation as a scholar. You can dabble in scholarship over the course of decades, if you care to, but if you're writing primarily as a vehicle for entering academia, the smart money says that you should act quickly.

Why else might you choose to write?

You might choose to write from the noblest of motivations: Write because you have a clever idea, and you want to share that idea with the world. You can help your readers with a legal issue, advance the development of the law, and get some personal pleasure out of sharing your thought. Those words may strike many readers of this column as insanity and only a few as either credible or enticing, but I swear that this motivated me (in part) to write over the years.

Write to help your clients. Suppose you're advocating on behalf of a client a legal position that some people perceive to be "as black as hell, as dark as night." Some law professor writes a liberal screed undercutting your client's legal position, and plain-tiffs' lawyers are attaching copies of that 40-page law review article as Exhibit A to crappy five-page briefs. You thus can't respond to all of the arguments in five pages of opposition, and you're not allowed to file a 45-page response. What do you do? Write your own law review article, and attach your article as Exhibit A to your five-page brief. Now the judge has two short briefs, and the judge can choose to delve into the issues more closely if the judge so pleases. (Again, I'm not making this up; I've written at least one article in part for that reason. Before you ask: No, I didn't charge the client for time spent writing the article. The client didn't commission the thing or ask me to write it. And I received personal benefits from having written the piece, including satisfaction and the possibility of attracting new business. Your blood doesn't always have to run green.)

Finally, write to develop business. This is self-evident: If you write articles, you are likely to be asked to write more articles and to give talks on the subjects about which you've written. You can send reprints of your articles to clients and prospects. At beauty contests, you can hand out copies of your articles. Writing articles is one part of a broader business development plan.

If you're writing to attract clients, what should you write, and where should you publish? First, write on substantive topics, not procedural or evidentiary ones. Clients hire "10b-5 lawyers" or "product liability lawyers;" clients almost never hire "removal lawyers" or "Federal Rule of Evidence 103 lawyers." Second, publish in the trade press, not the legal press or scholarly journals. If you're writing to develop pharmaceutical product liability business, aim for *Pharmaceutical Executive*, not the *National Law Journal* or the *Michigan Law Review*.

When you write, must you have anything to say? It depends. Try not to embarrass yourself by saying in print things that are either pablum or wrong. But, if you're writing solely to develop business, you don't need a novel legal thesis. Clients may be interested in articles that simply describe a recent development in a relevant area; you don't need a creative idea to crank out one of those articles. If you'd like to take it up a notch, then gin up a thesis—perhaps even one that's new or interesting. But that's hardly essential. I personally have written some articles that said new and provocative things and other articles that simply put my name in a public place, hopefully without causing me undue embarrassment.

What happens when you move in-house? Your motivations change. Business development is no longer part of your job; in-house lawyers don't write for that reason. If you're in-house, young, and considering a career in academia, then it makes sense to write a scholarly piece or two. If you have a thought that you'd like to share, then you may still get some satisfaction out of sharing it. You can write to help your client, although that may be trickier to do as an in-house lawyer than an outside one—for reasons of both politics and job responsibility. (Unless you're at the helm of researching and writing briefs—and many in-house lawyers are not—it's hard to crank out a scholarly article in a reasonable amount of time.)

Finally, the ultimate in navel-gazing: Why do I write this column? As always, my motivations are mixed: It's interesting to be involved in the public discussion. It's good for a company (such as mine) that serves as an insurance broker to law firms to have its name mentioned to tens of thousands of lawyers twice each week. It's good for our corporate law department if our lawyers maintain relatively high profiles, because that makes us a more attractive employer when we recruit new in-house lawyers. It's personally a good idea for me to maintain a relatively high profile, because people then remember that I exist. That's about it. (Okay, okay: I said I'd be completely honest. Writing this column has surely prompted sales of more than a few *Curmudgeons*, and this was a great vehicle for launching *Drug and Device Product Liability Litigation Strategy*. And, I confess, Lat pays me enough for writing these ditties that, after taxes, I can go out for one nice dinner a month. Like I said, our motives are always mixed.)

On the other hand, if you're an in-house lawyer and you speak publicly, be very, very careful. I, for example, cannot offend law firms (on either side of the "v."), because our brokers will place insurance for any law firm; I can't offend clients or potential clients. I cannot offend corporations, because we act as insurance brokers for most of the Fortune 500, and we'd love to help the rest. Those are overwhelming constraints. For example, someone recently asked me to write a post advocating a certain position about the "Stop Online Piracy Act," a fascinating legal topic that has fractured corporate America. Half the Fortune 500 would love the position I was asked to advocate, and the other half would be outraged. If I were to write that post, I'd infuriate clients and potential clients and have brokers with pitchforks storming my office door. That ain't gonna happen.

What about you—should you write? What motivates you? Write for personal satisfaction; you can't lose. If you're at a firm, write to develop business; over time, that may prove a worthwhile effort. If you're in-house (and thus not concerned with developing business), then choosing to write is a much closer call: The benefits are fewer and the risks more perilous. And one thing is certain: The rewards to in-house lawyers of writing will be far more ephemeral and far less green than the rewards to outside lawyers.

COMMENTS

KILROY: I have written over 500 comments on Above the Law. Should I put that on my resume?

BONOBO_BRO: Mark, if the craziest thing you considered doing during the 80s was retire to academia, you were doing it very, very wrong.
  –Bright Lights Big City Bro

THE INJUSTICE OF TRUST

I have two memos sitting unread in my inbox.

One of the memos is great; the other one is terrible. I know which is which. And, as I said, I haven't yet read either one of them.

Isn't trust terribly unfair?

Think about the many ways that establishing trust permeates a business relationship. Once the superior (whether that be partner, client, boss, or whomever) trusts the underling, the underling can do no wrong. And once the superior mistrusts the underling, the underling can do no right.

Which of the two unread memos in my inbox is great? The one from the guy I trust. All of his earlier memos have been great. They're crisp, incisive, intelligent, and lucid; the one that I haven't yet read is surely a thing of beauty, too. Which memo stinks? The one from the guy I don't trust. All of his earlier memos have left me gripping my head in agony, trying to figure out what in God's name this clown was trying to communicate and why anyone would think it was worth trying to communicate that drivel.

Trust permeates everything; it's terribly unfair. Trust infuses more than just the memos I haven't yet read. Trust permeates silence, too. How can trust permeate silence?

When I hear nothing about an ongoing event from the guy I trust, that's very good news: "The matter is under control. There's nothing for me to worry about. My trustworthy assistant is holding down the fort. How good of him."

When I hear nothing from the guy I don't trust, the silence takes on an entirely different meaning: "That matter is probably blowing up, and I'm not hearing anything about it from my subordinate. Why doesn't that clown report to me on a regular basis? I must make a note to follow up, so I'm not blind-sided by some development that I should know about, but don't. I really must remember to note on the next performance review my subordinate's inability to keep me apprised of important information."

That is the sound of silence—silence—infused with trust or mistrust.

Trust changes the presumption of guilt. When the client does something unspeakably stupid, there are two possible gut reactions. For the person you trust: "My subordinate is a meticulously good lawyer who gives fine advice. What a shame the client went off on a lark and did something stupid. We'll really have to get the moronic client under control."

For the person you don't trust: "Shoot! If only my subordinate had advised the client correctly, the client would have done the right thing. My inept subordinate didn't give the client sufficient guidance, so my subordinate induced the intelligent client to make a mistake."

Trust changes the reaction to errors. When the one you trust makes a mistake: "Ha!

The trusted one made a mistake. Well, no one's perfect. I'm kind of pleased to see that the trusted one finally butchered one. It means he's not God."

When the one you don't trust makes a mistake: "Again! How many times can this happen? Can we fire that moron yet?"

Trust changes even your reaction when caller ID tells you who's on your phone line. For the one you trust: "Ah. I'm about to speak to the trusted one. That means we'll discuss an issue worth raising, and he'll probably propose some solution, making my life easy."

But if you see the name of the one you don't trust looming on caller ID: "Shoot. I'm about to kill a half hour listening to that clown blather unintelligibly about some issue that doesn't even matter. Maybe I can avoid this torture by simply not answering the phone."

Trust is terribly unfair. It causes people to prejudge the quality of your work, forgive your errors, and interpret your silences even before you've done anything.

Given how the presence (or absence) of trust pervades a relationship, why do so many people seem to overlook the critical importance of building trust early and never doing anything to undermine that bond?

COMMENTS

EMPEROR_AGUESTUS: Shut up, gramps.

SERGEIBRIN: Typical biglaw-partner (or former partner) absolutist thinking. People are either 100% geniuses or 100% clowns. Why is this form of dysfunctional thinking so common in the legal profession?

TASKS VERSUS PROJECTS

Success—at a law firm, in-house, or in any professional services environment—requires a certain mindset. The mindset is this: "My job is not to take an order from my client (or boss) and fill that order, but rather to achieve things." Or, to put it differently, strive to execute projects, not simply to perform tasks.

Let's start with a silly example: You ask someone to call the plumber to get the sink fixed.

Three days later, you realize that you haven't heard back on this subject, so you ask, "Did you call the plumber?"

You hear back, "Oh, yes. I did."

"And?"

"The plumber hasn't returned my call."

Do you feel as though you received intelligent help with this project? Of course not—because the project was to get the sink fixed. You didn't really care whether your helper called the plumber, or e-mailed the plumber, or attracted the plumber's attention with smoke signals. So long as the sink got fixed, the project was completed.

But your helper chose not to think about the project and instead focused only on the task—making a phone call, whether or not anything came of it. Your helper completed the task and ignored the actual project.

Undertaking tasks, rather than executing projects, is exactly the way to fail in a professional services environment. Here's an example, from the legal world....

As a partner at a law firm, you might say to an associate, "The other side cited *Smith v. Jones* in its opposition brief. What's the story on that case?"

An order-taking associate returns a half hour later: "Here's a copy of *Smith v. Jones* for you to read."

Okay, but not particularly helpful.

A project-oriented associate returns six hours later: "*Smith v. Jones* hurts us. It holds X. But *Smith* is distinguishable in three ways: Ways one, two, and three. And *Smith* has been criticized by courts in two other states, and one later court expressly refused to follow the holding that hurts us. This small binder has a one-page outline of the things that I just told you, followed by highlighted copies of the relevant cases, with Post-it notes on the key pages."

Aha! Here's a person who took a project and acted as though it actually mattered.

This mindset applies to everything that anyone is asked to do in a professional services environment. When talking to a junior lawyer about a brief, a partner might say: "I had one thought when I was reading this. Please think about [thought]."

An order-taking person returns at the end of the day with a revised draft of the brief. The revised draft is identical to the original, except for one sentence in the middle paragraph of page seven, where the new idea has been added as a dependent clause. The changed sentence now reads: "Old text old text old text, [new thought], old text old text old text."

Okay—and maybe even correct—but not necessarily helpful.

A project-oriented person might return with one of several possible responses. Perhaps: "I considered your thought. I read the relevant cases and looked at our evidentiary record. I'm not sure that your idea works in this context. These are my concerns . . . . I was thinking of modifying your thought to add the new argument in a slightly different way. We might instead say . . . ."

Or perhaps the revised brief has a new sentence in the introduction highlighting the new idea, and the statement of facts now recites the facts needed to set up the new argument, and the brief has a new argument section "C" that lays out the new argument, complete with citations to helpful cases.

Aha! This person took a project and acted as though it actually mattered!

It's remarkable how long it takes some junior lawyers to realize that their job is not to do the minimum amount of work needed to get the partner off their back, but rather to help the partner accomplish something. Further along the career path, it's remarkable how many people think that projects can be blown off to avoid doing boring tasks. But the need to complete projects, rather than to perform tasks, never ends.

A client will ask the most senior partner at a law firm to help with something, and the partner succeeds only if the partner completes a project, rather than performs a task. The CEO can ask the general counsel to help with something, and the general counsel succeeds only by completing a project, rather than performing a task. And a big client may ask the CEO to do something; the CEO succeeds only by completing a project, rather than performing a task.

This isn't a matter of rank or hierarchy. It's a matter of attitude that infuses everything you'll ever do in a professional services environment.

Think about what the other person needs to achieve, and then cause that person to achieve it. Don't perform tasks. Execute projects, and people will beat a path to your door.

COMMENTS

SAD FROG: You just spent six hours on a task the assigning partner expected you'd spend thirty minutes on. Not only was your extensive case history too late to be of any help, all your time will be written off.

> **EPEEIST:** Exactly.
>
> I've worked for some more senior people who—to use the examples above by analogy—only wanted a copy of *Smith v. Jones*, not my analysis. Or only wanted my thoughts on the one issue/sentence identified, not a rewrite of the whole brief.
>
> The best bosses gave a time estimate when they gave the work (which told me how much work they were expecting me to do); if not, I had responsibility to ask, e.g., "did you just want a copy of the case, or an analysis" or if assigned by e-mail a quick response "Here's a copy of the case attached; if you wish I can do a memo

on it for you by this afternoon" or whatever.

LEARNED PAW: Or the partner realizes one paragraph into the memo you labored over for six hours that he meant to ask you to look at Smith v. *Hughes*, not Smith v. Jones.

GUEST: More likely, he meant for you do a memo on Smith v. Hughes but never noticed the error because he never read your memo.

GUEST: Knowing who you work with (both partners and clients) is also part of doing it right. That's a mistake that almost every first/second year makes at some point.

Spending 6 hours writing a full memo when the partner really just wanted you to print off the case and bring it to him, or alternatively, printing off the case and bringing it to him when he wanted a more comprehensive answer and knew the client would pay for it.

Yes, partners should strive to be more specific, but that doesn't help you when you get the assignment and don't know what to do.

LATINTHUNDER: *Think about what the other person needs to achieve*

And make sure that you don't interrupt this thought process by actually asking them what they want.

FORE PLAY: Executive summary: do your boss's job for him so he doesn't have to be distracted with trivial tasks like work or work-related questions as he labors at his real job (as he perceives it) on the golf course.

GUEST: Trolled, but it's a fair comment.

Particularly at smaller firms, your boss hires you to make his life easier, and to help him make money. If he has to spend more time (and/or money) supervising you than he would have had to take to do the work himself, then he hasn't gained much.

The relationship's attenuated in a very large firm, but the same really holds true. The partner assigns you work because he either can't do it himself or doesn't want to do it himself. (Unless it's summer clerk make-work.) It's part of your job to make his job easier, not make it harder.

TOTALHOSE: Did I receive intelligent help from this post? Of course not.

GUEST: I generally agree with Herrmann's advice. However, you need to take care not to go beyond the scope of your assignment. If you're fairly experienced and have an understanding with the person for whom you are working that you will simply "run with the ball" and fix the problem, by all means, *carpe diem*. But, if that's not the case, ask before going too nutso.

BRIAN: I think law school and bar exams already filter out people who can't function (do projects). This article just states the obvious.

GUEST: Good advice, Mark. I tend to think that some workers just "get" this and some don't, but if your article convinces even one timid, unassertive, gumption-deficient potted plant to take some initiative, then it's worth it.

Seriously, if you lack the initiative to EVER go above and beyond (and despite your own perfection, reader, you've WORKED WITH people who do), then please quit trying to act like a lawyer. You're a potted plant acting like a lawyer, and it's pathetic.

END

PROVIDE 'ADVANCE PRAISE' FOR 'INSIDE STRAIGHT— THE BOOK'!

I've relented.

Under extreme pressure from all quarters—well, my wife thought it was a good idea, anyway—I've committed to publish a compendium of "Inside Straight" columns in the form of a book. ABA Publishing tells me that, in June, you'll be able to hold in your hands *Inside Straight: [followed by a clever subtitle]*! (This obviously remains a work in progress.)

I have two items of good news about the forthcoming book and two requests for your help. First, the good news: The book will not simply be about me; it will also be about you! In addition to reproducing a collection of my columns, the book will include assorted "comments" that you, my readers, have appended to my posts. The book will thus answer many of your burning questions: Do I read the comments? Will I reproduce in the book the nastiest of the comments? (That raises the obvious derivative issue: Am I a self-loathing lunatic?) When I choose which comments to publish in the book, will "Bonobo Bro" make the cut? Will "Concerned Pastafarian"? Find out the answers to those questions—and more!—in *Inside Straight: The Book*!

The other good news is that David Lat has agreed to contribute a foreword to the book. Whatever you think of the quality of my writing, you know that Lat can write. The foreword alone is worth the entire price of the book!

So much for the good news; now, the requests for your help . . . .

First, the book needs a subtitle. We started with "Inside Straight: The Story of an On-Line Legal Column," but that doesn't do the trick. That subtitle doesn't tell a potential purchaser that the book provides (1) my ruminations about the legal profession, plus (2) intelligent conversations that occasionally break out in the comments to my columns, where readers debate issues of life and law, plus (3) the commenters' usual vicious attacks on me, my family, and the horse we rode in on. I'm currently leaning toward calling the book "Inside Straight: The Advice of a Blawger, the Vitriol of the Commenters, and the Wisdom of Crowds." That would tell a potential purchaser what's in the book, but I hate the word "blawger," which is both too obscure and likely to quickly fall out of fashion. So help me: Please suggest a subtitle for the book.

I also need your help on another front. Before a book is published, the author must solicit "advance praise" for the manuscript. "Advance praise" is those silly little blurbs raving about a book that appear on the back cover and first page or two of the published work. I figure that you, my loyal readers, may be a uniquely good source of "advance praise" for my book, so I'm asking you to contribute.

If you're a regular reader of "Inside Straight," then you have a pretty good sense of what the book is going to say. You should thus be able to provide a short (150 words or fewer) reaction to the manuscript for us to reproduce in the final work.

If you'd like to contribute advance praise, feel free simply to post your words as an anonymous comment below. We'll pick and choose from among your contributions and publish the best (attributed only to your screen name) in the book. (Actually, we may publish the worst of the advance praise, too. I personally might be tempted to buy a book if I popped open the front cover and read advance praise that said something like: "Herrmann, you idiot! You've wasted our time for 18 months on-line and now you're assembling that pablum into a book? What in God's name is wrong with you?")

If you'd prefer actual attribution of your reaction to the forthcoming book, then use the link provided below to send me an e-mail that includes both your praise and your name and contact information. We'll again pick and choose from among the suggestions that we receive, and we'll publish the most interesting in the book.

And that's not all!

I'm not simply going to reproduce in the book the advance praise that you provide. I'll probably also use this post—and these very words—as the final chapter in the book. That means that the book will have a pretty dull ending unless you, my readers, do your most creative work in the comments that you append to this post.

If this book is going to end with a bang, not a whimper, then it's up to you! Commenters, don't fail me now!

COMMENTS:

SUPRAMAN: Inside Straight: How I Got You, the Reader, to Pay for Columns and

Comments Available for Free On-Line

BRO_CAMEL: Inside Straight: Hey, Don't Walk Away Yet. At Least Read the Back Cover. C'mon, I Put A Lot of Work Into This. Oh Yeah? Well Eff You, Too!

SANTOSFLEISCHMAN: Inside Straight: But Outside? Pretty Into Dudes.

GUEST: Inside Straight: Clever Subtitle

GUEST: Inside Straight: Please Help Me Pay for My Son's Medical School Expenses

GUEST: You have to solicit advance praise. How embarrassing for you.

GUESTY: I bet this makes it into the book.

(INDÎCÀTING): Inside Straight: And Other Metaphors for the Low Probability of You Enjoying a Career In Law

HATER: Inside Straight: The Curmudgeon's Guide to Life After Practicing Law

MIDNIGHT BLUE: Mark Herrmann—You. Have. Got. To. Be. Kidding. Man, you are an embarrassment to in-house lawyers everywhere. (Which is impressive!)

GUEST123: Inside Straight: How I went online, took abuse and laughed all the way to the bank...

    PRESTIGIOUS PRESTON: When I got to the bank, I deposited the shiny roll of nickels that ATL paid me for my work in 2011.

GUEST123: Inside Straight: Advice Is Worth What You Pay, So Buy This Book!

GUEST 1: Inside Straight: The Annoying Ramblings of an Uber Douche

NON-IP ATTORNEY: Inside Straight: Ending with a Bang, Not a Whimper

JOHNNY STEC: tsk tsk...
    What an incorrigible gallery of miscreants!

ABOUT THE AUTHOR

MARK HERRMANN has done some things. He went to school—Princeton University and The University of Michigan Law School (*Michigan Law Review*, Order of the Coif). He clerked for a federal judge—The Honorable Dorothy W. Nelson of the United States Court of Appeals for the Ninth Circuit. He worked as an associate at a small law firm—Steinhart & Falconer in San Francisco. He worked for two years as an associate, and eighteen years as a partner, at a large law firm—Jones Day, in Cleveland and Chicago. Mark is currently the Vice President and Chief Counsel—Litigation at Aon, the world's leading provider of risk management solutions and human resources consulting.

Along the way, Mark found time to teach "complex litigation" for nearly a decade on the adjunct faculty of Case Western Reserve University School of Law. He also managed to write a book that was fun and highly acclaimed—*The Curmudgeon's Guide to Practicing Law* (ABA 2006), which was a finalist for a Benjamin Franklin Award in 2007. He co-authored two other books, but they were neither fun nor highly acclaimed—*Statewide Coordinated Proceedings: State Court Analogues to the Federal MDL Process* (Thomson West 2d rev. ed. 2004) and *Drug and Device Product Liability Litigation Strategy* (Oxford 2012). His articles have appeared in publications ranging from *The Wall Street Journal* and *Chicago Tribune* to the *Tulane Law Review* and *University of Pennsylvania Law Review PENNumbra*.

Mark's adult children, Jessica and Jeremy, are great, and his wife, Brenda Gordon, provides the inspiration (or at least the motivation).

INDEX